PROTESTANTISM—
ITS MODERN MEANING

David A. Rausch and
Carl Hermann Voss

PROTESTANTISM—
ITS MODERN MEANING

FORTRESS PRESS   PHILADELPHIA

Library of Congress Cataloging-in-Publication Data

Rausch, David A.
  Protestantism, its modern meaning.

  Includes bibliographies and index.
  1. Protestantism — History. I. Voss, Carl Hermann.
II. Title.
BX4805.2.R38 1987   280'.4'09   86-46413
  ISBN 0-8006-2060-7

3003D87   Printed in the United States of America   1–2060

To
David Joshua Rausch
Jonathan Daniel Rausch
Benjamin Joel Rausch

Teresa Voss Iuzzolino
Mark Joseph Iuzzolino

CONTENTS

FOREWORD

Protestantism — Its Modern Meaning is the third in a series of books
about America's major religious faiths. The first was *Judaism — An
Eternal Covenant* by Howard R. Greenstein, followed by *A Catholic
Vision* by Stephen Happel and David Tracy. While we underscore the
Jewish and Catholic roots of Protestantism and cannot fail to mention the interaction of these faiths in history, the other books discuss
the major events of their historical heritage. Thus, Vatican II is elaborated upon in *A Catholic Vision*, while the growth process of American Reform, Conservative, and Orthodox Judaism is left to
Judaism — An Eternal Covenant.

As do the other two volumes, *Protestantism — Its Modern Meaning*
gives proportionately more space to Europe and the Anglo-American
world. Because our readership will be basically in the English-
speaking sphere, the shift to movements in the United States, such as
Liberalism and Fundamentalism, is quite important. These movements are nurtured from European sources, but obtain a special
character in the American sphere which reaches out to the entire
world. For example, questions about Fundamentalism and Evangelicalism absorb a world community of scholars today, and our
survey provides an understanding of the origin and growth of these
complex movements. The nineteenth century was definitely the Century of Evangelicalism in the Anglo-American realm, and both
Liberalism and Fundamentalism spring from this religious milieu to
affect the world.

We believe that the modern meaning of Protestantism is grounded
in its historic meaning. Therefore, our book may be used as a survey
of this history, an overview that has high regard for the diverse
denominational and theological components of this complicated

movement. Nevertheless, *Protestantism — Its Modern Meaning* does not seek to catalogue every Protestant group or nation, but rather to bring Protestant principles and concepts to light through its history.

Therefore, while we are aware of the many missionary groups that spread the Protestant message throughout the world, the use of mass communication today, and the modern movements of liberation in the Third World, this volume does not cover such phenomena in detail. Rather, these events are acknowledged, and their theological and philosophical underpinnings outlined. To do otherwise in a volume of this size would deprive our readers of historical data that clarify the principles and components of Protestantism and, in our view, would be at best a shallow treatment of the complexity of worldwide Protestantism.

Instead, our Suggested Readings at the end of each chapter note relevant studies to guide the reader into specialized research. In addition, scores of pertinent primary sources are alluded to in this book in an effort to spark the imagination and further the educational process.

It is our hope that your journey into the realm of Protestantism will touch your spirit and revitalize your particular faith experience, as it has ours.

DAVID A. RAUSCH
Ashland, Ohio

CARL HERMANN VOSS
Jacksonville, Florida

1

WHAT IS PROTESTANTISM?

The year was 1529. Politics had drastically changed in the German territories. Roman Catholic princes who, three years earlier in the First Diet of Spires (Speyer), had supported the right of each German state to choose its own religious allegiance (Catholic or Lutheran), changed their moderate policy. They formed a strong majority with those Catholics who opposed such freedom of choice. The policy of tolerance toward Lutheranism was in jeopardy of being revoked by law in a Second Diet of Spires.

In the midst of the pomp and splendor of the Second Diet, a declaration was drawn up by the Lutheran princes emphasizing that the legal change would be acting against "conscience." "In such matters," they wrote, "we ought to have regard, above all, to the commandment of God, who is King of kings and Lord of lords." They resolved to "maintain the pure and exclusive preaching of His only Word, such as it is contained in the biblical books of the Old and New Testament," and entreated the majority to "weigh carefully our grievances and motives."

"If you do not yield to our request, we PROTEST. . . ," the signed declaration of the Lutheran princes concluded, "neither consent nor adhere in any manner whatsoever to the proposed decree, in any thing that is contrary to God, to His holy Word, to our right conscience, to the salvation of our souls, and to the last decree of Spires."

The reading of the declaration intensified the hostility between both parties in the Second Diet of Spires, and war loomed on the horizon. The minority princes announced that they were leaving the assembly the next day; and, because of their formal declaration of protest, these German Lutheran princes were called "Protestants." A

1

specific historical incident had inadvertently given a name to a growing religious movement and tradition.

While the detractors of these "protestants" may have seen only the negative aspects of the new movement, that is, protesting *against* Roman Catholic orthodoxy and polity, it is appropriate that the primary Latin meaning of the word "protestant" is "a bearer of witness on behalf of something." Indeed, Protestantism is more a witness than a denial.

No religious faith can live by its denials. Thus, Protestantism affirms and testifies to certain principles and concepts—principles and concepts evident even within the Luthern declaration of protest made by the minority princes at the Second Diet of Spires. These may be summarized in part as (1) individual conscience and freedom of religion, (2) grace and faith, (3) the authority of the Bible, and (4) the priesthood of all believers. Let us look briefly at these concepts.

Individual conscience and freedom of religion. The right of individuals to follow their conscience and to exercise freedom of religious belief is an important component of Protestantism. Much of the complexity and diversity among Protestants and Protestant denominations stems from this concept. "Acting against our conscience, condemning a doctrine that we maintain to be Christian . . . would be to deny our Lord Jesus Christ. . . ," the Lutheran princes asserted to the Second Diet of Spires.

Although Lutheranism in particular and Protestantism in general would at times be woefully intolerant toward those of other religious persuasions (even within their own religious community!), the principles of individual conscience and freedom of religious belief have been cherished by individual Protestants and groups throughout history. In fact, most Protestant groups have at one time or another appealed to these "God-given rights."

Protestantism has maintained that men and women, even *Christian* men and women, are at best imperfect. From the Protestant viewpoint, therefore, all human institutions fall far short of perfection. Even the church is defective and flawed, in constant need of God's reforming touch in each generation. The obligation of all Christians to follow their own moral sense in matters of faith and practice helps protect the Christian church from institutional dictatorship and spiritual stagnation. Protestantism would agree with

2

the Westminster Confession of Faith (1647) in its affirmation, "God alone is Lord of the conscience," for Protestantism stresses the freedom of human beings from the spiritual domination of people or institutions.

Grace and faith. Protestantism has always considered itself a religion of grace. A gracious God loved humanity and reached out to it through Jesus Christ. "Through Jesus Christ, our throne of grace and our only mediator," the protest document at the Second Diet of Spires affirmed. Humankind did not and could not merit such love. Only the heavenly Father could initiate such a process. While Protestants have historically differed about the nature of salvation and the interaction between God and humanity, *sola gratia* (by grace alone) has been a central axiom of the Protestant faith.

And in Protestantism, *sola fide* (by faith alone) is the human response to the grace of God. Martin Luther believed that "faith is a lively, reckless confidence in the grace of God"; and Protestantism has at least concurred that faith is indeed trusting and acknowledging the work of grace that God has provided. The result of such faith is commitment to the way of Christ — the realization of what Dietrich Bonhoeffer (1906–45) would refer to as "costly grace," Christ enduring the horrors of the cross to make grace a reality in one's life. The lives of dedicated Protestant women and men discussed in the following pages testify to the quality of that commitment.

Authority of the Bible. In the response to the Second Diet of Spires by the Lutheran princes, one notes the emphasis on the Bible's being the sole judge of religious dogma and practice. "There is no sure doctrine but such as is conformable to the Word of God. . . . Each text of the Holy Scriptures ought to be explained by other and clearer texts," it was asserted. "This holy book is in all things necessary for the Christian, easy of understanding, and calculated to scatter darkness," the protest declaration continued.

Although Protestants would historically contend with one another on its interpretation, Scripture has been viewed in the Protestant tradition as the absolute norm of the Christian faith. Protestantism has emphasized that the Bible's central message of grace and faith can be as clear to the average man, woman, or child as to the highly educated and intellectually astute. Therefore, the Scriptures were to be available to the individual who, with moral conscience and honest faith, would be free to draw from this wellspring for the human soul.

Ideally, the Bible was to be the only rule of faith for Protestant practice. The protest declaration explained that the Bible was "the sure rule of all doctrine and all life." Historically, however, various traditions, creeds, illuminations, and denominational teachings have fashioned the sixty-six books of the Protestant Bible into institutional molds that have sometimes differed greatly from one another. Protestantism's traditional emphasis on the right of the individual to interpret Scripture and freely practice his or her interpretation has contributed to this diversity, but also has breathed fresh spirit into the movement. For the Protestant, the Bible is the message of a gracious God to a beloved world—a world that God calls to follow in the way of Christ.

Priesthood of all believers. The diversity within Protestantism also results from the belief that the church is a fellowship of believers rather than an organization or institution. The protest declaration even questioned the Second Diet of Spires on what was meant by "the true and holy Church." The individual Protestant is viewed as a "priest." He or she has direct access to God without the assistance of a special earthly mediator.

Nevertheless, community is essential in Protestantism, and every believer is to act as a "priest" for other believers, that is, praying for one another, confessing to one another, helping one another. Protestantism freely admits that the church is a community of sinners—sinners who depend upon the grace of God daily. And yet it asserts that there is a greater unity of Christian believers, one that transcends denomination or local community. In this sense the church is a divine organism rather than a human organization. There are very few Protestant denominations that believe their particular human organization is the only church God has provided for the salvation of humankind.

Because of the priesthood of all believers, Protestantism views every vocation as sacred and refuses to divide into religious and secular Christian standards. The highest moral standard is to be applied to all vocations. Protestantism realized that not every Christian's vocation is a church-related vocation (pastor, missionary, etc.), but every vocation should be a sacred service to God. The intrinsic worth of every "child of God" and the need for a variety of consecrated

4

vocations in the Christian community is a principle of Protestantism that may at times have been neglected, but has impressively contributed to the dynamism of the Protestant faith.

JEWISH HERITAGE

One cannot consider the roots of Protestantism without acknowledging its indebtedness to Judaism. Jesus was a Jew. Those who first followed him were Jews. He chose only Jews as his disciples. Christianity was the child of Judaism, and Jerusalem was the center of Christianity in the early decades of the church. That early Christian believers were Jewish is evident in Acts 15, which records that at a Jerusalem council around 50 C.E. (two decades after Jesus' death) Jewish Christians debated whether or not Gentile converts should be under the Mosaic law. In other words, they were asking, Should the Gentiles become Jewish *before* they become Christians?

Only after great debate and a spirited speech by Peter, who had debated on the other side a few years earlier, did James the Just, the presiding elder of their congregation, express his judgment that they "not trouble those who are turning to God from among the Gentiles [i.e., not trouble them to become Jewish first], but that we write to them that they abstain from things contaminated by idols and from fornication and from what is strangled and from blood" (Acts 15:19–20).

The suggestions were very Jewish-oriented, and historical records reveal committed *Jewish* followers of Jesus. Recent scholarship has convincingly stressed what some scholars of the past had asserted, that is, that the apostles maintained their own Jewish identity and continued their Jewish practices, probably encouraging other Jewish believers to do so as well. Paul himself appears to have remained an observant Jew all through his life. A vibrant Jewish Christianity developed in Judea during the apostolic period and was considered by the Romans as a sect of Judaism.

Protestantism, as well as all Christendom, is indebted to Judaism for its emphasis on the Scriptures, the Hebrew Scriptures composing over three-fourths of the Protestant Bible (the remaining New Testament almost totally written by Jews as well). The great reverence and care with which these Hebrew Scriptures were kept by the "People

5

of the Book" should provoke gratitude throughout all Christendom. In fact, Protestantism has benefited so directly from the Jewish heritage, from worship services to church polity, that an entire treatise could be devoted to such a study.

EASTERN ORTHODOX AND ROMAN CATHOLIC HERITAGE

It must be remembered that all early Protestant reformers were Roman Catholics. They grew up within the confines of the mother church, some ordained as priests as in the case of Martin Luther. And yet until 1054, the Western Roman Catholic church and the Eastern Orthodox church were united. The early councils that formulated doctrinal positions to which Protestants would wholly adhere were the products of both East and West — all the early councils were held in the East. The Eastern Orthodox was a more mystical and philosophical tradition from which Protestantism would gain an insight into the Eastern origins of Christianity. They allowed their clergy, up to the rank of bishop, to marry, and Protestantism, too, would oppose the Western emphasis on celibacy. The Orthodox churches also claimed to be a family of self-governing churches held together by a bond of unity in the faith and thus, like Protestantism, would oppose the primacy of the papacy.

Nevertheless, Protestantism had much more in common with the West, and its roots are embedded deeply in Roman Catholicism. Protestant reformers were profoundly indebted to the formulations of Augustine. Concepts such as prayer, meditation, fasting, discipline, fellowship, and the importance of communion are rooted in the history of the Roman Catholic church. Theological debates in Protestantism reach back into a rich heritage of theological and philosophical discussion on the Bible and tradition which permeated the Western ecclesiastical milieu. Luther's earlier views on grace and salvation were in perfect harmony with Catholic tradition, and he even called for a general council in the spirit of conciliarism, until Johann Eck pointed out to him that Jan Hus was burned at the stake by order of such a Catholic council at Constance in 1415. Protestant liturgy and polity are so entrenched in Catholicism that Protestant groups that deviated from the traditional norm have from time to time accused their brethren of being "tainted with popery."

6

PROTESTANTISM TODAY

From these roots a vibrant Protestant movement thrives today. With approximately 293 million adherents in 212 countries, Protestantism comprises more than 6 percent of the population of the world. Eighty-two hundred denominations support tens of thousands of hospitals, charitable institutions, publishing houses, periodicals, schools, colleges, and missionary enterprises.

The modern meaning of this diverse movement is lodged in its historic meaning. As we view Protestant principles and concepts as they interact with and are molded by this history, let us remember that the journey of Protestantism has not ended; it continues.

SUGGESTED READING

Bouyer, Louis. *The Spirit and Forms of Protestantism*. London: Harvill Press, 1956.

Brauer, Jerald C. *Protestantism in America*. Rev. ed. Philadelphia: Westminster Press, 1965.

Brown, Robert M. *The Spirit of Protestantism*. New York and London: Oxford Univ. Press, 1961.

Forell, George W. *The Protestant Faith*. Philadelphia: Fortress Press, 1975.

Gerrish, B. A. *The Old Protestantism and the New*. Chicago: Univ. of Chicago Press, 1983.

Leonard, Emile G. *A History of Protestantism*. 2 vols. Toronto: Thomas Nelson & Sons, 1965.

Marty, Martin E. *Protestantism*. New York: Holt, Rinehart and Winston, 1972.

Tillich, Paul. *The Protestant Era*. Chicago: Univ. of Chicago Press, 1957.

Whale, John S. *The Protestant Tradition*. New York: Cambridge Univ. Press, 1955.

THE PRECURSORS
OF THE REFORMATION

"These people, although stupid and unlearned, traveled through the villages [preaching]," Bernard Gui (c. 1261–1331) complained in his *Manual of the Inquisitor.* "Summoned by the Archbishop of Lyons," he continued, "they refused [to refrain from preaching], declaring . . . that one should obey God rather than man."

Gui, a Dominican inquisitor in southeastern France, paid a backhanded compliment to the tenacity of this group of Waldenses as he recounted their history, condemnation, and execution under the Fourth Lateran Council of the Roman Catholic church in 1215. According to this conscientious eradicator of heresy, the former Waldenses "despised the prelates and clergy because, they [the Waldenses] said, they [the prelates and clergy] owned great wealth and lived in pleasures." "Disdain for ecclesiastical authority was and still is the prime heresy of the Waldenses," Gui continued. He then instructed his readers on the "false and crafty replies" of the Waldenses of his day and on the procedure for convicting them.

Gui's *Manual* is only one of thousands of historical documents that testify to individuals and groups within the Roman Catholic church who were attempting to reform the church long before the birth of Martin Luther. One must never forget that the early Protestants were Roman Catholics, and they built upon a foundation of reform history that spanned centuries. That these precursors were met with apathy, violence, and death in no way diminishes the importance of this early reform impulse.

THE NEED FOR REFORM

That the church needed to be reformed is commonly asserted by both Catholic and Protestant scholars. Popes of the medieval period increasingly asserted their absolute authority over princes as well as prelates, over kings as well as kingdoms, over the temporal as well as the spiritual. As they gained such supremacy, the church hierarchy became increasingly centralized and rigid. Secular impulses began to replace the spiritual.

Pope Gregory VII (1073–85) declared that "all princes shall kiss the feet" of the pope and that "he himself may be judged by no one." Pope Innocent III (1198–1216) brought the medieval papacy to the zenith of its power, declaring that "the royal power derives its dignity from the pontifical authority." He compared "the lesser" authority of kings to the moon, while likening "the greater" authority of the pope to the sun. Indeed, during his papacy, the kings of Europe were forced to submit to him. King John (1199–1216), for example, had to surrender England as a fief of the papacy in order to regain Innocent's favor after excommunication. John had dared to defy Innocent's choice of the archbishop of Canterbury, and Innocent proceeded to release all his Catholic subjects from their vows of obedience to John. Their first allegiance must be to the church. Thus, the spiritual authority of the church was turned into a lethal political weapon.

With the rising power of the nation-states and the loyalty of the populace to those states, however, such illustrations of papal supremacy lessened. When Pope Boniface VIII (1294–1303) asserted "temporal authority subject to spiritual" and emphasized that "submission on the part of every man to the bishop of Rome" was necessary for salvation, the much stronger King Philip IV of France (1285–1314) balked. He imprisoned the pope and plundered the papal palace. The papacy was completely disrupted and moved to Avignon under the watchful eye of the French monarch from 1309 to 1377 (commonly referred to as the "Babylonian Captivity" of the church). Upon its return to Rome, French cardinals disputed with Italians over who should be pope. During subsequent years (1378–1417), the Roman Catholic church had two popes and, for a few years, even three.

When the papacy returned intact in the fifteenth century, a Renaissance papacy emerged that was extremely secularized. Popes were strong, but immorality abounded. Some were excellent administrators, while others were warriors who could wage war against powerful nation-states. On the eve of the Protestant Reformation, Pope Alexander VI (1492–1503) bribed his way to the papacy and was so lacking in religious beliefs that he was accused of being an atheist. Indeed, he had at least three illegitimate children, appointing one an archbishop at the age of seventeen and a cardinal the next year. Amassing a great personal fortune, he was guilty of avarice, injustice, and cruelty as well as immorality. And yet he would periodically "bless" a crowd of 200,000 pilgrims in St. Peter's Square. His successor, Julius II (1503–13), sold even more benefices in order to build the papal treasury. Julius II personally led his own troops into battle against his foes, while Pope Leo X (1513–23) created new ecclesiastical offices to be sold to recoup massive amounts of money he had squandered on luxury.

Anticlericalism was rampant in the fourteenth and fifteenth centuries. The average European resented the excessive wealth of the upper-class clergy, and the secularization of the church hierarchy surpassed at times even that of European royalty. The church held large tracts of land and levied heavy taxes. Religious offices were bought and sold, the spiritual needs of the populace sacrificed to greed and avarice. Parish priests were sometimes lacking in education or, even worse, eliminated from some areas on a cost-efficient basis. When the Black Death raged in Europe during the Avignon years, with its incredible toll and accompanying despair, people tended to blame the lax churchmen for "God's judgment." The Babylonian Captivity with its Avignon aristocracy and the Great Western Schism with its multiple popes underscored the fact that the papacy did not intend to initiate any needed reforms.

EARLY ATTEMPTS AT REFORM

During the twelfth century, a cry arose that the church was too worldly and needed to be purified. Groups such as the Albigenses and Waldenses proclaimed values of simplicity, poverty, and morality in face of the papacy's climb toward the zenith of power. Peter Waldo (c. 1140–1218), a wealthy merchant in the city of Lyons, gave away all of his property which he had acquired by loaning money at high rates of interest and assumed a life of poverty. A deep religious experience had turned his thoughts to a "simple gospel" and he translated portions of the Bible into the local dialect in an effort to preach more effectively. As he preached in the streets to both rich and poor, scores of men and women began to follow him.

Unlike the Albigenses, who held to a form of Manichean dualism, these "Poor of Lyons" espoused traditional orthodoxy. Nevertheless, their insistence that all believers had the right to preach drew vehement opposition from the local clergy. The archbishop of Lyons ordered Waldo and his followers to stop preaching. When they persisted, they were banned from the city; and in 1184 Pope Lucius III (1181–85) included them among the sects that were excommunicated from the Roman Catholic church. Such pious persistence was viewed as an attack on the papacy and was resisted by persecution, torture, and death for adherents of those views.

Within the church itself, Dominic (1170–1221) and Francis of Assisi (1182–1226) formed orders of "begging" friars who lived active lives in the world while preaching and ministering to the needy. The Dominicans and Franciscans would soon be divided in their ranks over the extent to which they should pursue the zealous reforming tactics of their founders.

Universities were also bastions of the reforming trend. Philosophical thinkers, such as the Franciscan William of Ockham (c. 1285–1347) at Oxford University and Marsiglio of Padua (c. 1275–1342) of the University of Paris, challenged the authority the papacy claimed over the princes of the earth. Conciliarism, the view that general church councils should ultimately determine the doctrine and polity of the church, was conceived in such bastions of learning. Former University of Paris chancellor, Pierre D'Ailly (1350–1420), upon appointment as cardinal, argued that the pope was not essential to the church. In his tractate "On the Reformation of the Church," D'Ailly argued that bishops and priests received their jurisdiction directly from Jesus Christ and not through the pope. While believing that neither the pope nor a universal council was infallible, he insisted that all opponents must submit to the authority of the council. This view led to the death of Jan Hus (c. 1372–1415). The Council of Constance (1414–18) sincerely wanted to reform the church as well as combat heresy; but its reforming zeal was circumvented by the ensuing strength of the Renaissance popes.

MYSTICS

Throughout church history one finds emphases on knowing God and being immersed in God's presence. As the Roman Catholic church reached the zenith of temporal power with the subsequent decline in morals, a vibrant form of Christian mysticism appeared which aimed for direct union with God through a life of dedicated piety. Men and women who were a part of religious orders, such as the Dominicans, spearheaded enterprises of contemplation and devotion. However, the movement also included a dedicated lay witness in which women were predominant. Mystics like Mechthild of Magdeburg (1210–80) devoted their lives to prayer, study, and charity, yet never took monastic vows. With the help and encouragement of her Dominican confessor, Mechthild wrote *The Flowing Light of God*.

In Germany, one of the best-known mystics was the Dominican Meister Eckhart (c. 1260–1327). Like Martin Luther three hundred years later, he was a native of Thuringia and was known for his keen intellect and exemplary conduct. A product of the Universities of Paris and Strasbourg, he lectured in both cities, but soon became one of the most popular preachers in Germany through his work with nuns and lay people devoted to piety and the practice of good works. Meister Eckhart asserted that God transcends all human knowledge and experience, and only by an act of grace generates God's word in the soul that is pure. Thus, God and humankind are united in the ground being of the soul, empowering men and women for the highest good.

The last years of Eckhart's life were marred by the accusation of heresy and investigation into controversial statements in his writings. He admitted that he was "capable of error, but not of heresy," because error depended upon finite understanding while heresy was an act of will. Like most mystics, he remained devoted to the church and its hierarchy. Nevertheless, his emphasis on the individual's direct communion with God and responsibility for living a pure life unintentionally encouraged a detachment from the existing ecclesiastical hierarchy. It was an attempt to reform the church through the individual Christian's life; and it is little wonder that some emphases in the sermons of Eckhart's disciple, Johann Tauler (c. 1300–61), were highly regarded by Luther.

On the other hand, the mystic Catherine of Siena (1347–80) became politically involved to further the spiritual reform that had taken place in her life and that of her followers. A Dominican tertiary, a layperson who belonged to a third order after monks and nuns, she had gathered a circle of friends from among the clergy and laity who respected her deep insight and unwavering devotion. During the Avignon papacy, she convinced Pope Gregory XI to bring the papacy back to Rome in 1377 and worked tirelessly to reunite the church during the subsequent Great Western Schism. Although so frail that she often fainted during the Eucharist, she fearlessly denounced clerical immorality and spoke boldly at the papal court. Her letters and treatises emphasized the importance of becoming a vessel of God's love.

John Wycliffe

If most mystics simply ignored the power politics and theological intricacies of the Roman Catholic church in their inward reformation of the soul, a more radical and forthright reformist approach may be seen in the life of scholar-statesman John Wycliffe (c. 1330–84). A renowned philosopher at Oxford University, he had begun to lecture on theology by 1371, during the Avignon papacy. On various occasions he worked for English governmental officials, conferring with papal authorities and entering into negotiations with a papacy clearly dominated by the French.

Wycliffe's written works on the Bible were the only complete commentary issued in this period, and they seem increasingly to have drawn his attention to the doctrine of the church. He became opposed to the hierarchy of the Roman Catholic church, and in the mid-1370s wrote his treatise "On Civil Dominion." In this work, he argued that all authority, including that of the church, came from God and was dependent upon the grace of God. Priests and bishops who were immoral or worldly could lawfully be deprived of their property and position by the civil government.

His success with the Avignon papacy differed significantly from that of Catherine of Siena. Pope Gregory XI condemned Wycliffe's position in a papal bull in 1377, listing nineteen errors and naming Marsilius of Padua as one of Wycliffe's misguided forebears. This only served to strengthen Wycliffe's hostility toward the papacy, and his subsequent writings declared that the papal office had no foundation in the Bible. Wycliffe emphasized that if a man was to be chosen as supreme pontiff, he should be the man of greatest virtue. He also asserted that the Bible was the only valid criterion for doctrine and that it should be put back in the hands of Christian believers who were actually the "body" of Christ's church. The multiple popes of the Great Western Schism, two warring "vicars of Christ" during Wycliffe's latter years, only confirmed his evaluation of a reprobate papacy.

Pope Gregory XI had ordered that "John [be] seized and jailed . . . under careful guard in chains. . . . " However, such an act required the cooperation of the civil authorities, authorities who agreed with Wycliffe's assessment of unwarranted papal taxation and excessive possessions by church institutions. Wycliffe was protected from harm, but was later forced into retirement when he denied the doctrine of transubstantiation. He wrote that the presence of Christ in the Eucharist was sacramental and spiritual, but the elements did not change into the literal physical body and blood of Christ.

Wycliffe had begun his spiritual journey in an effort to convince the church to return to the purity and simplicity he found in his Bible. He dreamed of an era when the poor would be helped and the devoted, not the wealthy bureaucrats, would be the leaders. He ended his journey by calling the papacy "a poisonous weed" and viewing the two popes who warred as "dogs snarling over a bone." He had called into question the central doctrines of the Roman Catholic church, and as a heretic was so hated that the Council of Constance ordered his bones exhumed and burned three decades after his death. His followers, often called Lollards ("mumblers" of prayers), held to many of the precepts of the Protestant Reformation a century before Luther.

Jan Hus

The writings of Wycliffe had a profound effect on the life of the dean of the philosophical faculty at the University of Prague, Jan Hus (c. 1372–1415). Appointed rector and preacher of the famed Bethlehem Chapel, Hus was impressed with Wycliffe's denunciation of the worldliness of the clergy and the corruption throughout the church. He devoted his life to a practical reform of the church, cautiously following Wycliffe's precepts on "righteous stewardship" without accepting his radical views on the Eucharist. Although he did not oppose the doctrine of indulgences, he vehemently denounced the sacrilegious manner in which they were sold to finance the papacy.

During the struggle among three "popes" in the Great Western

Schism, Hus was ordered to stop preaching at Bethlehem Chapel. The chapel had become the center of reformist ideology and a bastion of Czech nationalism. Hus refused to obey and was ultimately excommunicated. In the ensuing effort to defend himself, Hus was encouraged by Holy Roman Emperor Sigismund (1361–1437) to attend the Council of Constance and was guaranteed safe passage both ways. He hesitated because of the charges against him, but was urged by his king to clear up the matter. Less than a month after his arrival, he was imprisoned in a Dominican monastery dungeon and was tried for heresy as an adherent of "Wycliffism."

At first, he successfully defended himself; but Cardinal Pierre D'Ailly (see above, p. 12), a conciliarist reformer in his own right, insisted that Hus obey the council and recant the articles brought against him. Hus refused to do this on the ground that he did not hold to any of the charged heresies in the first place. To abjure would be to perjure himself. Asked by a bishop, "Do you wish to be wiser than the whole Council?" Hus replied, "I do not wish to be wiser than the whole Council, but I pray, give me the least one of the Council who would instruct me by better and more relevant Scripture, and I am ready instantly to recant!" The council, however, viewed him as an obstinate heretic, a disciple of Wycliffe who would not bow to the authority of the conciliar movement, and ordered him burned at the stake.

Hus had asserted that the Bible was supreme, an authority to which pope, council, and Christian must all bow. That his moderate reformist goals shared by the council members themselves could not be tolerated under the intricate legalism of the ecclesiastical hierarchy demonstrates the degree to which Catholic officials had become rigid. In death Hus became a Bohemian hero to a degree he could have never attained in life. Some of his followers insisted that the laity receive both the bread and the wine in the Eucharist, while others declared that they rejected everything that could not be supported by the Scriptures. A number of Catholic crusades against the rebellious Bohemian church were repulsed and served merely to fan the flames of reforming fervor. Only a negotiated peace, including communion with both bread and wine, brought part of the church back into the fold of Catholic Christendom. Some never accepted the agreement at all.

CATHOLIC HUMANISTS

Several forces of reform came together to produce a prolific Christian humanism that attempted to transform the Roman Catholic church. First of all, the nominalists, those who believed that there were no universal essences in reality, challenged the rigid "total" systems of the scholastics. For example, William of Ockham was led to challenge such systems because of his belief that universals were only a convenience of the human mind. In William's estimation, an arrogance of reason in matters of faith had led to scholastic arguments that reflected the scholastics' own purposes rather than the character of reality. He believed that theology could ultimately be based only on faith and not on fact. Therefore, through grace and not knowledge, he accepted the teachings of the Roman Catholic church. Through nominalism, the well-defined dogma that buttressed the fortress of papal supremacy was cracked, and the supposed unity of the church was jeopardized.

Second, the Renaissance added to such a complication with its emphasis on the individual and excellence in secular vocation in *this* world. As a force for change, it fostered love for the liberal arts and critical analysis. The Italian philologist Lorenzo Valla (1407–57) demonstrated that the Donation of Constantine was an eighth-century forgery and could not be used to support the claims of the papacy to temporal power since the time of Constantine. Valla also emphasized the differences between the Latin Vulgate and the early Greek manuscripts. The humanists' love for the classical tradition would lead to the collection of ancient manuscripts and a return to the original languages of the Bible.

In the fourteenth century a third force arose that affected Christian humanism. A devotional movement of lay-centered piety originated in the Low Countries and was destined to have a significant impact for reform in northern Europe. Centered around the Dutch mystic Gerhard Groote (1340–84), this *Devotio Moderna* movement was exemplified by the religious society, the Brethren of the Common Life. The society consisted of both clergy and laity, and its members sought to live totally dedicated to Christ, to participate in active good works and philanthropy, and to dwell in a community dedicated to holiness, simplicity, and honesty. Lay ministry was encouraged, and schools were later established to provide a general, as well as a religious, education without fee. Member Thomas à Kempis's (1380–1471) small devotional book, *The Imitation of Christ*, is still read today, stressing personal virtue in modeling Christ and the positive love of Christianity that inflames the heart.

The *Devotio Moderna* movement suggested that study should emphasize love and devotion to God, rather than the speculative theologizing and systems of the scholastics. This movement and nominalism seem to be linked in Gabriel Biel (1420–94), who joined the Brethren of the Common Life in old age. A German born at Spires and a follower of William of Ockham, Biel declared that reason could neither demonstrate that God was the First Cause of the universe nor make a distinction among the attributes of God. He emphasized that the reality of the Trinity, as well as any theological dogma, could be found in the realm of faith. Partially responsible for founding the University of Tübingen, he was professor of theology there until 1484.

The worth of the individual was at the center of the Christian humanist movement. Although it differed from place to place, Christian humanism applied the Renaissance concepts of classical studies, individualism, excellence, vitality, and versatility to a pious life devoted to God. Because man was created in the image of God, the Christian humanists asserted that man possessed dignity even in his fallen state. A Sermon-on-the-Mount piety from Matthew 5 – 7 was coupled with academic excellence and cultural awareness.

Desiderius Erasmus (c. 1469–1536) was taught by the Christian humanist Alexander Hegius (1433?–98) at the Brethren of the Common Life school at Deventer, and went on to become the leading Christian humanist of the Reformation era. In his *Enchiridion* (1503), Erasmus emphasized that the way of piety was to follow the life of Christ, and the state of one's heart was more important than external service through ceremony. In his *In Praise of Folly* (1509), he railed against ecclesiastical and civil abuse, declaring that what in the eyes of the world is the greatest folly (the way of Christ) was in actuality the highest wisdom.

Working on his critical edition of the Greek New Testament, which appeared in 1516, Erasmus underscored his deep respect for the Christian Scriptures. In the introduction, he proclaimed that "the

Holy Scriptures" should be read by the "layfolk" and publicly wished that the Bible could be translated into the languages of the common people. "I should like all women to read the Gospel and the Epistles of Paul," he also wrote in an age of male chauvinism, asserting that Christ did not desire his teachings to be obscure. Erasmus was sympathetic toward Luther's cries for reform during the early years following the posting of the Ninety-Five Theses (1517), but he balked as he became aware of more volatile language and drastic actions that he believed would divide the Roman Catholic church. Until his death he remained an advocate of reform *within* his church.

TIGHTENING THE PRESSURE VALVE

The Catholic precursors of the Protestant Reformation described in this chapter criticized in varied ways their beloved church and advocated its reform. In their views and calls for reform, one notes many, if not all, of the principles and concepts affirmed by the Protestants. With one accord they cried out against clerical abuse and excessive wealth. Themes of individual conscience, freedom of religion, grace, faith, the authority of the Bible, and the priesthood of all believers are found in varying degrees in this Catholic reform movement. So potent were their pleas for reform, piety, and charity that modern Catholic scholars maintain the church would have reformed itself *from within* without the divisiveness of the Protestant movement.

Nevertheless, they were confronted with a church hierarchy that met such reform from within with apathy, persecution, violence, and execution. Instead of loosening the intense pressure for reform, the Roman Catholic church elected not only to ignore it but also to oppose it energetically. Thus, the church became like a giant boiler ready to burst. Instead of releasing the pressure through reform and change, the papacy and other hierarchical figures elected to screw the valves even tighter. The resulting Protestant Reformation that divided the church was the explosion, the critical additional pressure provided by a little-known priest and university professor, Martin Luther.

19

SUGGESTED READING

Hall, Louis B. *The Perilous Vision of John Wyclif.* Chicago: Nelson-Hall, 1983.

Leff, Gordon. *Heresy in the Later Middle Ages.* 2 vols. Manchester: Manchester Univ. Press, 1967.

Oberman, Heiko, A. *Forerunners of the Reformation: The Shape of Late Medieval Thought.* Philadelphia: Fortress Press, 1981.

Ridolfi, Robert. *The Life of Girolamo Savonarola.* London: Routledge & Kegan Paul, 1959.

Spinka, Matthew. *John Hus: A Biography.* Westport, Conn.: Greenwood Press, 1978.

———. ed. *Advocates of Reform, from Wyclif to Erasmus.* Philadelphia: Westminster Press, 1953.

Spitz, Lewis W. *Renaissance and Reformation.* 2 vols. St. Louis: Concordia Pub. House, 1980.

Tuchman, Barbara W. *A Distant Mirror: The Calamitous 14th Century.* New York: Alfred A. Knopf, 1978.

Wakefield, Walter L., and Austin P. Evans, eds., *Heresies of the High Middle Ages.* New York: Columbia Univ. Press, 1969.

3

THE REFORMATION

There was nothing radical in Martin Luther's posting of the Ninety-Five Theses on the door of the Castle Church at Wittenberg. He was calling neither for a break with Rome nor a fight against the pope, but only for a debate about abuses he felt the pope himself would denounce. The Theses contain statements such as "If the pope knew" (thesis 50) and "If pardons were preached according to the spirit and mind of the pope all these questions would easily be disposed of" (thesis 91).

In addition, the debate topics were written in Latin, not for the general public, and were tacked to the door of a church that housed approximately eighteen thousand relics that could cancel millions of years in purgatory, funding that underwrote the finances of the University of Wittenberg where Luther taught. Pilgrims who first copied the Theses viewed "authentic" feathers dropped by angels, pieces of Mary's girdle, and a twig from Moses' burning bush.

Nevertheless, in a few weeks, Luther's Theses were publicized all over Europe, tapping a pent-up resentment against the church which Luther could not have anticipated. Luther had unwittingly called the church's most lucrative form of fundraising a fraud. He believed in the doctrine of indulgences, but was totally against the abuse of the doctrine by the wicked and greedy. Little did he realize that the pope had in fact condoned their methods and was skimming some of the profits for himself.

That his act could set off such violence and separation only underscores the fact that the Reformation milieu was ready for explosion. Political, economic, and social factors combined to inflame the religious and intellectual tinder in a way that would not have been possible decades earlier.

THE ENVIRONMENT

Politically, the early sixteenth century had witnessed the growth of national consciousness among citizens and the rise of nation-states and absolute governments on a level unparalleled in medieval history. The feudal system had crumbled in France, England, and Spain, and the German territories that lacked such freedom seethed with discontent. Kings, dukes, and princes vied with the Roman Catholic church for political dominance in their lands, and some would choose the fledgling Protestant movement to express their territorial particularism.

Economically, these leaders questioned how they could be absolute in their domain when the richest and strongest institution was the church. The massive wealth of the church and its tax base was coveted by the powerful as much as it was despised by the lower classes. On the other hand, church properties could not be taxed; and the vast economic empire controlled by the papacy led to price fluctuations, depression, and unemployment. A great economic gulf separated the emerging middle class from the aristocrats.

Socially, these factors led to unrest and rebellion. Peasant rebellions occurred even before Martin Luther's time. Since the church was basic to medieval society, the whole social fabric was questioned when the church was questioned. The emergence of towns and cities spelled the death knell for the manor, and the price revolution of speculation and industry dispelled the medieval claim that the clergy was the "head" of society, the nobility the "arms," and the peasantry the "feet"—a hierarchy supposedly dictated by God. "Individualism" and "religious freedom" were not only the rallying cries of the Renaissance; they quickly became fundamental principles of Protestantism.

The Age of Exploration with its more precise navigation aids and better sailing ships not only opened up new missionary enterprises for the Roman Catholic church but also contributed to new ideas and expressions that infused the Reformation spirit. Inventions such as the printing press and movable type encouraged the spread of ideas. Martin Luther soon learned the power of the printed word and geared his writing to the language of the common men and women. The German territories on the eve of the Reformation were intensely religious, and the Lutheran Reformation was to have an enormous impact on church history.

THE LUTHERAN REFORMATION

In spite of the many luminaries of the Protestant Reformation, Martin Luther (1483–1546) stands out as *the* reformer. He is the man whose protest came at a critical juncture of history and whose Lutheran Reformation contributed to the multifaceted dynamic of Protestantism.

Born in Eisleben in Saxony, Martin Luther was the son of a peasant who had used a mining career to rise to the middle class. Eventually, his father owned several foundries and was able to support Martin's education toward a law career at the University of Erfurt. Although he received his bachelor's degree in 1502 and his master's in 1505, Martin turned from the lucrative course his father had planned for him and entered the Augustinian monastery in Erfurt. During a summer lightning storm he had cried out to St. Anne for help, vowing to become a monk if spared. He kept his word, and with an unusual range of gifts became one of the most devoted members in that austere order. In 1507, he was ordained a priest and soon was overcome with a sense of unworthiness, gripped by terror as he held the very body and blood of Christ in the Mass.

Johann von Staupitz (c. 1460–1524), vicar-general over the monastery, became his mentor. When Luther's excessive penance and monastic discipline endangered his health, von Staupitz persuaded him that such guilt was not part of the Christian life. The young priest was encouraged to pursue further biblical studies and received his doctorate in 1512. He was appointed professor of theology at the University of Wittenberg, which had been founded in 1502. This university would be his home for the rest of his life and became a central component in the Lutheran Reformation.

In young Luther's mind, the "justice" of God had been linked to severe punishment and retribution. He felt overwhelmed by the demands of such a God, subconsciously identifying them with the excessive discipline of his parents. As he began teaching and embarking on further study, however, he came to the realization that the "justice of God" was actually linked to the "grace of God." Through Jesus Christ, a gracious God had reached out to mankind in spite of the fact that men and women did not deserve such love. Luther began to understand passages of the Bible that he had feared, such as Rom. 1:17 ("For in it [the Gospel] the righteousness of God is revealed from

23

faith to faith; as it is written, But the righteous man shall live by faith [Hab. 2:4]"). In his own words, such a realization led him to be "born anew" and the gates of heaven seemed to be "opened." The "justice of God" no longer filled him with "hatred" but with "great love."

To Luther, faith was a person's response to the grace of God, a life-transforming force that had created "a different spirit and a different mind" in that person. His young friend and colleague at Wittenberg, Philip Melanchthon (1497–1560), would later formulate such thoughts in the Augsburg Confession (1530) and its Apology (1531). To Melanchthon, good works were bound to flow from the new relationship between God and humankind, and he uses the Latin terms *regeneratio* (to be born again) and *vivificatio* (to be made alive again) to express the new life God's grace gives to the believer. Luther stated that he preferred "the books of Master Philippus" to his own and, indeed, Melanchthon became one of the gentler spirits in a violent, argumentative age.

As Pope Leo X sought to blunt the effects of the Ninety-Five Theses and the subsequent Lutheran movement, Luther's thinking progressed and matured into many of the concepts and principles that became central to Protestantism. As early as 1520, he published important essays that asserted the clergy was not above the laity and the church was not above the state. He also declared that every Christian as part of the body of Christ is important and that the vocation of baker or housewife is as sacred as the life of a monk. While a gracious God offered salvation as a free gift, Luther instructed, Christians are bound to love God with all their hearts and to love their neighbors as themselves. Such faith, Luther asserted, is declared in the authoritative Scriptures that are interpreted by one's conscience and is an absolute trust in God rather than a trust in political or ecclesiastical leadership.

Martin Luther's passion for truth and justice is an appealing aspect of this Protestant spirit and at times he was able to rise above his culture. On other occasions, his harsh and often vulgar phrases were deeply rooted in the psyche of the populace and more appropriate for the banter of the tavern. His humanness is both appealing and frustrating — encompassing the curse, blessing, and test that face the modern Protestant today.

For example, in a culture and church where hatred of Jewish

24

people was widespread, Martin Luther seemed to be a breath of fresh air. In his treatise *That Jesus Christ Was Born a Jew* (1523), he took a firm stand against mistreatment of Jews throughout the history of the church and advocated a new relationship with them. He reminded his readers that Jesus Christ was a Jew and sadly recounted the horrors that the medieval church had heaped on Christ's kin. "If I had been a Jew and had seen such dolts and blockheads govern and teach the Christian faith, I would sooner have become a hog than a Christian," Luther wrote. The Jewish people viewed the Lutheran Reformation as an opportunity for religious freedom, an opportunity to be treated as human beings.

Alas, Luther expected Jewish people to convert to Christianity once they heard a Christian gospel free from "papal paganism." Soon he became irritated with them, complaining about their stubbornness and beginning to use the caricatures of his day. In 1543, at the end of his life, he wrote three derogatory treatises against Jews which anti-Semites would quote for the next four hundred years. So revolting were his statements that Julius Streicher, Adolf Hitler's hate-sheet editor and propagandist in *Der Stürmer*, cited Luther at his Nuremberg trials to justify his actions.

Luther's failure to rise above the anti-Semitic statements and actions of the early church fathers and the medieval church has left the task to other individual Protestants. Some Lutheran thinkers, such as Dietrich Bonhoeffer (1906–45), stood firmly against anti-Semitism, realizing that religious hatred totally ignores Christ's command to love one's neighbor, and is a cancer in the body politic. Luther had inadvertently set some guidelines for this, both in his theological principles and in his belief that the church must be continually reformed and renewed.

THE SWISS REFORMATION

Ulrich Zwingli (1484–1531) led the movement for reformation in the Swiss cantons, especially the German-speaking area of Zurich. Educated at the Universities of Vienna and Basel, he received his bachelor's (1504) and master's (1506) degrees from the latter institution. Steeped in the Humanist reform tradition, he applied reason and intellect to the study of the Scriptures. He came to view the Bible as the supreme authority in matters of faith and practice. Deeply indebted to Erasmus and later influenced by Luther, Zwingli was ordained a priest in 1506; by the time he had arrived in Zurich in 1518, he had acquired a reputation as an expository preacher. With the help and support of the city government, Zwingli was able to institute a Protestant Reformation in Zurich by 1525.

Casting aside outward religious symbols that were not "supported by the Bible," Zwingli differed from Luther by rejecting all material elements that did not meet this standard. Musical instruments were eliminated from the churches and images were banned. The Mass was turned into a "love feast," where both the bread and the wine were passed around to communicants at a white-clothed table in place of an altar. Education was regarded highly, and Zwingli made sure that both a public school and a seminary were located in the city.

A powerful speaker of keen intellect, Zwingli was able to draw other scholars and Humanists to his theological views, including Oecolampadius (1482–1531), soon to become a leading reformer in Basel. In fact, Oecolampadius's path to Protestantism indicates the numerous influences at work in the early sixteenth century. He had contact with both Melanchthon and his granduncle Johann Reuchlin (1455–1522), the outstanding Catholic Hebraist and devout Humanist of the era. Reuchlin had stood boldly against a Hebrew Christian, Joseph Pfefferkorn, who in alliance with the Dominicans had attempted to burn Jewish literature; later Reuchlin had successfully recommended his grandnephew Melanchthon for the teaching post at Wittenberg.

In 1515, Oecolampadius met Erasmus and assisted him in the publication of his Greek New Testament. Three years later as a priest in Augsburg, he was deeply influenced by Luther's teaching, then spent some time in a monastery, and in 1523 was a lecturer in Bible at the University of Basel. By that time, he had become a close friend of Zwingli, instituting many of the Zurich reforms in Basel and preaching for the Protestant cause. He joined Zwingli in responding to Luther's *Larger Confession of the Lord's Supper* (1528) with a defense of the symbolic view of the communion.

One of the key areas that separated Zwingli and Luther was, indeed, their respective views of the presence of Christ in the bread and wine during the Eucharist. While both Reformers condemned the Catholic view of transubstantiation (the belief that the elements changed into the literal body and blood of Christ during the "sacrificial" Mass) and affirmed that *both* the bread and the wine should be a part of the Lord's Supper, Luther insisted that Christ was bodily present in the eucharistic act "in, with, under, around, and behind" the elements. To Luther, Christians literally partook of bread, wine, *and* the body of Christ during communion. He bitterly opposed Zwingli's views that the sacrament of communion was merely a symbol of the spiritual reality of Christ. When both men were brought together at the Marburg Colloquy in 1529 by Philip of Hesse (1504–67) in an attempt to resolve their differences and unite German and Swiss Protestants, Luther insisted from the outset, "The words of God are to be adored and observed with awe. God commands [in Matt. 26:26]: 'Take, eat; this is my body.' I desire a persuasive proof from sacred Scripture." He then wrote in chalk on the table, "*Hoc est meum corpus*," that is, "This is my body."

Although illustrious Reformers such as Oecolampadius, Melanchthon, and Martin Bucer (1491–1551) of Strassburg joined Luther and Zwingli in the discussions, this issue, as well as a basic personality clash between Zwingli and Luther, stymied any possibility of unifying the Reform movement. When Bucer reportedly asked Luther "to confirm that we teach correctly" on the issues of trinity, justification, and baptism on which they agreed, Luther declined to do so. "Will you recognize me as brother or do you think that I err so that I can overcome them?" Bucer pleaded. "Your spirit and our spirit do not go together," Luther reportedly answered in part. He then explained that those who would not accept "the words of Christ" blasphemed the faith.

Within two years, Zwingli lay dead on the battlefield, a victim of the controversy between Catholic and Protestant cantons. The question of Christ's presence during communion continued to be a major issue of debate between Lutherans and the "Zurich Consensus," who became known as the "Reformed."

Bucer untiringly endeavored to discover a way to state the doctrine in a form that both sides could accept, but was unsuccessful. He also attempted, in the 1540s, to bring Catholics and Protestants back together and even mediated in some Anabaptist controversies. His theological contributions did have some effect on the English Reformation (he taught at Cambridge at the end of his life), but realized their greatest potential in a young theologian seventeen years his junior—John Calvin.

John Calvin (1509–64), born in France, was the son of a notary who worked for the Bishop of Noyen. Trained as a Humanist, he was steered by his father into church service at an early age to pay for his education and was led subsequently to a lucrative career in law. John Calvin's first book, *Commentary on Seneca's Treatise On Clemency* (1532), did not even mention religion.

Nevertheless, within two years Calvin had experienced a "sudden conversion" and became a part of the Reformation movement in France. His publication of the first edition of the *Institutes of the Christian Religion* (1536) was popular, but because of the persecution of Protestants under Francis I (1517–47) it made life in France dangerous for him. On his way to Strassburg, he was invited to stay in Geneva and, except for a three-year period, Geneva was his home for the rest of his life.

Although a second-generation reformer of the Protestant movement, Calvin has been often regarded as the "systematizer" of the Reformation because of his expansion of the short six-chapter *Institutes* into a large seventy-nine-chapter comprehensive systematic theology (fifth edition—1559). He also wrote numerous commentaries on books of the Bible. While systematizing Reformation emphases on the authority of the Bible, justification by faith, and the priesthood of all believers, Calvin's great stress on the complete sovereignty of God led him to assert that God *eternally elected* some to be believers and that election *preceded* faith. While this "predestination" was meant to be a liberating doctrine, it was much more rigidly interpreted by some of his successors.

Calvin interpreted the presence of Christ in the communion much as did his friend Martin Bucer, that is, midway between Zwingli's and Luther's viewpoints. Martin Luther regarded highly the early publication of the *Institutes*, and Calvin subsequently joined Bucer and Melanchthon in attempting to unify the Protestant movement. During his lifetime, the *Institutes* enjoyed a widespread influence throughout Europe and his impress on Protestantism continues unabated to this day. The *Institutes* devote large sections to the role of civil government and the believer's relationship to the state.

Interpretations of Protestant reformers' views toward church and state would dominate succeeding generations of prelates and rulers.

CHURCH AND STATE

In light of the turmoil engendered by the Roman occupation of Palestine in the first century C.E., Jesus had remarkably little to say about civil government and his followers' relationship to the state. And yet, what he had to say contradicted future formulations of a Christian state concept. The apostle Paul made no intimation that Christians should even be entertaining the thought of making the pagan Roman Empire a "Christian" republic. The early Christians had simply viewed earthly power as an antithesis to the kingdom of God.

Ironically, when the opportunity for a Christian state came in the fourth century with the rise of Constantine, church leaders succumbed to the favors of the state. By the end of that century, the union of church and state had resulted in the dominance of the church. Even Augustine of Hippo (354–430), who had supported religious liberty when he was among the oppressed, changed his mind when his brand of "orthodox" Christianity was supported by the state. He charged the state to "compel" men and women to conform to his interpretation of Christian doctrines. Asking the state to punish "heretics," he rationalized this compulsion as Christian kindness, "for what is a worse killer of the soul than freedom to err?" His teaching would influence the stand of not only the medieval church, but the Protestant Reformation as well.

In spite of Protestantism's emphasis on individual conscience, most early Protestant groups accepted the sovereignty of the state, that is, Lutherans, the Zurich Consensus, the Reformed, and the Anglicans. In the sixteenth century, this alliance resulted not in the dominance of the church, but in the dominance of the state. Like their forebears in the fourth century, Protestant leaders were the victims of circumstance. While the principles of Protestantism championed the cause of religious liberty, the reality of the Reformation was unprecedented intolerance and cruelty by Protestants and Catholics alike.

As Augustine had, Luther changed when the circumstances were in his favor, unable in practice to rise above a medieval mentality.

29

While facing excommunication and execution, Luther insisted that the state must not bind any law on Christians nor should it be called upon to support theological stances. He knew well the effect of religious intolerance because Charles V (1500–58), the Catholic Holy Roman Emperor, had charged after the Diet of Worms (1521) that Luther's views were a "cesspool of heresies" and he must be hunted down. Luther had presented his case of individual conscience to Charles and the assembly, declaring, "I cannot and I will not recant anything, for to go against conscience is neither right nor safe. God help me. Amen. Here I stand. I cannot do otherwise."

Whisked away by his friends to Wartburg Castle and assured of safety under the protection of Frederick the Wise, Elector of Saxony (1463–1525), Luther not only translated the New Testament into German but also cemented his relationship with the German princes. In 1528, the state gained final control of both religion and education in the German territories. The dignity and splendor of the First and Second Diets of Spires (1526 and 1529) underscored the fact that Luther had the support of a rising German nationalism among princes and populace. Even the Swiss city of St. Gallen signed a protest and appeal to the emperor on April 25, 1529, supporting Protestant principles.

Secure under the protection of secular rulers and directly in a pact with the state, Luther began to insist that "heretics are not to be disputed with, but to be condemned unheard" by fire and sword. Even Melanchthon, who is so often the sweet spirit of the Lutheran movement and who early on opposed severe methods against religious dissenters, changed his view to support state persecution of heretics and those who would foster "new opinions." The concept of the "Christian state" had become a postulate of their theology.

In Zurich, Zwingli viewed his mission as spanning the temporal as well as the ecclesiastical. Every stage of his religious reform had to be endorsed by the civil authorities and promoted by political power. Groups that sought to transmute his Reformation principles of individual conscience and biblical authority to a dimension beyond the civil sphere, such as the Swiss Brethren (see below), faced Zwingli's religious wrath and persecution by the "republican" officials of Zurich.

The latter-day reformer, John Calvin, initially pleaded for religious toleration from the Catholic nation-state of France. "They charged me with two of the worst crimes—heresy and schism," he lamented in a letter to Cardinal Sadoleto, "and the heresy was, that I dared to protest against dogmas which they received." When the possibility existed of turning Geneva into a Protestant Christian city, however, Calvin progressively came to emphasize the visible "dominion" of the saints.

In contrast to Luther, who progressively acquiesced to state control of religion, Calvin treated church and state as one single community organized in two distinct ways. While both were to be submitted to the "sovereignty of God," the state's obligation was to render service to the church and "God's dominion" of the earth. Magistrates were seen to be invested with divine authority and to represent the person of God. And yet, although he constantly pointed to the divine right of rulers, for Calvin the church in reality functioned as the real master in determining the state's character and goals.

In his established "theocracy" at Geneva, therefore, Calvin insisted that it was not only proper to put "heretics" and "blasphemers" to death, but declared culpable those who believed such actions to be unjust. During his rigid rule, criticism of the clergy was included in the crime of blasphemy. In spite of attempts by revisionists to explain away the murder and atrocities committed under Calvin at Geneva, he was neither tolerant nor democratic in our modern understanding of those terms. Egalitarian democracy was not an idea favored by Calvin, and pluralistic society would find it impossible to survive under his dictums. The Unitarian Michael Servetus (1511–54) was only one of the most famous of those executed at Geneva. He was burned to death, although Calvin had argued that beheading him would have been more humane.

In the union of church and state in the sixteenth century, Protestant principles were bent and distorted. The conventional clichés of an egalitarian society were often present on the theoretical level; but Protestant leaders found themselves uncritically accepting a sordid situation. Their "freedom of worship" turned in many cases to exclusive privilege, and some Protestant leaders became drunk with new-found power. In some cases, they succumbed to the state's all-absorbing interference in religious affairs. The English Reformation, for example, was intricately intertwined with the personality and problems of one man, King Henry VIII (1491–1547). A staunch defender of the Catholic faith, he led the nation out of the realm of

Rome when Pope Clement VII hesitated to annul his marriage of more than twenty years to Catherine of Aragon. He divorced Catherine anyway and married his mistress, Anne Boleyn. The Act of Supremacy of 1534 made the King of England supreme over the Church of England.

THE RADICAL REFORMATION

Little wonder then that by 1535, fifty thousand Anabaptist Protestants had been put to death with the blessings of Luther, Zwingli, Calvin, and Henry VIII (as well as the Roman Catholic church). The Anabaptists plagued these Protestants because they called into question the union of church and state, they maintained that the Protestant Reformation had not gone far enough, and they asserted their right to interpret the Bible by their own individual conscience. Although they were nicknamed Anabaptists (again baptizers) because they denied the validity of the infant baptism upheld by the major Protestant groups and insisted upon adult "believer baptism," they felt the title to be inappropriate. They believed that their baptism (often by immersion) was their first, and only valid, public confession of faith. In tragic mockery, many of them were drowned by their opponents.

Although most Anabaptist groups were pacifists, they were felt by a majority of Protestants, who were still fighting against Catholic armies, to be a dangerous, subversive sect. Protestant leaders also rationalized that a proliferation of Anabaptists might lead to anarchy. In spite of other differences, both the Catholic and Protestant leaders agreed at the Second Diet of Spires that Anabaptists were heretics worthy of death and therefore supported the Catholic emperor's edict against them. The only German prince unwilling to implement the emperor's edict was Philip of Hesse.

This early struggle is clearly evident in Zurich. Zwingli had never intended to progress with his reforming effort beyond the dictates of city officials. As they were convinced of the accuracy of his teaching and the need for reform, he supported them in their implementation of new regulations and directives "of the spirit." He did, however, encourage his adherents to go directly to the Bible as their spiritual source and advocated the Protestant principle of individual conscience.

One of Zwingli's converts, Conrad Grebel (c. 1498–1526), a well-educated Humanist and aristocrat, took his mentor at his word and began to study the New Testament diligently in Greek. He concluded that both the mass and infant baptism were unscriptural. Joined by others in a home Bible study, Grebel emphasized that Zwingli was progressing much too slowly in reforming Zurich because he insisted on the approval of the city council before implementing reforms. He and his friend, Felix Manz (c. 1498–1527), the son of a Zurich canon, tried unsuccessfully to convince Zwingli to renounce infant baptism and establish a church on the New Testament model without state support and paid clergy. In 1525, Zwingli opposed them in a public disputation before city council. The council declared Zwingli's viewpoint to be in accordance with the law and decreed that *all* children were to be baptized. Those who would not obey this decree would suffer imprisonment and banishment.

Defying the ban, Grebel baptized Georg Blaurock (c. 1492–1529) in Manz's home. Blaurock then baptized the others present. Both Manz and Grebel were imprisoned for their actions; but their quiet testimony of interpreting and following the Bible by individual conscience won many to the Anabaptist cause. These acts of defiance forced the city council to pass more stringent laws in 1526, including death by drowning for those who "rebaptized."

Grebel was so weakened by his imprisonment that he died shortly thereafter. Manz was drowned early in 1527 in the Limmat River, a Protestant martyred by Protestants. Blaurock was banished from the city the same day Manz was sentenced. He then traveled through central Europe as an evangelist, winning thousands to the Anabaptist cause.

On his way to death, Manz is recorded to have praised God that he could die "for the sake of truth." He emphasized that those who followed Christ would have to suffer and sang out in a clear voice just before he was dropped into the water, *"In manus tuas, Domine, Commendo spiritum meum"* ("Lord, into Thy hands I commend my spirit").

Soon thereafter, a group of Swiss Brethren met at Schleitheim on the border to "make known in points and articles to all who love God that as concerns us we are of one mind to abide in the Lord as God's obedient children, sons and daughters, we who have been and shall be separated from the world in everything, completely at peace." The

33

ensuing Anabaptist document, largely the work of Michael Sattler (1490–1527), became known as the Schleitheim Confession of 1527.

Although intensely persecuted by both Catholics and Protestants, the Anabaptist movement underscored concepts of individual conscience, freedom of religion, grace, faith, biblical authority, and the priesthood of all believers that Protestantism would treasure as its intrinsic heritage. This "radical" Reformation was in many ways echoing precepts taught by the dominant groups of the "magisterial" Reformation. In subsequent centuries, Protestantism would learn to rise often above sectarian disputes over baptism, church polity, and communion. State churches would become a phantom of the past.

WOMEN

The plight of women during the Reformation era was akin to that of medieval society. Often they were treated as lower-class citizens and restricted from leadership functions in politics and in the church. Men dominated the printed word, and detraction of women had been a male sport for millenniums. In spite of this, the influence of women on the early Protestant movement must not be minimized, for their influence was felt at every level.

Women of wealth and nobility, such as Elizabeth of Braunschweig (1510–1558), supported the Protestant cause with generous gifts of time and money. Others, such as Elisabeth of Brandenburg (1485–1545), were quickly impoverished and abandoned because of their brave stand. In 1523, when those around her refused to speak out against the forced recantation of a young professor at the University of Ingolstadt for his espousal of "Wittenberg theology," noblewoman Argula von Grumback (c. 1492–1563) wrote a spirited letter of protest, replete with scriptural references. Other women followed her lead.

Women of royalty, such as Elizabeth I (1533–1603), for forty-five years queen of England, were among the few involved in national administrative functions by virtue of their office (see chap. 4). Other noblewomen, however, encouraged their husbands to espouse Protestantism, ensuring the longevity of the fledgling movement. Most had to manipulate the political structure "from the outside," as women had done for centuries.

Nevertheless, the translation of the Bible into the common language of the people and the availability of such printed copies provided women with the opportunity to steep themselves in the Scriptures. In spite of the laborious duties of mothering families of ten or more and tending to numerous household duties, these women diligently read their Bibles and could give their inquisitors and judges an interpretive battle on any point of theology, as many trial documents attest.

Most of the Reformers married, and the importance of the women in their lives is amply illustrated. For example, Luther referred to his wife, Katherine von Bora (1499–1550), as "My Lord," and declared, "In domestic affairs, I defer to Katie. Otherwise I am led by the Holy Ghost." He called one of his favorite books of the Bible, *Galatians*, "My Katherine von Bora," and had no qualms about indicating the influence she had in his life since their marriage in 1525. Besides keeping the reformer as healthy as possible and carefully managing the household funds which Luther easily let slip through his fingers, she strengthened his resolve at times to answer polemical attacks and was not loath to put up a good argument herself when she differed with him theologically.

Katherine had been a nun, and it was not uncommon in the Protestant movement for former priests and nuns to marry. These devotees to God brought a strong religious consecration to their union, a "meeting of the minds" for their cause. Children from such families became the backbone of future Protestant generations, providing both leaders and thinkers.

It was among the Anabaptists, however, that the common women's role in the spiritual enterprise sprang forth. In most Anabaptist groups, women had the same rights as men, a number assuming pastoral responsibilities as well as administrative duties. Women joined this movement in great numbers, and the incredible steadfastness of these under intense persecution from both Catholic and Protestant authorities is staggering. Many died bravely for their faith, looking toward a day when freedom of religion and individual conscience would be practiced in deed as well as word.

Today, the women of Protestantism continue to struggle with concepts of liberation and equality as they seek to fulfill their role in the movement. As that role is debated and defined in numerous social arenas and vocational areas, the historic groundwork laid by the brave women of the Reformation era must not be forgotten.

CATHOLIC REFORMATION

As the brushfire of reforming Protestantism swept across Europe in the 1500s, it appeared to many that nothing could stop it from throwing the whole Western church into division and chaos. By mid-century, however, the Roman Catholic church had not only stemmed the Protestant "explosion" but had nearly accomplished its own reform.

As we have seen in the precursors to the Protestant Reformation (chap. 2), the spirit of reform had been kindled in the church even before Luther. This preliminary corps helped the Catholic church to counter Protestantism, a movement it viewed as divisive and heretical. Whereas cries for reform had fallen upon deaf ears in earlier decades, the Catholic church now set about with purpose cleaning up abuse and corruption.

In Spain, Queen Isabella (1451–1504) determined to restore the church to its former glory in the latter quarter of the fifteenth century. Using the devoted Francisco Jiménez (c. 1436–1517), a man who abhorred corruption and was revered for his spiritual depth, she instituted a rigorous reform throughout the Spanish church. Clergy were educated, their vows were strictly enforced, and charitable institutions were given new impetus. Convents and monasteries became bastions of spiritual renewal. Even the corrupt Pope Alexander VI was enlisted to give the Queen and her confessor the power they needed to accomplish such religious reform.

Pope Alexander VI sought strong political connections with the Spanish Reformation because Spain was expanding into a powerful nation-state during this period. Closer to home in Florence, however, he deplored the reforming Dominican friar, Girolamo Savonarola (1452–1498), who would not bow to Alexander's request to join in war against France. The fiery preacher, who had been gladly accepted as spiritual leader of the city-state, lost his popularity as Pope Alexander exerted political and economic pressure on Florence. Arrested, Savonarola was tortured by papal inquisitors who could not obtain a confession of heretical guilt. He finally was declared a heretic and schismatic in general, and was hanged. His body was then burned, and his ashes were scattered to erase all traces of his existence. Ironically, his possessions became relics, and his reform sermons were long remembered, adding another thread to the reform trend throughout the church.

In Spain, too, intolerance reigned. In cleaning up morals and abuse among Christians, Queen Isabella also caused Jews and Muslims to suffer and die for their beliefs. The infamous connotation of the Spanish Inquisition and the expulsion of Jews and Moors from Spain in 1492 are only two of the survivals of the fanatical, cruel "devotion" of Isabella and Jiménez. Nevertheless, Spain became the seedbed of the Catholic Reformation, and Jiménez as archbishop of Toledo continued the reform after Isabella's death. It has been suggested that if Jiménez had been in the German territories rather than in Spain, Luther would have had no reason to affix the Ninety-Five Theses on the door of the Wittenberg Church. The spark would not have had the tinder to ignite the flame.

Reforming Catholic orders were established that breathed vitality and piety into the church as well. The Oratory of Divine Love was founded the same year Luther posted the Theses (1517); an Italian order dedicated to service to the poor, brotherhood, prayer, and reform, it was later used by Pope Paul III (1534–49) to investigate clerical immorality. Reformist Pope Paul IV (1476–1559) was a member of this order. The Theatines (1524) was an offshoot of this group dedicated to strict discipline in serving the poor and was intensely involved in reforming clergy and nobility. Many reform bishops would arise from this order.

The Society of Jesus, founded by Ignatius of Loyola (1491/95–1556), was dedicated in 1534 to education and missions. Its chief goal was to restore the Catholic church to its former glory, and it was committed to absolute obedience to the reforming papacy. Loyola's *Spiritual Exercises* emphasized each person's free will to choose to serve God totally. Receiving its final form in 1548, it had an immense effect on Catholic piety for the next four centuries.

Women led the movement for Catholic reform. Mystics, such as Teresa of Avila (1515–82), combined a deep spiritual experience with a traditional devotion to the church. Lay men and women were joyous as the renewal was being accomplished in their church; and women especially performed the tedious tasks of nursing the sick and caring for the poor. The Ursulines, an order of women founded in

1535, was dedicated to meeting the needs of the sick, helping the poor, and educating girls.

Prodded by reform from within and without, traditional Catholicism called for a general council to solidify the reform impulse and centralize it. Pope Paul III enlisted an assembly of theologians, national representatives, and clergy in December 1545. This Council of Trent would meet sporadically for eighteen years through the rule of five popes. In 1564, Pope Pius IV invoked the Tridentine Profession of Faith ratifying and encapsulating the findings and actions of the council, a monumental task of great significance.

At the Council of Trent, Catholic reformers carried the day, instituting reforms in the moral and disciplinary realm that revived the respect and allegiance of the common people. Scripture and tradition were affirmed as the foundation of this Christian community, the pope mediating as the final authority in conflicting interpretations.

In regard to Protestantism, however, the Council of Trent did not move toward reconciliation. Although church leaders such as Gasparo Contarini (1483–1542) and Reginald Pole (1500–1558) argued for concessions and reunion, the decrees of the council were extremely critical of Protestants. Not a single concession was made to the Protestant movement. The break was irreparable.

THE REFORMATION ERA AND
PROTESTANTISM

Taken in its variegated forms, the Reformation era was a landmark for Protestantism. Not only did it receive its name and identity during this period, but the principles so intrinsic to the meaning of Protestantism today were at the same time visible, dynamic ingredients during the Reformation. Certainly, the violent, intolerant age of the sixteenth century covered, and sometimes smothered, the light of those principles. In an era that believed religious uniformity was necessary for the healthy existence of nations and duchies, Protestant principles of individual conscience and freedom of religion lay dormant only to be reawakened in verbal barrage against the Roman Catholic church. Sadly, the principle of the priesthood of *all* believers lost out at times to sectarian triumphalism and political expedience. And yet, the Reformation underscored the fact that the principles of Protestantism were too dynamic to be encompassed by a single era or church polity. Protestant principles simply transcended the historical reality of Protestantism itself. As Paul Tillich (1886–1965) was later to affirm, "What makes Protestantism Protestant is the fact that it transcends its own religious and confessional character, that it cannot be identified wholly with any of its particular historical forms."

Thus, Protestantism would come to evaluate every expression of religion and culture in light of its concepts and principles. It would even critically evaluate the Reformation era.

SUGGESTED READING

Bainton, Roland H. *Erasmus of Christendom*. New York: Charles Scribner's Sons, 1969.
———. *Here I Stand: A Life of Martin Luther*. Nashville: Abingdon-Cokesbury Press, 1950.
———. *The Reformation of the Sixteenth Century*. Boston, Beacon Press, 1952.
Bireley, Robert. *Religion and Politics in the Age of Counterreformation*. Chapel Hill, N.C.: Univ. of North Carolina Press, 1981.
Clebsch, William A. *England's Earliest Protestants, 1520–1535*. New Haven, Conn.: Yale Univ. Press, 1980.
Davies, C. S. *Print and Protestantism, 1450–1558*. New York and London: Oxford Univ. Press, 1976.
Dickens, A. G. *The Counter-Reformation*. New York: W. W. Norton, 1979.
Grimm, Harold J. *The Reformation Era, 1500–1650*. 2d ed. New York: Macmillan Co., 1973.
Littell, Franklin H. *The Free Church*. Boston: Beacon Press, 1957.
Manschreck, Clyde L. *Melanchthon: The Quiet Reformer*. Nashville: Abingdon Press, 1958.
Oberman, Heiko A. *The Roots of Anti-Semitism in the Age of Renaissance and Reformation*. Philadelphia: Fortress Press, 1984.
Olin, John C., ed. *The Catholic Reformation: Savonarola to Ignatius Loyola, 1495–1540*. New York: Harper & Row, 1969.
Oyer, John S. *Lutheran Reformers Against Anabaptists*. The Hague: Martinus Nijhoff, 1964.
Rilliet, Jean Horace. *Zwingli: Third Man of the Reformation*. Philadelphia: Westminster Press, 1964.
Spitz, Lewis W. *The Protestant Reformation*. New York: Harper & Row, 1984.

Stauffer, Richard. *The Humanness of John Calvin.* Nashville: Abingdon Press, 1971.

Wendel, Francois. *Calvin: The Origins and Development of His Religious Thought.* New York: Harper & Row, 1963.

Williams, George H. *The Radical Reformation.* Philadelphia: Westminster Press, 1962.

Yoder, John H., ed. *The Legacy of Michael Sattler.* Scottdale, Pa.: Herald Press, 1973.

4

PURITANISM AND PIETISM

Emperor Charles V, born in 1500, was heir to an empire greater than that of Charlemagne. Self-confident and brave, his blue-grey eyes and prominent chin suggest an imperial challenge in a portrait from the early 1520s. Dedicated to the Roman Catholic church, he knew that he alone was in a political position to guarantee the unity of Christendom; and he dedicated his resources and talents to that end.

War with France and the Turks and contention with other rebellions kept him from crushing the growing Protestant movement. By the time he was able to give it his full attention, its roots were too firmly established. Military force and imperial pressure for a general council could not mend the breach within the church, and the emperor's portrait in 1548 depicts him as weary and prematurely aged. His eyes are still alert, but a certain resignation shows through. Charles's life spanned almost a half-century of religious, social, and political upheaval which had left its mark.

Having failed in his attempt to reunite his treasured church, Charles abdicated and returned to Spain. Tired and discouraged, he built a modest villa next to a monastery. After lengthy negotiations with the German princes, the best he could accomplish was the Peace of Augsburg (1555).

The Peace of Augsburg established the principle of *cuius regio, eius religio,* literally, "whose region, his religion." It stated that each prince determined the religion of his territory, and a Catholic prince who converted thereafter to Protestantism would forfeit his title, lands, and privileges. Church property that had been taken by the Protestants was to remain in their possession, but further confiscation was not to be tolerated. Catholics and Protestants were also compelled to promise that they would remain at peace with one another, and both groups were assured by the empire that their rights would remain secure. Although conflicts would later break out, the Peace of Augsburg was a recognition of the fact that Europe was not unified politically, socially, or religiously. Ultimately this treaty became a landmark in Western history.

By the summer of 1558, Charles was dying, In his last painful weeks, he adjured his son Philip to deal harshly with two nests of "Lutheran heresy" that had appeared in his beloved Spain. Almost to his last breath, this problem consumed him. It was as though Charles's failure in the German territories alerted him to the potential strength of Protestant principles and ideals. He died on September 21, 1558, imbued with the medieval spirit of devotion and faith to the end. Contemporary Europe knew that a great man had passed, and that a new era had begun.

SCHOLASTIC ORTHODOXY

After Luther's death in 1546, Philip Melanchthon took his place as leader of the movement, participating in negotiations and disputations. Doctrinal disagreements were plentiful in Lutheran circles. Debate raged over such issues as the role of faith and works in the justification process, the elements in the Lord's Supper, and the preaching of the law or the gospel in the churches. Lutheran theologians soon divided into two major camps: Philippists, the followers of Melanchthon; and the more conservative strict Lutherans.

Melanchthon deplored such division and controversy. He had often worked for compromise and unity, and these arguments and divisions served only to remind him of his inability to unify the reform movement. At his death in 1560, a note was found in which he explained why he was not afraid to die. One of the reasons he cited was that he would be set free "from the fury of theologians."

The Lutheran controversies were settled later in the Formula of Concord (1577); and the *Book of Concord* (1580) combined this Formula, Lutheran creeds, catechisms, and articles of faith into a complete statement of Lutheran theology. In subsequent decades, Protestant theologians, Lutheran and Reformed, would achieve harmony in their obsessive pursuit of *total systems* of doctrine, much like those the medieval scholastics had sought. This "Protestant Scholasticism" aimed at uniformity of truth but, in some cases, degenerated into a rigid confessionalism and dogmatic exclusivism that ran counter to the authentic spirit of Protestantism.

For example, the Synod of Dort (1618-19), one of the most famous meetings in the history of the Reformed church, condemned the theology of Dutch Reformed pastor and professor, Jacob Arminius (1560-1609). Issuing a mandatory five-point Calvinist program — total depravity, unconditional election, limited atonement, irresistible grace, perseverance of the saints — it sentenced some pastors in the Arminian party in the Netherlands to life imprisonment. Others were excommunicated and forced to leave the country.

About the same time in Lutheran circles, Georg Calixtus (1586-1656), professor of theology in Helmstadt, attempted to reconcile factions of the Christian church by arguing for a consensus of the "fundamentals" of the Christian faith. The scholastics of Lutheran orthodoxy, however, rejected his pleas for Christian unity, labeling him a "syncretist." In recent times, Calixtus has been hailed as a forerunner of the modern ecumenical movement.

Doctrinal formulation and uniformity in Lutheran and Reformed circles established standards and norms upon which future religious discussion and Biblical analyses would be based. The proponents of scholastic orthodoxy sincerely sought God's truth for their particular tradition. Yet such orthodoxy turned the theology of Martin Luther or John Calvin into such a strict system that either reformer might have had difficulty recognizing the "spirit" of his own Christian faith in the cold calculations of his "followers."

THE PURITANS

Within the Anglican church, too, such changes and controversies were occurring. In an age of reform and doctrinal formation, some individuals in the Church of England believed that the English Reformation had not gone far enough. During the later sixteenth century, under Elizabeth I's reign (1558-1603), those who sought the "purification" of the worship and ceremony of Anglicanism from Roman Catholic influence succeeded in uniting. While they differed in their timing, tactics, and ultimate goals, they were all dissatisfied with the established order.

By the 1590s, Queen Elizabeth enacted a statute against those who "obstinately refuse" to attend Anglican services and who "deny, withstand, and impugn her majesty's power and authority in causes ecclesiastical. . . . " Persons over sixteen years of age who preached or wrote against the Anglican church or assembled in their own church services were to be imprisoned. Acts were also passed against nonconforming Roman Catholics. By the end of Elizabeth's reign, the Puritan was viewed as an odd, hypocritical, seditious individual.

The circumstances of Henry VIII's break with Rome had precipitated these difficulties for Elizabeth. Henry's secession from the church was strictly political, for he had been a staunch Catholic. The Act of Supremacy (1534) had made the sovereign of England supreme head of the Church of England; but it must be remembered that Henry's Six Articles (1539) were extremely Catholic in nature. They advocated transubstantiation, the withholding of the cup in the Eucharist, celibacy of the priesthood, vows, private masses (even for the dead), and auricular confession.

Under Edward VI (1547–53), Protestantism was favored more, and the Forty-two Articles (1553) replacing the Six Articles were decidedly Protestant in content. The Book of Common Prayer (1549), however, seemed to satisfy neither the Roman Catholics nor the Protestants. Queen Mary I, Mary Tudor (1553–58), reinstated Catholicism and the Six Articles. Nicknamed "Bloody Mary," she persecuted so many Protestants that by the time of her death all England was ready to rebel.

Queen Elizabeth, therefore, had to steer a middle course among numerous opposing factions. Her Supremacy Act of 1559 made her "supreme governor" over the Anglican church, and a revised Book of Common Prayer was instituted in the same year. Her Thirty-Nine Articles (1563) became the foundation stones of Anglicanism, repudiating purgatory, the papacy, and relics. By 1570, Pope Pius V (1566–72) had excommunicated Elizabeth as "a heretic and an abettor of heretics," but there was no one to enforce this edict. The Anglican church was well established under Elizabeth's stable and effective rule. Conformity to that church's episcopal power was viewed as essential to the nation's social and political fabric.

Puritans like Thomas Cartwright (1535–1603) were led by their consciences to "purify" this system. A professor of theology at Cambridge University, Cartwright advocated a Presbyterian form of church government with the abolition of "popish" offices (such as archbishops) and the election of pastors by their people. Insisting upon a return to the Biblical norms of church worship, Cartwright opposed kneeling for communion and making the sign of the cross. Deprived of fellowship in the state church, he lost his teaching position and was persecuted. Nevertheless, forty years after his death, English Presbyterianism blossomed; and the Westminster Confession of Faith (1647) was adopted. The confession became one of the foremost documents of orthodox Calvinism in English-speaking countries.

Advocates of a more congregational form of church government, such as Henry Jacob (1563–1624), charted a course for English Congregationalism that later developed the Savoy Declaration of Faith and Order (1658). Although imprisoned under James I (1566–1625) and banished to Holland for ten years (1606–16), Henry Jacob founded the first Congregational church in England in Southwark, London, in 1616. He insisted that Christian congregations have the right to manage their own internal affairs and to choose their own pastors — hence, Congregationalism. By the 1660s, Congregationalism was more powerful than Presbyterianism in England.

Both Cartwright and Jacob sought reforms *within* the confines of the Anglican church. Other groups, however, were convinced that the Anglican church could never be "purified." These "separatist" Congregationalists aimed to set up their own church by a voluntary covenant with one another. They believed the Biblical principles they had delineated should be introduced immediately and with one accord. In addition, a splinter group from Henry Jacob's congregation went to London in 1633, advocating immersion in baptism and a stricter Calvinism. The Particular (Calvinist) Baptist movement owes its formation to this group.

Nevertheless, others joined the Calvinistic persuasion and thus became a significant factor in the House of Commons in Parliament during the early seventeenth century. Under James I, son of Mary Stuart, Queen of Scots, tensions between Puritans and the Anglican church increased. James hated the Presbyterians of Scotland where he had reigned as James VI until the death of Elizabeth. He had sought to impose various forms of the episcopacy over the Presbyterian structure in Scotland made more rigid by reformer John Knox (c. 1514–72). Although James initially tolerated Puritanism in England when he succeeded Elizabeth in 1603, he was firmly committed to the episcopal form of church government. This was immediately evident in the Hampton Court Conference that he convened in 1604. The conference was called ostensibly to provide a forum between the Anglican bishops and the Puritan leadership, but most of the Puritan demands were dismissed. Both parties did agree that translation be undertaken of a Bible for the English-speaking world. The subsequent Authorized Version of 1611, often referred to as the King James Version, became the Bible of English-speaking Protestants for nearly three centuries. James ordered that a copy be chained in every church in the kingdom, thus making it available to all people.

Both Puritans and Anglicans insisted on the Bible as their criterion in doctrine and forms of worship. Article 20 of the Church of England's Thirty-Nine Articles, for example, declares that "it is not lawful for the Church to ordain anything that is contrary to God's word written." Nevertheless, their differences as to how those Scriptures were to be interpreted and enforced grew wider. The struggle between the groups came to a climax in the reign of Charles I (1625–49). Charles lost both his throne and his life in the resulting Civil Wars (1645 and 1648), and the Puritans were able briefly to enforce their form of government under the Commonwealth of Oliver Cromwell (1653–58). Anglicanism and the episcopal system ultimately prevailed. A century later, however, the "Glorious Revolution" brought William and Mary to the throne in 1689; and they decreed religious toleration to anyone subscribing to the Thirty-Nine Articles and swearing loyalty to the monarchs.

THE NEW WORLD

As Puritanism increased in political power in England, English Protestantism was having an important effect on the eastern seaboard of North America. Dissident Puritans found that they could emigrate to America to escape England's archbishops and England's jails. They would attempt to follow their conscience in perfect obedience to God and God's written word, the Bible.

Some had come by way of the European continent. In Leyden, Holland, for example, a separatist group from England sent members from their church to America. These 101 Pilgrims sailed on the Mayflower, establishing Congregationalism in their new colony of Plymouth in 1620. During the next twenty years, over forty thousand

Puritans who were harassed in England fled to America. In the Massachusetts Bay Colony, nonseparatist Congregational Puritans who had no intention of leaving the Church of England gradually shifted into a separatist Congregationalist position. Therefore, New England's Puritans, both separatist and nonseparatist, were soon gathered under a new denomination — Massachusetts, Connecticut, and later, New Hampshire, would be Congregational colonies.

This early period of the history of the United States was dominated by Protestantism. English stock was predominant in the colonial period, and even most of the immigrant groups were Protestant. Catholics were concentrated mainly in Maryland, and by the latter decades of the 1700s were still fewer than twenty thousand in a nation of two and one-half million.

Furthermore, Calvinism shaped colonial religious attitudes. Both the Anglicans who settled in Virginia and the Puritans of New England were greatly influenced by Calvinism. They shared a strong sense of destiny — a belief that God had prepared them as God's agents in the New World. They were to undertake a noble experiment of establishing the kingdom of God on earth, especially in their particular colonies.

Unfortunately, their own desire for freedom of religion did not preclude them from intolerance toward anyone who might deviate from their prescribed religious polity and practice. In the Massachusetts Bay Colony, for example, it was evident that the Puritans had come for their own liberty — not "liberty for all." Believing that the Bible was the rule of life and that the church could reproduce the New Testament model, they sought to enforce a society that reflected their particular interpretation of the will of God. The early Puritan church was a withdrawn and exclusive fellowship, where examination of one's life was both rigorous and frequent. The lines of demarcation between church and state were often blurred. Roger Williams (c. 1603–84) and Anne Hutchinson (1591–1643) were only two of the most famous who were expelled from this colony for blasphemy in the 1630s.

Williams had refused to serve as a pastor in Boston, claiming that civil magistrates were given too much power over an individual's relationship with God. He also insisted that the Indians were deprived of their land unjustly, and *The Bloudy Tenent of Persecution for Cause of Conscience* (1644) advocated religious toleration for all. Although he later went on to be a "seeker," he formed the first Baptist church in Providence, Rhode Island in 1639. The Baptist movement in the United States traces its beginnings to this church.

Other Protestants, however, continued to force their way into exclusive colonies, providing a background for the pluralism that would later be 'characteristic of the new nation. Quakers, Presbyterian Scots, Lutheran and Reformed Germans, French Protestant Huguenots, as well as small enclaves of Roman Catholics and Jews, persistently created a religious mosaic out of intended parochial enclaves. By the time of the Revolutionary War, no single religious polity was strong enough to unite all of the American settlements. In fact, most of the population were not members of a single denomination or church, a fact of great importance in the formation of the American Republic.

PURITAN HERITAGE

In the Puritan Protestant heritage one finds an intense spirit of political liberty and a genuine love of individual freedom in spite of an accompanying intolerance. They had a firm confidence in God's overriding providence and a strong emphasis on faith and works. They sincerely pursued justice and were not afraid to apply their religious beliefs to the political arena.

While attempting to break from the mold of medieval tradition and practice, the Puritans were able to build bridges toward an understanding of the modern world. In the area of marital relations, for example, the Puritans affirmed that marriage was a sharing not only of the spiritual but also of the sensual, recognizing that the sensual had an important part to play. Furthermore, the Puritans were not enemies of learning, but rather believed that "Satan deluded the educationally illiterate." By 1671, all of Puritan New England had a system of compulsory education. Harvard College was founded in 1636 to prepare a literate ministry, enhancing the well-educated Congregationalist pastorate from Cambridge and Oxford.

To the Puritans, theology crowned a pyramid built upon the liberal arts. This included history, literary enterprises, and science. Later Puritans were personally involved in the scientific enterprise. Cotton Mather (1663–1728) wrote America's first treatise on medicine. In

1721, this Puritan minister tried to persuade Bostonians to be immunized against smallpox.

In literature, English Puritan poet John Milton (1608–74) published *Paradise Lost* in 1667, after many years of pamphleteering for the Puritan political cause that ended in the Civil War, and he also served in Cromwell's government. Puritan preacher John Bunyan (1628–88), illiterate until his wife taught him to read, was imprisoned intermittently from 1660 to 1672, but while in jail wrote *Pilgrim's Progress* (published 1678, 1684), still a popular best seller.

PIETISM

While Puritanism attempted to reform the ecclesiastical order through political means, Pietism avoided politics; for Pietism emphasized an individual expression of heartfelt religion that would cultivate a spreading spirituality—a spirituality that would change the church from within.

Pietism challenged the Protestant status quo. It pointed out that Protestant scholasticism and credal formation had drained the life of the church and had produced a hard shell devoid of the very essence of Bible-centered morality. It insisted that intellect and will alone could not lead Protestants to a meaningful relationship with God and neighbor. The love and joy of an emotional commitment to God were also necessary. The Pietist believed that the standards and goals of Scripture and the life of Christ must of necessity be manifest in the dedicated lives of his followers.

Such emphases on "heart religion" were not without antecedents. Some Puritans certainly cultivated religious introspection and emotion. Roman Catholic precursors abounded; and in Judaism, the Hasidic movement was to flourish on such emphases. Lutheran Johann Arndt's *True Christianity* (c. 1606) used medieval mystical sources extensively to assert that orthodoxy was not enough to attain true Christianity. Arndt held that communion with God was much more than credal formation and advocacy. Good works and a holy life were just as important.

Seven decades later, in the midst of an age of orthodoxy and Protestant scholasticism, Philip Jakob Spener (1635–1705) was asked to write an introduction to a new edition of sermons by Arndt. The

49

resulting *Pia Desideria* (Pious Desires) in 1675 became the bulwark of a Pietist revival. A Lutheran pastor who had been deeply impressed by Luther's 1520 essays on the spiritual priesthood of believers, Spener sought to "complete" the Lutheran Reformation. That his plea struck a responsive chord in the populace was due at least in part to the fact that, as in Luther's day, people were incensed at the laxity in the church and cried out for reform. As in Luther's day, too, critical attack would swiftly come from all quarters of the hierarchy, embroiling Spener in controversy for the rest of his life.

Pia Desideria blamed the spiritual decline in Protestant Germany on many different groups and classes, while insisting that a true Reformation had to be the product of every class of Lutheran. Part 1 dealt with the "corrupt conditions" in Lutheranism. The "sins and debaucheries" of the Lutheran civil authorities were not far removed, in Spener's estimation, from the abuses of the Reformation period. They even obstructed the good work proposed by "decent ministers."

In addition, the defects in the clergy consumed Spener. While there were some open scandals, Spener pointed out that many of the clergy did not really understand or practice true Christianity. The work of the church, from care of the needy to spiritual enhancement, suffered while pastors labored to stuff their minds with a theology that missed the simplicity of Christ and his teachings. Theologians occupied themselves with meaningless scholastic exercises, accused Spener. While they preserved the foundation of faith from the Scriptures, he noted that they built on the "wood, hay and stubble" of human inquisitiveness and entirely blocked "the gold" (an allusion to 1 Cor. 3:12).

Spener wrote that without a quality leadership, average church members led mediocre lives. Public regulations meant more to them than the precepts of Christ. Personal welfare and goods far outweighed concern for neighbor (and for God). Vices, such as drunkenness, overwhelmed both the rich and the poor. Spener insisted that the Jewish community was offended at such laxity in the Christian religion as were Catholics and other groups. He noted that they saw no reason to adopt such a hypocritical and negligent religious system.

In his second section, Spener emphasized the possibility of better conditions in the Lutheran church. He was optimistic that the church could be truly reformed and possess true Christianity. In fact, he believed that the church must pursue this goal even if it appeared to be distant.

The third section of *Pia Desideria* gave six concrete proposals — with detailed explanation — to correct conditions in the church. Many of these reasserted principles and concepts that Protestantism had affirmed in the past. They were a definite heritage left to Protestants in the modern age, and they gave an excellent indication of Pietist solutions.

His first proposal was to adopt a more extensive use of the Bible, to read and practice its words. The second proposal insisted that the doctrine of the spiritual priesthood of all believers be exercised. All Christians should be active in the ministry of the church. There is a spiritual function, he maintained, to every vocation.

In proposal three, Spener asserted that Christians must be taught that the key to Christian faith and life consisted in *practice* rather than in knowledge. The spiritual life of individual Christians would have to be cultivated if Christian growth were to take place. One should incline oneself to Christian love toward one's neighbor. The fourth proposal elucidated this theme, urging restraint and love in religious controversies. His plea for toleration was significant in an age of intolerance, and he clearly pointed out that not all theological disputes were useful and good, a concept with important implications for modern Protestants.

The fifth proposal asked that there be more quality of piety and devotion in pastoral candidates. Spener advocated reform in the educational system for ministers. He felt that the spiritual life of the professor was the key to such an enterprise, including the practice of piety and denial of self among teachers. Spener contended that without such attention to practical piety, as well as scholastic exercises, pastoral students might become adept at a "philosophy of sacred things" without understanding the higher theology of communion with God.

His sixth proposal implored ministers to preach sermons that edified the people and could be understood by them. Rather than technical discourses, instruction in the practical fruits of faith and the godly life should always be preached. The Christian religion consists of the inner self, Spener explained. If one merely corrects "outward vices" and practices "outward virtues," one is not more than an "ethical heathen." True love of God and neighbor are awakened by penetrating the heart, piercing to the depth of the soul.

Spener concluded his *Pia Desideria* with the challenge that the "heart of Christianity" be preached with simplicity and power. His message not only struck a chord in his day, but is reaffirmed daily in modern Protestantism. In our fast-paced age of scientific achievement and computer science, we are continually reminded of the need of dealing with the inner self, suffering the consequences of emotional breakdown and spiritual dearth by neglecting such principles. Protestantism reaches out to the needy through dedication to such principles, remaining relevant to modern men and women through the depth of its character.

PURITANISM AND PIETISM

The seeds planted by the Puritan and Pietist movements flowered in later decades as cross-fertilizing developments in the Enlightenment period. These influences, coupled with the Enlightenment itself, emerged as a rich pattern of varied trends and new directions in the now burgeoning era of modern Protestantism.

Puritanism has been characterized as being "austere" and "intellectual," while Pietism has been contrasted as "congenial" and "emotional." Puritanism is said to emphasize faith and works, while Pietism emphasizes love and joy. The movements developed so many facets of a belief system and such diversity in membership that stereotypes and contrasts of this sort do not bear intellectual scrutiny. Pietists insisted on good works, while some Puritan groups and leaders created intense religious emotion. A few Pietist groups became narrow-minded and bigoted, just as did some of their Puritan sisters and brothers.

In the formative years of modern Protestantism, Puritans and Pietists complemented one another. While neither movement was without problems and intransigent attitudes, their combined contributions to the Protestant heritage are incalculable. German Pietism was ecumenical in spirit, alive to the issues of worldwide Christianity. English Puritanism developed critical analyses, devoting its attention to ultimate issues concerning God's will for society and church. Its devotion to justice, combined with Pietism's depth of conscience, helped to form the attitudes still characteristic of today's Protestantism.

SUGGESTED READING

Collinson, Patrick. *The Religion of Protestants: The Church in English Society, 1559–1625.* New York and London: Oxford Univ. Press, 1982.

Demos, John Putnam. *Entertaining Satan: Witchcraft and the Culture of Early New England.* New York and London: Oxford Univ. Press, 1982.

Halbrooks, G. Thomas, ed. *Pietism.* Nashville; Broadman Press, 1981.

McLoughlin, William G. *New England Dissent, 1630–1833.* 2 vols. Cambridge, Mass.: Harvard Univ. Press, 1971.

Miller, Perry, and T. H. Johnson. *Puritans: A Sourcebook of Their Writings.* New York: Harper & Row, 1963.

Morgan, Edmund S. *The Puritan Family: Religion and Domestic Relations in Seventeenth-Century New England.* New York: Harper & Row, 1980.

Seaver, Paul S. *The Puritan Lectureships: The Politics of Religious Dissent, 1560–1662.* Stanford, Calif.: Univ. of Stanford Press, 1970.

Simpson, Alan. *Puritanism in Old and New England.* Chicago: Univ. of Chicago Press, 1961.

Spener, Philip Jakob. *Pia Desideria.* Philadelphia: Fortress Press, 1964.

Stannard, David E. *The Puritan Way of Death: A Study in Religion, Culture and Social Change.* New York and London: Oxford Univ. Press, 1977.

Stoeffler, F. Ernest, ed. *Continental Pietism and Early American Christianity.* Grand Rapids: Wm. B. Eerdmans, 1976.

———. *The Rise of Evangelical Pietism.* Leiden: E. J. Brill, 1965.

Zaret, David. *The Heavenly Contract: Ideology and Organization in Pre-Revolutionary Puritanism.* Chicago: Univ. of Chicago Press, 1985.

5

THE AGE OF
ENLIGHTENMENT

During the Reformation period and throughout the Puritan and Pietist stages of Protestantism, great advances were made in the field of science, especially in astronomy, physics, and mathematics. Nicolas Copernicus (1473–1543), a Polish astronomer and contemporary of Martin Luther, challenged the prevalent view of an earth-centered universe. He asserted that the sun was the center.

Galileo Galilei (1564–1642), the great Italian scientist, used the telescope to support Copernican theory and proved that "heavenly bodies" were much like the earth. When in his book *Dialogue Concerning the Two Chief Systems of the World* (1632) he insisted that the earth was not the center of the universe, he was tried by the Holy Office of Inquisition. The Roman Catholic church made him recant his "heresy." Although he was sentenced to life imprisonment for viewpoints "dangerous to the Christian faith," he was permitted to live under house arrest until his death.

Thus the Scientific Revolution seemed to some to be in direct conflict with the Age of Faith. In reality, early pioneers in European science were often devout Christians, some even members of the clergy. In spite of the church's initial opposition, an era was blossoming that would usher in the modern period—an era in which Protestantism would play a major role.

Such was the life of Sir Isaac Newton (1642–1717). An Anglican of deep piety, he believed that his scientific discoveries were communicated to him by God. His chief aim, he stated, was to understand the Bible better; and in his early years he helped to distribute Bibles to the poor. He had interests in biblical chronology, church history, and prophecy, as well as mathematical science; and he spent considerable time relating science to religion. In his *Principia Mathematica* (1687), he not only interpreted the laws of gravitation, but suggested that various forces of attraction and repulsion operate between particles. This allowed for the view that the universe was mechanical, even at the microscopic level. It was a test-tube type of phenomenon that could, and should, be measured and interpreted.

Newton became a towering figure in seventeenth- and eighteenth-century thought, revered by believers and skeptics alike. Although the educated upper class could not fully understand his treatise, nor could the uneducated masses, his ideas were passed on by other admiring writers. The *philosophes*, the best minds of intellectual France in the era of the Enlightenment, almost worshiped him. Voltaire (1694–1778), who helped to spread Newton's fame throughout Europe, called him the greatest man who ever lived. The mystique of Newton permeated the 1700s, Voltaire exclaiming that Newton taught people "to examine, weigh, and calculate, but never to conjecture."

DEISM

Newton's discoveries, as well as those of other scientists, had significant religious implications; for example, if the universe is mechanical, what role does God perform? In an era reacting to cold orthodoxy and Protestant scholasticism, the response was wideranging. Some individuals abandoned their religious faith while others adopted a more impersonal view of God.

Deism became the "thinking man's religion." Deists insisted that God exists; but after giving the universe its initial impetus, God was less personal in the functioning of the world and the life of humankind. Some deists declared that God wound up the universe like a clock and let it operate by itself. While deists varied in their personal beliefs, they ushered in a movement that appealed to reason and reasonableness. A rationalistic form of Christianity began to develop.

The stage for this process had been set by individuals such as Oxford University professor John Locke (1632–1704). Educated for the Anglican ministry and knowledgeable in chemistry and medicine, his study of René Descartes (1596–1650) awakened his interest in philosophy. His philosophic system became a mixture of Christian rationalism and empiricism.

In his *Essay Concerning Human Understanding* (1690), Locke depicted the human mind as a blank slate, *tabula rasa*, a sheet of white paper "void of all characters, without any ideas." Knowledge came from sense experience and self-reflection. Such knowledge, according to Locke, was never absolute or final, but probable and reasonable. Thus he spoke of the "reasonableness" of Christianity, argued for the existence of God, and maintained that the law of God gave people their rule of morality.

Locke's place in Protestant theology is clearly demonstrated in his *Reasonableness of Christianity* (1695). In this treatise he affirmed that the essence of Christianity is the acknowledgment of Jesus Christ as the Messiah, but declared that reason is the final criterion in ascertaining the truth of the Bible. Locke admitted that Christian dogma was incapable of irrefutable proof but insisted that Christ confirmed a moral law already apparent from nature, a law enforced by rewards or punishments in another world. The broader implications of this thought are found in his social contract theory, which postulated an ethical society of those who voluntarily accepted a set of moral principles advantageous to society and self. Thus government was not absolute, but rather was to be instituted, reformed, and replaced by the consent of the governed. Champions of republican principles drew heavily from Locke, and even the Declaration of Independence of the American colonies used his confidence in natural law to make a case for natural rights.

While extremely popular, Locke denied that he was a deist. In fact, he claimed that he did not want to dispense with Scriptures as revelation and devoted the last years of his life to the study of the Bible. Nevertheless his philosophical and theological thought provided a bridge to the natural religion of deism — a deism that denied any direct intervention by God in the natural order and criticized the Scriptures Locke held dear.

BIBLICAL CRITICISM

As the appeal to reason strengthened, both the church and the Bible came under attack. Deism itself had stimulated the critical study of all religious ideas, and it built upon a scientific criticism engendered decades before.

English statesman Francis Bacon (1561–1626) was the seventeenth century's great popularizer of scientific ideas. Making an eloquent appeal for the scientific method, he was one of the first philosophic writers of early modern Europe to use the inductive method of logic. He railed against a priori speculation and imitation of the ancients, criticizing Christian scholastics for their "small variety of reading," limited knowledge of history, and worthless "webs of learning" based on proof texts.

Skeptic Thomas Hobbes (1585–1679) went much further, declaring that nature was a machine. All that counted was matter and motion. He castigated popular views of the Old Testament, proclaiming that the Pentateuch was not written by Moses. Believing that the Bible should be treated as any other book, he noted that most of the Old Testament Scriptures were written much later than the events they narrated.

In Jewish circles, Baruch Spinoza (1632–77) affirmed that the Bible was full of errors and contradictions if the texts were interpreted literally. Insisting on a rational reading of Scripture, he denied the personal God of Christians and Jews. The nature of things, he commented, is not to be understood through the Bible; but, rather, the Bible is to be understood by the nature of things. He was expelled from the synagogue in 1656 for heretical views.

This approach of applying the methods of textual criticism to the Bible, methods that had been reserved for secular documents, created an entirely new dimension of biblical criticism. For the first time since the foundation of the church, the Bible came under bitter attack. Richard Simon's *Critical History of the Old Testament* (1675) claimed that the biblical texts had been corrupted by copyists. Furthermore, he denied miracles, asserting that they were contrary to the new scientific evidence that confirmed the "regularity" of the universe.

The progression of such thought, however, is best viewed in the life of Pierre Bayle (1647–1706), the son of a Protestant pastor in France. Studying with the Jesuits and attending the University of Toulouse, he converted briefly to Roman Catholicism. Returning to the Protestant faith, he went on to study in Geneva, where he was impressed with the writings of Descartes.

When he later taught in a Protestant academy in Sedan, he published *Thoughts On The Comet* (1682), explaining that comets did not foretell disasters but were purely natural phenomena. The book also held that atheists were less dangerous than idolaters and that a society of atheists could be more moral than a society of religious practitioners of superstition. His statements supporting the view that a lack of religiosity did not necessarily lead to bad conduct attracted great attention. Although he was expelled from his religious community, his book passed through many editions.

In subsequent works, Bayle condemned the religious traditions of both Catholics and Protestants. He rejected the idea that human nature was basically evil, and insisted that the Bible should be interpreted by individual conscience. When in 1685 Louis XIV (1638–1715) revoked the Edict of Nantes which had granted freedom of religion to the Huguenots (French Protestants), Bayle asserted that such lack of toleration could lead only to deism or skepticism. He explained that a state that tolerated many religions was blessed in its moderation. An intolerant state was cursed.

In 1687 Bayle's *Historical and Critical Dictionary* was published. It has been referred to as the Bible of the eighteenth-century Enlightenment. Consisting of a wide range of biographical articles on figures in religion, history, and philosophy, along with a few assorted topical articles, the *Dictionary* shook the foundation of the ecclesiastical world by declaring both the Protestant and Catholic churches to be "cruel." It submitted some of the most prestigious of biblical heroes to rigorous examination. While most of the damaging information was placed in long notations, the biblical accounts were interpreted by Bayle to be "preposterous" in many cases, and the Bible was criticized as a "cruel and immoral" book, at times venerating "evil ones" rather than justice and order.

Such biblical criticism would grow in intellectual circles, creating a movement that demanded attention by friend and foe alike. Protestantism would encompass the entire spectrum, and the rise of religious liberalism in the nineteenth century would owe a great debt to those fledgling efforts at biblical analysis.

EIGHTEENTH-CENTURY ENLIGHTENMENT

As the appeal to reason strengthened in the 1600s and critical analyses abounded, Germany produced a towering figure in the field of philosophy, devoted to the cause of harmony and peace. Gottfried Wilhelm Leibnitz (1646–1716), the brilliant son of a philosophy professor at Leipzig University, has been referred to as the true originator and founder of Enlightenment philosophy. He is also regarded as the founder of the modern German philosophic tradition. Leibnitz defended the freedom of each individual to pursue his or her own moral and intellectual growth. An irenic spirit, he tried to promote peace between Protestant and Roman Catholic theologians as well as endeavoring to unite the fragmented Protestant groups. He was devoted to the cause of international peace.

Although he was a rationalist, he disliked Newton's mechanistic view of the universe and was not content with Descartes's dualism in regard to "spiritual substance" mysteriously interacting with "material substance." Furthermore, he denounced Spinoza's philosophy as lacking in divine purpose and creativity, and declared that Spinoza had with impunity attacked personal immortality.

Leibnitz interpreted God as a free and rational being, a being who could have created any type of world. God, in Leibnitz's estimation, therefore created the best of all possible worlds, one in which men and women are rewarded and punished according to their conduct. A precursor of Enlightenment optimism, Leibnitz explained that God was not responsible for evil, but that evil was the direct result of human freedom. He was the first writer to use the term "theodicy," which means "a vindication of divine justice in the face of the existence of evil." His book *Theodicy* appeared in 1710 as a reply to Bayle's *Dictionary*, and in it he explained that the existence of evil is a necessary condition of the existence of the greatest moral good. In this work he also demonstrated the harmony of faith and reason.

Believing that Christianity was the summation of all religious systems, in his *Monadology* (1714?) Leibnitz contended that beyond the divisible physical atoms were spiritual force centers he called *monads*. Although independent of each other, these monads are brought into a rational organization through a predetermined harmony arranged by the mind and will of God. This philosophical system allowed Leibnitz to defend with modification traditional proofs of God's existence and to uphold some of the scholastic principles attacked by other philosophers. In fact, he believed his doctrine of substance brought into harmony both the transubstantiation and consubstantiation views of the Eucharist.

Leibnitz's influence was deeply felt in eighteenth-century France, where the *philosophes* as publicists for the "enlightened" intellectual outlook were prevalent. The central concepts of reason, humankind's inherent goodness, and the mechanistic universe spread to an essentially literate, educated middle class in France and Britain. While *philosophes* such as Voltaire would help to undermine absolutism in government (monarchy) as well as absolutism in religion, their concepts were not entirely new. In fact, the vigor and extent of their publication is a key ingredient in their influence. For example, Voltaire's thought was heavily indebted to English deists, yet he scarcely wrote a paragraph that was not a criticism of some abuse or a recommendation of some reform. He was widely read by the educated classes. He believed that natural religion was "engraved on all men's hearts" and declared that God must exist as an explanation for the universe. He also believed that good and evil must have a "final sanction" in a world of future rewards and punishments. And yet he opposed organized Christianity, attacked the Bible, called the Jews of biblical times a "horde of Asiatic bandits," and called Jesus a "good fellow, a coarse peasant, and a fanatic like George Fox," founder of the Quakers.

Using the standards of science and common sense, the *philosophes* of the Enlightenment added a new dimension to the intellectual spectrum. Whereas the Humanists of the Renaissance had appealed to the authority of classical writers and the reformers had referred to the authority of the Bible, the *philosophes* found their basis for truth in the use of reason and the laws of nature. In doing so, they would incessantly challenge Christian faith and practice; and their cry for autonomy would lead to a reexamination of authority and tradition. The Age of Enlightenment would end in political upheaval accompanied by a measure of philosophical skepticism. In regard to theology, many *philosophes* sought to prove that humanity had developed beyond the need for both Protestantism and Catholicism.

THE HISTORICAL JESUS

Indeed, even Jesus of Nazareth was not immune to the piercing inquiry of the Enlightenment. In Germany, Hermann Samuel Reimarus (1694–1768) was the first to begin seriously to investigate the question of the historical Jesus. Once a teacher of philosophy at Luther's Wittenberg, he was influenced by English deism and spent most of his life in Hamburg as a professor of Oriental languages. He was not well known during his lifetime and his writings, which attacked the historicity of biblical sources, shocked the world only when portions of them were published by Gotthold Ephraim Lessing in 1774.

Reimarus proposed that Jesus actually thought of himself as a political messiah. Planning to set up an earthly kingdom in which he would reign, Jesus sought to deliver the Jews from the Roman yoke. When his plans went awry and he was killed, his disciples stole his body, invented the resurrection, and created the myth about the returning messiah.

Gotthold Ephraim Lessing (1729–82), the son of a Lutheran pastor in Saxony, replaced his Lutheran scholasticism with the Enlightenment philosophy while studying in Leipzig and Berlin. Elevating reason to primacy in the human experience, he insisted that the life of the historical Jesus might well be different from the portrayal in the Bible and church tradition. He claimed that historical events could neither be demonstrated nor accurately used to prove any biblical truth. To Lessing, religious truth was of a different order from historical events; and he called upon his colleagues to adopt natural religion.

He was severely criticized for publishing Reimarus's writings but defended himself by explaining that humankind had entered the third stage of educational development, a stage beyond "childish guidelines" of faith and morality. In *The Education of the Human Race* (1780), he wrote that the first stage of education was that of childhood, that is, Old Testament guidelines with promised rewards and punishments. The second stage was that of New Testament ideals of sacrifice and self-surrender. The adult stage was geared to reason and its accompanying responsibilities.

Whatever the stage, Lessing's publication of Reimarus's work opened the floodgates to the "Lives" of Jesus abundantly published in the nineteenth century, and also produced an avalanche of literature against biblical sources and the historic faith.

THE AMERICAN ENLIGHTENMENT

The French *philosophes* had only a marginal effect on early colonial American Protestantism, and French skepticism never really captured the American spirit. The thought of Newton and Locke, however, left a clear impression on eighteenth-century American culture; and their sense of balance and order in the universe was deeply embedded in colonial institutions, including the church. Many colonists believed Newton and Locke when they insisted that religion was necessary for good order and a stable, moral society. Science attracted the attention of laity and clergy alike, and the literature from England caused great excitement on college campuses. Most early colonists thought of themselves as "enlightened" English Protestants.

The Enlightenment's emphasis on the progress of humankind adapted well to the optimistic vision of the colonial frontier and with the kingdom of God concepts of American Puritanism. Colonists came to believe that the New World was meant to be special and that America *had* to be more progressive than other countries. Protestantism captured the spirit of reason, seeking to counter the rational arguments of its critics with rational answers. A delicate balance was maintained between liberty and order, revelation and nature, passion and reason. Many eighteenth-century American Protestants would view earlier ages as superstitious and ignorant, while insisting that their present age was morally and intellectually progressive, attuned to liberty and truth. Principles of democracy became intertwined with this American Enlightenment, and the Protestant work ethic sought to define progress in terms of success as well as self-determination.

By the time of the American Revolution, Enlightenment emphases had been fused in the colonial psyche with universal themes of human rights and freedom dictated by "the laws of God and Nature." A secular optimism and revolutionary civil religion permeated the rising nation and drew diverse segments of the population into a "moral" crusade against England. The crisis of 1775–76 drew together an odd mixture of compatriots, from deists to staunch Calvinists, in bold commitment to national independence and patriotic harmony.

It is important to note that in such an atmosphere of enlightenment compromise, the Declaration of Independence did not resort to laborious argument from Scripture, but asserted that the truths about humanity and government were "self-evident." The end of government was "the pursuit of happiness" and not the restoration of virtue or restraint of evil.

As these same men began to frame the American Constitution, they realized that the history of the early colonies had been a failure with respect to religious liberty. Religious colonists, most of them Protestants, had come for their own liberty, but not for the liberty of others. Both Anglicans and Puritans had required landholding and church membership in "good standing" as requirements for voting, and those who were not members of the dominant religious group in the colony were still required to pay tithes. The Founding Fathers acknowledged that, as a plethora of groups and belief systems inundated the thirteen colonies and fought for their own religious rights, a "Christian Commonwealth" or "Protestant Commonwealth" would not do. Even strict Calvinists had learned that persecution and restriction did not insure religious zeal.

In the Massachusetts Bay Colony, for example, a Reforming Synod had to be called in Boston in 1679 to catalogue the sins and problems among the "visible saints" in their fifty-year-old "Christian Commonwealth." Ironically, even with their stringent rules and their "laws of God" enforced, the catalogue included "inordinate affection to the world," "lack of community concern," "sinful angers and hatreds," and "excess of pride in spiritual matters." The colonists of Massachusetts Bay had to admit the failure of their "holy," deliberate spiritual experiment.

Furthermore, the framers of the American Constitution realized that their own personal religious beliefs were threatened under such an intolerant system. Indeed, few of them could have been members "in good standing" in the Massachusetts Bay experiment. "Is uniformity attainable?" Thomas Jefferson questioned in his *Notes on Virginia* (c. 1782), and responded: "Millions of innocent men, women and children, since the introduction of Christianity, have been burnt, tortured, fined, imprisoned; yet we have not advanced one inch towards uniformity. What have been the effects of coercion? To make half the world fools, and the other half hypocrites. To support roguery and error all over the earth."

The commencement of the enlightened American experiment in freedom and pluralism, although incomplete in practice with regard to Jews, Catholics, blacks, and women, was to serve as an example to the rest of the world. The *Constitution of the United States* guaranteed that this country would not become a "Christian" state or a sectarian enclave. Article VI insisted that "no religious Test shall ever be required as a qualification to any Office of public Trust under the United States," and the First Amendment to this Constitution added that "Congress shall make no law respecting an establishment of religion, or prohibiting the free exercise thereof." Such attitudes were in harmony with the individual conscience and freedom of religion principles of Protestantism, as well as with the legacy of the Enlightenment.

The Enlightenment's emphasis on compromise is reflected throughout the Constitution and indicates the sincerity and boldness of the Founding Fathers. Yet this same emphasis that *all* things could be settled by compromise glaringly underscores a major shortcoming of the enterprise. Refusing to use the words "slave" or "slavery," the Constitution provided that "persons held to service or labour" should be returned to any state from which they had escaped. Apportionment for representatives and for taxes counted every free person and three-fifths of "all other persons." Furthermore, in an effort to garner Southern votes, the slave trade was not prohibited until 1808. Enlightened Northerners and Southerners realized that they had maintained an immoral institution, which they abhorred, for the sake of "compromise." This would lead to the deaths of their grandchildren and great-grandchildren in a subsequent civil war. More important, it would scar and blemish the opportunity for immediate freedom and personal liberty for all Americans.

Throughout the eighteenth century there was no massive movement against Christianity in the American colonies. In fact, the criticism and skepticism of some of the Enlightenment publicists never caught on — it was out of place in a moving, expanding frontier. Nevertheless, the challenge to traditional orthodoxy within Protestantism was not without adherents. Imbued with rationalism and devoted to a spirit of compromise, a nascent Unitarian movement arose in New England in the latter eighteenth century. Standing between the deists and the orthodox, Unitarians contended that humankind was good and could continue to progress if regulated by an enlightened conscience. They also believed, however, that without such conscience evil could gain the upper hand over human nature.

To these early American Unitarians, the doctrine of the Trinity was "unscriptural tritheism," and yet they maintained that they were firmly in the Christian tradition holding to Jesus "as the only appointed Saviour of mankind." They emphasized God's love and the mission of Christ rather than predestination and eternal damnation. Ebenezer Gay of Hingham, Massachusetts (1696–1787) has been called the Father of American Unitarianism. His *Natural Religion as Distinguished from Revealed* (1759) intricately balanced the philosophy of Newton and Locke with the thought of Calvin and scriptural authority. Charles Chauncy (1705–87), pastor of the First Church in Boston for sixty years, became the leading liberal voice in New England in the eighteenth century and was perhaps the most distinguished of the early Unitarian leaders.

As the religious philosophy of the Unitarian movement gradually matured, liberal emphases on the moral progress of society and of human intellect emerged, together with an insistence on the abolishment of prejudice and bigotry. William Ellery Channing's (1780–1842) sermon at the ordination of Jared Sparks on May 5, 1819 in Baltimore is usually regarded as the chief manifesto of American Unitarianism. Channing called for an American reformation in the Protestant churches, concluding that "much stubble is yet to be burned, much rubbish to be removed, many gaudy decorations, which a false taste has hung around Christianity, must be swept away." He declared that "the conspiracy of ages against the liberty of Christians may be brought to an end" and that "Christianity, thus purified from error, may put forth its almighty energy, and prove itself, by its ennobling influence on the mind, to be indeed 'the power of God unto salvation.' "

Insisting on a purifying vision of God, Channing's composite writings reveal the biblical, mystical, and rational aspects of American Unitarianism's diverse heritage. And yet the Enlightenment strands of progress, reason, and reasonableness are never far from his central focus. Unitarianism became the religion of the educated, the refined, the wealthy; and the leaders of society on the eastern seaboard in the early nineteenth century delighted in its insights.

IMMANUEL KANT'S CRITIQUE

"Do we now live in an *enlightened age?*" Immanuel Kant (1724–1804) rhetorically questioned in his 1784 essay, *What Is Enlightenment?* "No," he answered, "but we do live in an *age of enlightenment.*" Earlier, in his preface to *Critique of Pure Reason*

(1781), he had explained: "Our age is, in especial degree, the age of criticism, and to criticism everything must submit."

Ironically, Kant's criticism of rationalism provided a shattering blow to the philosophical system of the Age of Reason and profoundly influenced the course of nineteenth- and twentieth-century thought. A professor of mathematics and natural philosophy at the University of Königsberg in East Prussia, he had been a rationalist until reading the critique of empiricism by David Hume (1711–76). Kant came to believe that there could be neither purely objective knowledge nor innate ideas. In his *Critique of Pure Reason*, he carefully illustrated that the claim of Enlightenment publicists to speak in purely rational and objective terms was sheer illusion. Since the human mind structures and categorizes the data that the senses provide, what one really "knows" is not things as they *are* but rather things that the mind can grasp through mental molding. One cannot know reality as it is, Kant insisted, and one should honestly acknowledge the limitations of the human mind and of reason.

Kant's position also led him to reject many of the arguments for God; for example, the scholastic argumentation from causation or design. Yet he himself did not deny God's existence. He simply believed that by reason one could not prove such a thing. Nevertheless, in his *Critique of Practical Reason* (1788), he did conclude that there was a "practical reason" that differed in process from "pure reason." His *categorical imperative* for ethics was to "act in such a manner that the rule for your action can be made a universal rule." Thus Kant severed the universal moral law from its ground in nature and based it squarely on individual freedom and responsibility. His *Critique of Judgment* (1790) was a firm testimonial to his movement beyond the Enlightenment's rational ideal to the ultimate individuality of judgment and action.

Kant's philosophy molded Protestantism to a great extent, an impress that some have compared to Aristotle's influence on Roman Catholicism. He saw clearly the finitude of humankind and the difficulty of transcending the limits of that finitude. Protestant theologians of the nineteenth and twentieth centuries had to take his work into account, and many of the Protestant movements of the nineteenth century would be influenced by his thought. And yet, to understand Kant was to go beyond him — a principle that was not lost on his nineteenth-century successors from Albrecht Ritschl (1822–89) to Walter Rauschenbusch (1861–1918) and the Social Gospel movement.

CROSSCURRENTS: PIETISM AND REVIVALISM

There were other philosophical and theological crosscurrents that countered the Age of Enlightenment and challenged its basic premises. For Protestantism, the reaction to these countermoves to theories of reason, progress, and natural law had more influence on the personal piety of the average man and woman than the Enlightenment itself.

One crosscurrent was a continued emphasis on Protestant scholasticism, that is, holding firm to credal formulation and theological systems to the point of a cold, rigid, and sterile orthodoxy. As we have seen, the events of the Enlightenment were in partial reaction to such rigidity and lack of emotional warmth. Men and women were seeking a religious heritage that would meet their emotional and spiritual as well as their intellectual needs.

Romanticism, a movement that permeated most forms of art and literature, was another current, the secular ally of both Pietism and Revivalism. This movement arose in the eighteenth century in opposition to the cold, calculated, and unbending appeal to reason by the *philosophes*. It opted for human emotion, the value of feeling, and the importance of the subconscious.

Among the French *philosophes*, Jean Jacques Rousseau (1712–78) was the great proponent of Romanticism. He believed that society had corrupted the natural goodness of humanity and only through a better society could men and women be improved. This "noble savage" view of humankind insisted that conscience must be the guide for human beings and called on men and women to return to the simplicity of nature. Proposing a civil religion with a few dogmas, such as the existence of God and the punishment of the wicked, Rousseau did not totally reject reason; but he would not give it absolute control over natural emotions. Although he recommended reading the Bible, he believed neither in a church nor in a revelation outside of nature.

Romanticism was especially popular with literary figures of the eighteenth and nineteenth centuries. American Ralph Waldo Emerson (1803–82) preoccupied himself with man and nature, while the Schlegel brothers in Germany, August Wilhelm (1767–1845) and Friedrich (1772–1829), were teachers of Romanticism as well as writers. In England, William Wordsworth (1770–1850), Lord Byron (1788–1824), Percy Bysshe Shelley (1792–1822), and John Keats (1795–1821) were all inspired by the movement. Samuel Taylor Coleridge (1772–1834), the precocious son of a Devonshire Anglican clergyman, was an influential Romanticist. He opposed the prevalent mechanistic view of the universe, considering everything and everyone as an organic whole, members of one another.

To Coleridge, Christianity was a "revealed" religion, not a higher form of common sense. He castigated those "who read the Scriptures, when they do read them in order to pick and choose their faith. . . . for the support of doctrines which they had learned beforehand from the higher oracle of their own natural common-sense." He found nothing appealing in the dry biblicism of Protestant scholasticism; and his religious philosophy, like his mind, was always growing and changing.

Notwithstanding his struggles of faith and morals, Coleridge's lectures and writing influenced his secular world and enhanced the Romantic spirit of subjectivism, emotionalism, sensualism, mystery, imagination, and illumination. Economist and philosopher John Stuart Mill (1806–73) considered Coleridge one of the most original and penetrating thinkers in all of Europe. And yet, for Protestantism as a whole, the closely related Pietist and Revivalist movements had a more widespread impact than either rigid scholasticism or subjective Romanticism.

PIETISM

Pietism, while centered in the Lutheran church, was exceedingly influential in other areas of Protestant thought and activity. As an attempt to awaken the church from its lethargy, it countered the static scholastic exercise of fruitless argument that dominated the Protestant theological scene. Pietism centered on the heart of the individual Christian, emphasizing introspection of one's inner being as well as emotive expression of a meaningful relationship with God.

As has been shown in the previous chapter, foremost among its leaders was Philip Jakob Spener (1635–1705) who, in Frankfurt am

Main, decided in 1670 that he wanted to combat the sterile intellectualism of the prevailing orthodoxy of the day and therefore initiated within the church a succession of meetings between pastors and laity for Bible study, prayer, and fellowship. These *collegia pietatis* resulted in a widespread religious revival in many parts of Germany, and are the forerunners of the small cell meetings still used for counsel and fellowship in many Protestant churches today. In *Pia Desideria* (1675), Spener outlined a plan for the reconstruction of the church modeled after early Christian communities. Despite the opposition of the orthodox clergy in the Lutheran church, Spener's criticisms and ideas were influential in Germany as well as in many other parts of Europe. Inevitably, Pietism brought new life to Protestantism.

Spener's ablest and most devoted disciple was August Hermann Francke (1663–1727). Through his effort, the city of Halle became the focal point of Pietism. Like Spener, Francke focused his attention on the urgent need for an earnest study of the Bible. He firmly believed that the lay members of a church should have a role in the church's spiritual influence and ministry. His most bitter opposition came from those who would not agree that only persons understanding and experiencing a personal regeneration were truly Christian. The orthodox, who had felt threatened, counterattacked; but they achieved little success. The Pietist movement continued its efforts and was quite successful. Even after Francke's death, not only northern and central Germany were touched by the movement, but also Scandinavia, Switzerland, and other parts of Europe. Pietism also gained adherents among the German Reformed. F. A. Lampe (1683–1729) was the central figure of Reformed Pietism, spreading the movement through his preaching, books, and hymns.

The foreign missions movement was stimulated by Pietism, especially through the work of Count Nikolaus Ludwig von Zinzendorf (1700–1760), who was both a benefactor and a bishop of the newly revived Moravian church. Both the University of Halle and the Francke Institute of Education had a lasting impact throughout nearby lands as well as in Germany, and they contributed a strong current of Pietist strength to Prussian education. Immanuel Kant was raised in a Prussian Pietist home, while both Friedrich Schleiermacher (1768–1834) and Søren Kierkegaard (1813–55) were indebted to the Pietist movement as elaborated in the next chapter.

Spener could not have anticipated the power of the ripple effects in ever-increasing strength that projected his Pietist thought across a growing world. The results in both religious and secular life have been incalculable; and the secular world, knowing little of this humble man and his posterity of followers, is still unaware of the enormous impact of Pietism on our world today.

REVIVALISM

It has been argued that Pietism was actually a "revival" within Germany and Scandinavia, a revival that spread to England and New England as well. So important was the crosscurrent of revivalism during the Age of Enlightenment that famed church historian Roland Bainton (1894–1984) insisted: "What saved Christianity at the close of the eighteenth century was the miracle of the new birth in evangelical revivals."

Revivalism was also a crucial tide during the first half of the eighteenth century. No single event illustrates revivalism's spiritual quickening throughout the Western world better than the Great Awakening in America. Paralleling Pietism's period of strength, the precursor of the Great Awakening seems to have begun in a local revival that occurred in the churches of Theodore J. Frelinghuysen (1691–1747). A Dutch Reformed pastor with Pietist leanings, Frelinghuysen had been assigned in 1720 to a circuit of four Dutch Reformed churches in the Raritan Valley of New Jersey. Dismayed by the nominal religiosity of his parishioners, who showed no evidence of deeper spiritual experience, he embarked on a program of reform, personal counseling, and evangelistic preaching. Opposition was heated; but a genuine revival resulted.

By 1726, this revival had reached its peak. Conversions to Christianity and deeper faith commitments were so frequent that Frelinghuysen gained the respect and support of other Dutch Reformed pastors. He also encouraged and instructed Presbyterian pastor Gilbert Tennent (1673–1746), and a revival of spiritual awakening began to stir Tennent's congregation as well. Soon, intense local revivals spread throughout the area.

Jonathan Edwards (1703–58), pastor of the Congregational church at Northampton, Massachusetts, was to experience the same unexpected "spiritual awakening" in his congregation. Educated at Yale in Calvinist orthodoxy, he was deeply concerned with the low morals of the youth in his town. He began meeting with them and personally counseling them about the Christian faith. After preaching a series of sermons on justification by faith, sermons that detailed the lack of human ability in the salvation process, he saw a spirit of Christian love permeate Northampton. Conversions increased, and revival spread by 1736 to every corner of the Connecticut valley. Edwards's account of this revival, *Narrative of the Surprising Work of God in the Conversion of Many Hundred Souls in Northampton,* was published in London in 1737 and in Boston in 1738. Englishmen John Wesley and George Whitefield both read it and, by their own account, this book had an important effect on their thinking.

Many similar local revivals occurred in New England; but it was not until 1740 that a general outbreak of revival spread throughout the colonies. Oxford graduate George Whitefield, who had adopted a style of open-air preaching, arrived in Philadelphia in November 1739. Only twenty-four years old, he had an unusually clear and strong voice which provoked deep emotion in his audience. Great crowds began to throng his meetings in 1740 as he preached from New York to Georgia. Whitefield spent time with Jonathan Edwards, and Benjamin Franklin (1706–90) published his sermons.

Other leaders emerged as well; and the general colonial population, from pastors to educators to laymen and laywomen, were caught up in the revivalist movement. A Great Awakening had taken place—an awakening that not only increased religious sensitivity and contributed to significant Protestant church growth, but also provided social cohesion and a national consciousness among the American people. The masses were reinforced in their conviction that God had a special destiny for America.

In England, Anglican John Wesley (1703–91) led a revival that resulted in the Methodist church. A devout clergyman, he was instructed in the necessity of personal conversion by Moravian Peter Boehler (1712–75) as he sought "a closer walk with God." Boehler encouraged Wesley to continue preaching until he was assured he had "saving faith," and when that happened to continue preaching *because* he had such faith. Later, at a meeting in Aldersgate Street, London, Wesley explained that his heart was "strangely warmed" as he listened to a reading from Luther's *Preface to the Epistle to the*

Romans. He felt that a fire for God was kindled in his life that could never be put out.

Invited by his friend George Whitefield to preach in his absence to the working people of Bristol in the open air, Wesley was gradually convinced that God could indeed work outside church buildings. He became the main leader of the growing Methodist movement in England, a group of societies organized to meet spiritual and social concerns. Believing that the whole world was his parish, Wesley traveled over 250,000 miles, mostly on horseback, in the last fifty years of his life, preaching forty thousand sermons largely in the industrial North and Midlands. In England alone, he left eighty thousand followers at his death, with thirteen hundred preachers in numerous societies. In America, the sixty thousand followers at his death would develop into one of the faster growing Protestant denominations of the nineteenth century. This was ironic, for Wesley never intended to break with the Church of England and, in fact, remained a member of that church. His brother, Charles Wesley (1707–88), became the most gifted and prolific of all English hymn writers. Charles composed more than six thousand hymns and was known as the "sweet singer of Methodism."

Revivalism conveyed a vital Christianity that encouraged the response of the whole human being, emotional as well as intellectual, to a Christian gospel of repentance and spiritual rebirth. It demanded consecration and a reformed life, and left little room for pure rationalism or cold orthodoxy. As a powerful crosscurrent to the Age of Enlightenment, revivalism changed seventeenth-century Protestant Puritanism into nineteenth-century Protestant Evangelicalism.

SUGGESTED READING

Ahlstrom, Sydney E., and Jonathan S. Carey, eds. *An American Reformation: A Documentary History of Unitarian Christianity.* Middletown, Conn.: Wesleyan Univ. Press, 1985.

Artz, Frederick B. *Enlightenment in France.* Kent, Ohio: Kent State Univ. Press, 1968.

Cragg, Gerald R. *The Church and the Age of Reason.* Baltimore: Penguin Books, 1961.

Engell, James. *The Creative Imagination: Enlightenment to Romanticism.* Cambridge, Mass.: Harvard Univ. Press, 1981.

Gay, Peter. *The Enlightenment.* 2 vols. New York: W. W. Norton, 1977.

Hazard, Paul. *European Thought in the Eighteenth Century.* Cleveland: World Publishing, 1963.

Heimert, Alan, and Perry Miller, eds. *The Great Awakening: Documents Illustrating the Crisis and Its Consequences.* Indianapolis: Bobbs-Merrill, 1967.

Hunt, Margaret, and Margaret Jacob, eds. *Women and the Enlightenment.* New York: Haworth Press, 1984.

Krieger, Leonard. *Kings and Philosophers, 1689–1789.* New York: W. W. Norton, 1970.

May, Henry F. *The Enlightenment in America.* New York and London: Oxford Univ. Press, 1976.

Outler, Albert C., ed. *John Wesley.* New York and London: Oxford Univ. Press, 1964.

Reill, Peter H. *The German Enlightenment and the Rise of Historicism.* Berkeley and Los Angeles: Univ. of California Press, 1975.

Stoeffler, F. Ernest. *German Pietism During the Eighteenth Century.* Leiden: E. J. Brill, 1973.

6

THE CENTURY OF EVANGELICALISM

"What! Have you found me already? Another Methodist preacher!" exclaimed the shocked settler who had just pitched his tent on the ground of his future western home in 1814. "I left Virginia to get out of reach of them, went to a new settlement in Georgia, . . . but they got my wife and daughter into the church. . . . I was sure I would have some peace of the preachers, and here is one before my wagon is unloaded!"

The Methodist missionary, Richmond Nolley, looked the bewildered man straight in the eye and counseled: "My friend, if you go to heaven, you'll find Methodist preachers there; and if to hell, I am afraid you will find some there; and you see how it is in this world; so you had better make terms with us, and be at peace."

MODERN EVANGELICALISM

The nineteenth century was the great age of the modern Evangelical movement. Protestantism was permeated with the revivalistic spirit, and its compulsion to spread the message of the gospel to every corner of the earth was fervent and aggressive. Its goals went beyond revamping society. Indeed, optimistic nineteenth-century initiatives were to remake the world.

The term "evangelical" (pertaining to the gospel or good news) had been used to describe Lutherans in their assertion of Protestant principles during the Reformation era and soon had been commonly applied to all German Protestants, Lutheran and Reformed. By 1800, the word connoted a broader, ecumenical spirit that influenced the Protestant movement in Britain and America. Evangelical enthusiasm to "spread the gospel" and "win precious souls to Christ" soon

75

recaptured portions of the German churches as well, and spread through France, Holland, and other parts of Europe.

In the United States, the mainline Protestant churches considered themselves "evangelicals" and called themselves "evangelicals." A century ago, Episcopalians, Methodists, Presbyterians, and Baptists were *all* within the framework of evangelicalism. Their eschatology (their view of the future) was largely *post*millennial. In other words, they believed that the Protestant Christian church would bring in "the millennium," a thousand-year period of peace and prosperity, and that through the auspices of Protestantism the world would be "Christianized." They believed the world would become progressively better, and *then* Jesus Christ would return to earth. Postmillennial Evangelicalism was socially acceptable, and it dominated the culture of the nineteenth century.

ENGLISH REVIVAL AND REFORM

As England moved into its industrial revolution in the 1700s, Evangelicalism was a small minority movement within the Church of England. Although some lower church clergymen supported the work of Wesley and Whitefield, revivalism met with considerable resistance from the higher church clergy. Through the leadership of Evangelicals such as Charles Simeon (1759–1836), vicar of Holy Trinity Church, and Isaac Milner (1750–1820), a professor of science, Cambridge University became the training center for Evangelical clergy. Revivalism also spread in Scotland and Wales.

Gradually the British middle classes were drawn to the movement, as well as some gentry and aristocrats. William Wilberforce (1759–1833), Tory Member of Parliament, became an influential Evangelical layman of the upper middle class; and by the nineteenth century, Evangelicalism was the most vital religious force in England. The first Evangelical to become a bishop in the Church of England was appointed in 1815, and such distinguished Evangelical Anglicans as Lord Shaftesbury (1801–85) and William E. Gladstone (1809–98) were leading political personalities.

English Evangelicals achieved their most notable successes in philanthropic endeavors and social reform. Wilberforce, for example, joined other Evangelicals in fighting for the abolition of the slave trade, and in 1807 Parliament issued the Abolition Bill. Wilberforce joyfully wrote in his journal (March 22, 1807): "How wonderfully the providence of God has been manifested in the Abolition Bill! . . . Oh, what thanks do I owe the Giver of all good, for bringing me in His gracious providence to this great cause, which at length, after almost nineteen years' labour, is successful!" Subsequent laws and treaties led most other Western nations to abolish slavery. In some instances, the British Navy was used to enforce newly enacted abolition legislation.

A member of the Clapham sect, a group of politically active Evangelicals centered in the London suburb of Clapham, Wilberforce was also influential in the formation of the Church Missionary Society for Africa and the East in 1799 and the British and Foreign Bible Society in 1804. His book, *Practical View of the Prevailing Religious System of Professed Christians in the Higher and Middle Classes in This Country Contrasted with Real Christianity* (1797), sold extremely well for four decades of the 1800s.

The Clapham group, like many English Evangelicals, worked through voluntary societies as well as through governmental action. They formed Bible societies, missionary societies, and Sunday schools. Among the working classes, they promoted schools for the poor, distributing Bibles and religious tracts. Inspired by Wilberforce and the Clapham group, Hannah More (1745–1833) was a prolific author of Evangelical religious writings and during this period attained celebrity status. The "Old Bishop in Petticoats," she found that her series of *Cheap Repository Tracts* (c. 1788) achieved a wide readership; and the tract became a notable feature of British Evangelicalism.

THE SECOND GREAT AWAKENING

In America, in the early 1800s, a westward migration was taking place that in retrospect was phenomenal. The churches of the United States were increasingly concerned about the unevangelized and unchurched population flowing beyond the mountains and past the Mississippi River. Missouri became a state in 1821, and a rush to the Pacific Ocean was initiated.

With an evangelical fervor, Protestantism was awakened from a post-Revolutionary War lethargy to minister actively to these masses. Looking longingly at the spontaneous Great Awakening of 1740,

77

revivalists sought to produce another spiritual awakening through preaching and missions. Baptists and Methodists quickened religious interest in the new territories, and even the more staid New England Congregationalists experienced scattered revivals in the 1790s. By 1800, revivals and great religious enthusiasm were occurring from western New York to Tennessee.

Quite unpredictably, Yale University experienced in 1802 a religious revival which spread to other college campuses. Timothy Dwight (1752–1817), a respected Congregational minister, author, and educator, became president of Yale in 1795. Grandson of Jonathan Edwards and a champion of conservative Calvinism in New England, Dwight became a supporter of revivalism among the educated elite. Preaching a series of chapel sermons in 1802 to promote godliness among the student body, he was amazed at the explosive response. As a result, one-third of the student body professed conversion and dedicated their lives to serve God unreservedly. Dwight was convinced that revivals could stem infidelity, and his support of Evangelicalism brought many other New England leaders into the revivalist camp. Students from the Yale revival, such as Lyman Beecher (1775–1863) and Nathaniel W. Taylor (1786–1858), carried on the Evangelical tradition and spread its influence.

In the western territories, revivalists were more emotional, pressing for quick decisions among a transitory population. Techniques of revivalism took shape that affect Protestantism to this day. In 1801, the famed Cane Ridge revival broke out in Kentucky. Assemblies of the faithful or "camp meetings" had been organized in the area by the fiery Presbyterian minister, James McGready (1758?–1817). Joined by Baptist and Methodist ministers who preached for days, audiences were convinced, "reduced to tears," and "slain in the Spirit" from the revivalist messages.

At Cane Ridge, "preaching stands" were erected at different areas of the grounds, and even those who came to carouse and gamble were converted by the preachers. "Falling, jumping and jerking" sometimes took place with an enthusiasm that greatly disturbed conservative Presbyterians. In 1805, the General Assembly of the Presbyterian church indicated that this "confusion" was not to be tolerated, and an Old Light (antirevivalist measures) versus New Light (upholding revivalism measures) schism developed. Methodists and Baptists, in contrast, incorporated the camp meeting into their Protestant tradition; and within a few years hundreds of camp meetings were taking place throughout the country. Permanent conference centers, camp grounds, and summer resorts, such as Chautauqua in New York State, also were developed.

Controversial as they were, the revivalists' "new measures" were to shape Protestantism in America and affect the Evangelical movement throughout the world. Opponents had to come to grips with the enthusiasm and conversions that resulted from these spectacles. Methodism, which was not afraid of such "boisterous behaviors" and was on the forefront of frontier missions, became the largest denomination in the United States in the nineteenth century.

In addition, Protestant Charles G. Finney (1792–1875), a newly converted lawyer from Adams, New York, extended the revivalist measures of this western Second Great Awakening to the northern urban areas. Using the tactics of a trial lawyer, he sought to convict his audiences of their sinful ways and to convince them to come forward to an "anxious bench" to pray for or testify to their conversion. Finney also encouraged women to speak and to pray in the churches, and in the Evangelical revivalist movement women occupied an important place.

THE BENEVOLENT EMPIRE

A resurgence of revivals from 1857–59 underscored the fact that the power and prestige of Evangelical Protestantism dominated the culture and institutions of nineteenth-century America. Revivalism even created a political ethos for Protestantism that affected the way the British and American populace voted for many years. As will be shown in chapter 9, it stimulated the abolition movement in the United States as well as in Britain.

Characterized by an ecumenical spirit, Protestantism gave birth to a multitude of voluntary societies and missionary enterprises, some of which continue to this day. Often drawing membership from an interdenominational base and carrying out their activities with little church or state control, Protestant cooperative agencies throughout the world sought to reform society and perhaps eventually purify the world. The American Board of Commissioners for Foreign Missions (1810) sent thousands of missionaries to distant parts of the world. In Germany, the Inner Mission organized by J. H. Wichern (1808–81), a Hamburg pastor, was concerned with the plight of destitute children. Wichern believed that such works of love would unite all classes in Christian community, an effort that blossomed into a number of philanthropic enterprises.

In addition to the British societies and movements discussed earlier, America promoted other associations. The American Bible Society was organized in 1816 and by 1820 had distributed nearly 100,000 Bibles. The American Tract Society (1823?) followed in the footsteps of British efforts, and soon had distributed one million tracts, children's books, and devotional literature. The American Education Society (1826) expanded from funding scholarships for poor theological students to a movement for male and female education throughout the United States. English endeavors to promote Sunday schools in the latter eighteenth century (note the English Sunday School Union of 1803) influenced similar efforts in Philadelphia and then in New England. In 1824, the American Sunday School Union was formed, providing a national organization to establish Sunday schools for the children of the nation. Later, the International Sunday School Association (first conference 1875; formally incorporated 1907) would give a boost of enthusiasm to the enterprise through the incorporation of lay leadership. It is important to note that these societies were intricately connected to Evangelical Protestantism, and through interlocking directorates sought to move in a harmonious and concerted fashion of interdenominational cooperation and influence.

In addition to the American abolition movement that will be discussed later, American Protestant societies sought to influence every citizen toward moral good. The American Society for the Promotion of Temperance (1826) and the American Temperance Union (1836) under a growing female leadership became a springboard for women's rights, as well as, for a time, successful in passing prohibition laws in various states and the adoption of the Prohibition Amendment a century later.

For example, Frances E. C. Willard (1839–98), president of Evanston College for Ladies (later absorbed by Northwestern University), became president of the National Woman's Christian Temperance Union in 1879 and of the World's Woman's Christian Temperance Union in 1891. She helped organize the Prohibition Party in 1882, and was extremely active in the Association for the

Advancement of Woman (founded 1873). As arguments over the woman's role in Protestant churches became more animated in the late nineteenth century, Frances Willard reminded the American public in 1888 that "there are in the United States five hundred women who have already entered the pulpit as Evangelists, and at least a score (exclusive of the 350 Quaker preachers) who are pastors, of whom several have been regularly ordained." She pointed out that the Methodist, Baptist, Free Baptist, Congregational, Universalist, Unitarian, and Society of Friends churches had ordained women, and "in face of so much prejudice," shared letters from some of those women describing their successful ministries.

Dubbed by historians a worldwide "Benevolent Empire," thousands of Protestant societies worked with the handicapped, sought reform in medical and mental health facilities, and fought for individual freedoms. As the challenge of immigration and poverty increased, Protestant philanthropic enterprises expanded to solve these problems. Protestantism incorporated social, economic, political, intellectual, and religious reform as part of its basic lifeblood — as part of its mission. Its mission transcended revivalistic Protestantism to include Jews, Catholics, Unitarians, Antirevivalists, secularists, and others in its errand of mercy. And, while its optimism was utopian and its methods were sometimes paternalistic and elitist, its impulses and purposes are an integral part of the modern meaning of Protestantism.

SECTARIANISM

The ecumenical spirit of early Evangelical Protestantism eventually waned and even the word "denomination," originally an *inclusive* term, took on new connotations. John Wesley's proclamation, "From real Christians, of whatever denomination, I earnestly desire not to be distinguished at all," became less of a standard; sectarianism increased.

In America, Princeton's Samuel Miller (1769–1850) had declared that "it would never occur to us to place the peculiarities of our [denominational] creed among the fundamentals of our common Christianity," and Albert Barnes (1798–1870) insisted in 1840 that "the Church of Christ" was not exclusively under Episcopal, Baptist, Methodist, Presbyterian, or Congregational "form," but all were "to

81

all intents and purposes, to be recognized as parts of the one holy catholic church."

Nevertheless, Princeton Seminary's Charles Hodge (1797–1878), professor of theology for fifty years, wrote in *Biblical Repertory and Theological Review* as early as 1836 words that foreshadowed a shift in the interpretation of Protestant denominationalism. He declared that "no such thing exists on the face of the earth as Christianity in the abstract. . . . Every man you see is either an Episcopalian or a Methodist, a Presbyterian or an Independent, an Arminian or a Calvinist. No one is a Christian in general."

Such divisions within Protestantism engendered far greater prejudice toward those outside the Protestant fold. In the United States, nativist impulse (fear of the stranger) permeated the Century of Evangelicalism, tarnishing the image of inclusive cooperation and benevolent empire. A key paradox in the history of immigration to the United States is that while newcomers were welcomed as cheap labor, they were scorned and abused for being "different."

The rapid and obviously belated movement of the United States into the Industrial Revolution and its expansion of territory definitely mandated new settlers and cheap labor. Without immigrants, most felt that Evangelical Protestant America could not grow and prosper; and by the latter decades of the nineteenth century, Americans actively recruited European, Asian, and Latin American peoples. This immigration would not only change the British dominated stock of the colonial period, but would also change the religious complexion of Protestant America. In 1882, nearly 800,000 immigrants came to America's shores. While this was the peak year for immigration in the nineteenth century (1907 with nearly 1.3 million was the peak year in the twentieth), the United States received a total of 27 million immigrants between 1880 and 1930.

An important source of conflict between native-born and immigrants in the nineteenth century was religion. In earlier decades, Americans objected to the infusion of Irish Catholics. "Protestant America" worried that the Pope in Rome would rule if the Irish population increased, and "Irish Need Not Apply" signs were posted by employers. Anti-Catholic tracts abounded, and nativist attitudes at times flared into mob violence. In 1834, an angry mob burned an Ursuline convent on the outskirts of Boston. Even respected Americans, such as Samuel F. B. Morse (1791–1872), the inventor of the telegraph, spread wild rumors of a Jesuit plot to take over the United States. In like manner, the Evangelical Alliance formed in London in 1846 to "confess the unity of the Church of Christ," and to foster worldwide "brotherly love" through Evangelical principles, received great impetus from the anti-Catholic, nativist sentiment of its American leaders. By the 1850s, the Order of United Americans or the nativist Know-Nothing party, primarily bound together by the anti-Catholic sentiment of its Protestant constituency, had scored some political victories.

Many immigrants who had expected a land of opportunity and progress were unprepared for the often hostile reception accorded them. They clung together for protection and for survival. None of the immigrant groups escaped denigration and persecution. Germans were accosted for drinking beer, Jews had to face vicious anti-Semitism, and Greeks were physically attacked. Poles were called "stupid animals," and Italian immigrants were said to be "criminal by nature." Chinese on the West Coast, the "Yellow Peril," incurred the abuse and violence of natives and immigrants alike. Blacks must also be considered under the rubric of the "immigrant experience," although they were forced to immigrate; and caricatures and stereotypes of blacks will be considered in chapter 9. By the Civil War, there were 4.4 million black slaves in the United States.

As in colonial America, however, the new immigrants persisted in spite of the difficulties. From ethnic neighborhoods that included extended family, church, schools, and newspapers, immigrant children and grandchildren moved into the mainstream of American life, enriching the quality of culture and religious experience. The mosaic of American Protestantism would profit from the diversity of immigrant Protestant groups and from the challenge presented by other religious, cultural, and ethnic traditions.

In the first place, immigrants generally infused an Old World spirit into the New World's Protestantism. Among Protestants, Lutheranism benefited the most from the growing immigrant tide, and by the end of the first decade of the twentieth century, Lutherans were the third largest Protestant group, Methodists and Baptists being the first two. The Reformed churches (Dutch, German, and Hungarian) were bolstered as well, and even small enclaves of Mennonites felt the influence of Protestant immigration.

In regard to the challenge, Protestant America was increasingly becoming a pluralistic religious unit. The Jewish community expanded from a quarter of a million adherents in 1880 to three-quarters of a million in 1900. Eastern Orthodox Christians would number 200,000 by 1915, and even Buddhism would establish a foothold on American soil. Roman Catholicism gained the largest number of new immigrants and by the turn of the century accounted for over 15 percent of the population of the United States. Protestantism would have to respond to both the intellectual and social challenges of such changes. A maturity and broadening would occur in the innovative, though often painful, process.

TRENDS IN PROTESTANT THEOLOGY

In the nineteenth century, Protestantism in northern Europe exhibited new currents of thought and creative theological systemization that have had an important impact on modern philosophy, history, and literature. The center of Lutheranism was Germany, which had the largest body of Protestants on the Continent, and as a center of intellectual inquiry, German Protestantism held a position of leadership in the field of theology and religious philosophy. Dominated by the universities, German intellectual life promoted academic freedom and religious speculation. Although criticized for its lack of a sense of crisis and taunted as an "empire of the air" (Britain, it was said, had the sea and France the land), the richness and variety of German religious thought fascinated contemporary thinkers—a tribute to a Protestant enterprise where one viewpoint never dominated. In the land of the Reformation, a theological revolution took place in the nineteenth century.

Friedrich Ernst Daniel Schleiermacher

Schleiermacher (1768–1834) has been called the Father of Liberal Protestant Theology. Born in Breslau, the son of a Reformed army chaplain and educated in the Pietist tradition by the Moravians, he continued his education at the University of Halle in 1787, encountering the philosophy of Kant, but struggling with the cold rationalism of his age. An excellent speaker, he was appointed Reformed preacher at the Charité in Berlin, where he was affected by the Romantic movement. He believed that this movement was a humanizing influence that saved him from the doubt in which

84

rationalism had chained him. His *Speeches on Religion to the Cultured Among Its Despisers* (1799) defined religion as "sense and taste for the infinite." For Schleiermacher, religion was not a form of knowledge or a system of morality, but was grounded in feeling rather than reason. He sought to show his friends in the Romantic movement that religion must occupy an important place in human life.

He became dean of the faculty of theology at the University of Berlin, and in his subsequent and more mature work, *The Christian Faith* (1821–22), Schleiermacher elaborated upon his definition, describing religion as a "feeling of absolute dependence," a fundamental expression of human need. He proclaimed that all other activities of humankind, including science, art, and moral philosophy, were incomplete without religion. For him, the purest expression of religion was to be found in Christian theism, "God-consciousness," the provision of redemption through Jesus Christ. Pointing out that Jesus' disciples were drawn into Jesus' God-consciousness prior to their belief in the resurrection, he contended that an individual's experience of conversion comes through participation in the corporate life of the church.

All Christian doctrines that could not be directly related to the feeling of absolute dependence were expendable from Schleiermacher's viewpoint — they did not belong in the theological enterprise at all. He thus contributed to a critical approach in that no external authority, that is, Bible, church, or creed, could take precedence over the God-consciousness of the believer. Karl Barth (1886–1968) would criticize Schleiermacher for reinterpreting historic doctrines of the church and compromising the Christian faith; but American liberal Protestants of the latter nineteenth century were strongly influenced by his precepts.

Georg Wilhelm Friedrich Hegel

Hegel (1770–1831) was a colleague of Schleiermacher whose work overshadowed Schleiermacher's during their lifetimes. Born in Stuttgart, he studied philosophy and theology at Tübingen. In 1818 he was appointed to the chair of philosophy at the University of Berlin, where, as an eloquent lecturer, he soon gained many disciples.

Hegel insisted that reality be seen as a whole and declared that the *process* of reason was reality itself. His method of exposing incompleteness or contradictions of thought was to pose a "thesis" and question it by means of an opposite, "antithesis," in order to achieve "synthesis." Viewing Christianity as the synthesis of human religious development, Hegel underscored the importance of history as an expression of the Absolute, God. All reality was the expression of the divine mind, the dynamic thought of the Spirit of God. Even the political sphere was but a moment in the Spirit's mind.

To Hegel, the state was humanity's highest social achievement, a universal expression of family love. It was the highest revelation of the "world spirit." Hegel paved the way for both the Second Reich of Bismarck and the Third Reich of Hitler as well as the historical dialectic of Karl Marx by declaring that the state "has the supreme right against the individual, whose supreme duty it is to be a member of the State." While he predicted that Germany's great hour lay in the future and her mission would "regenerate the world," he viewed this historical fruition as a release from narrow dogmatism or partial systems. The state would become the "Kingdom of God," where an ordered moral life would abound.

Hegel's followers were criticized for trying to fit all areas of reality into his system, and many of them certainly believed that every problem could be solved through the system. For example, Ferdinand Christian Baur (1792–1860) introduced the Hegelian system to the study of early church history and the origins of Christian doctrine. He theorized that Peter represented the ancient theological system of Judaism (thesis), which Paul opposed in his "purer" gospel theology (antithesis), from which the postapostolic theology of Christianity emerged (synthesis).

Baur's student David Friedrich Strauss (1808–74) shook the theological world to its foundations in his two-volume *Life of Jesus* (1835). Strauss questioned the historical accuracy of the Gospel accounts of the life of Jesus, arguing in Hegelian fashion that religion presented the truth, but only in an incomplete and inadequate form. Criticized even by Baur for his weakness in historical literary analysis of the biblical documents, Strauss progressed in biblical criticism until he eventually accepted a Darwinian view of faith. His final work, *The Old and the New Faith* (1872), rejected belief in a personal God, insisting that too little is known about the historical Jesus to determine religious feeling. As we shall see in the next chapter, Protestant Liberalism would have to grapple with such constructs.

Although Hegel's followers would split sharply into left and right factions, and his system would suffer critical rebuke, Hegel brought critics and admirers alike back to the importance of history and the historical process. With regard to the study of theology and philosophy, even of the Bible itself, historical perspective would become central to proper interpretation.

Søren A. Kierkegaard

Kierkegaard (1813–55) was a Danish Lutheran theologian who questioned Hegel's system and who for a time sought refuge in Berlin. For Kierkegaard, the basis of Christianity was not its reasonableness or its system, but rather was rooted in faith. Through faith, man could know God directly. Faith to Kierkegaard, however, meant decision and commitment; risk and denial of oneself. He criticized Christendom for the "crime" of "playing at Christianity," insisting that Christian existence was a constant struggle to become, of acting on the truth.

In the midst of a theological trend to humanize God, Kierkegaard underscored the transcendence of God. He took little interest in the historical criticism of his day, but quoted uncritically from the Biblical sources themselves. Kierkegaard believed that in Jesus Christ, God has acted, and God gives faith as a gift because God truly transcends human history. Salvation and grace occur in "the moment," the encounter of God and individual.

Kierkegaard's emphasis on the subjectivity of truth (in contrast to Hegel's objective theory of knowledge) and his belief that true Christianity centers on a person's very existence, not merely on the intellect, have been interpreted by some as an origin of twentieth-century existentialist thought. Certainly, existence as a constant struggle, the struggle to become, is found in Kierkegaard, as well as themes of subjectivity, dread, despair, and hope. Existentialism would travel a path different from Kierkegaard's with respect to these themes; yet their continuing attraction for intellectuals definitely shows philosophical theology's debt to him.

Nevertheless, it is perhaps his critique of the human condition and of the theological enterprise that has undeniable implications for the modern meaning of Protestantism. In his criticism of the church of his day, Kierkegaard reminded his readers that individuals and their God must not be lost in theological extrapolations and systematic

87

haggling. Furthermore, the institution and organization of the church must always be open to question, and the mirror of social responsibility and "costly faith" in the midst of a comfortable society is to be held high by Protestantism itself.

TOWARD LIBERALISM AND FUNDAMENTALISM

The nineteenth century presented many challenges to Protestantism — challenges that actively guided the movement into the twentieth century. Industrialization, immigration, and urbanization presented social and economic dilemmas that demanded response, yet seemingly defied solution. A number of the new religious movements (see chap. 10) first appeared in this century and would demand their fair share of respect from the Protestant churches. Biblical criticism and Darwin's theory of evolution would require a creative theological response, and Protestant missions in the Third World would soon force a global perspective beyond Western mentality. Twentieth-century fascist and communist movements would test the constructs of nineteenth-century Protestantism, as would a rapid expansion of scientific knowledge and technology.

Both Liberalism and Fundamentalism arose within this vast theological and social sea of nineteenth-century Evangelical Protestantism. The next two chapters deal specifically with the complex development of these movements. One must be constantly reminded, however, not to build a false polarity between these movements. Extreme religious viewpoints do exist, both right and left, but there are in actuality a spectrum of parties within Liberal and Conservative Protestantism as well as in denominational groupings. Groups such as "evangelical christocentric liberals" and "moderate confessional conservatives" defy strict categorical structures.

SUGGESTED READING

Carwardine, Richard. *Transatlantic Revivalism: Popular Evangelicalism in Britain and America, 1790–1865.* Westport, Conn.: Greenwood Press, 1978.
Cross, Whitney R. *The Burned-over District: The Social and Intellectual History of Enthusiastic Religion in Western New York, 1800–1850.* New York: Harper & Row, 1965.

Dieter, Melvin E. *The Holiness Revival of the Nineteenth Century.* Metuchen, N.J. and London: Scarecrow Press, 1980.

Hardesty, Nancy A. *Women Called to Witness: Evangelical Feminism in the Nineteenth Century.* Nashville: Abingdon Press, 1984.

Jay, Elisabeth. *The Religion of the Heart: Anglican Evangelicalism and the Nineteenth Century.* New York and London: Oxford Univ. Press, 1979.

McLoughlin, William G. *The American Evangelicals, 1800–1900: An Anthology.* New York: Harper & Row, 1968.

————. *Revivals, Awakenings, and Reform.* Chicago: Univ. of Chicago Press, 1978.

Ruether, Rosemary R., and Rosemary S. Keller, eds. *Women and Religion in America: Volume 1, The Nineteenth Century.* New York: Harper & Row, 1981.

Smith, Timothy L. *Revivalism and Social Reform: American Protestantism on the Eve of the Civil War.* Baltimore: Johns Hopkins Univ. Press, 1980.

Welch, Claude. *Protestant Thought in the Nineteenth Century, 1799–1870.* Vol. 1. New Haven, Conn.: Yale Univ. Press, 1972.

7

PROTESTANT LIBERALISM

Arno C. Gaebelein (1861–1945) sat in the 1899 meeting of several hundred New York Evangelical ministers of the Methodist church in a state of shock. The speaker, S. Parkes Cadman (1864–1936), had boldly proclaimed that the "absolute inerrancy and infallibility of the Bible are no longer possible of belief among reasoning men." He illustrated this by noting that half of the pages of the Old Testament were of "unknown authorship" and that the New Testament contained "contradictions."

To Gaebelein's horror, the Methodist Evangelicals present applauded Cadman's remarks. "When I protested and suggested that charges should be brought against a man who uttered such unwarranted attacks upon the Book of books," Gaebelein wrote in his autobiography, "I was told by high [Methodist] officials not to be hasty about this, 'for,' as one said, 'sooner or later we must fall in line with these results of scholarly Biblical Criticism.' "

In the Century of the Evangelical, Protestantism in America was brought face to face with biblical criticism, its largest denomination dividing into liberal and conservative wings over the issue. As a pastor and member, Arno C. Gaebelein severed his connection with the denomination immediately, becoming a leader in the rising Fundamentalist-Evangelical movement (see chap. 8). Others, such as his friend Leander W. Munhall, a Methodist Bible Conference speaker, stayed within the denomination as a proponent of Conservative Evangelicalism, trying to convince Gaebelein to do likewise.

DARWIN'S CHALLENGE

As has been shown in earlier chapters, the tide of biblical criticism among European intellectuals had been rising throughout the eighteenth and nineteenth centuries. While in the eighteenth century Enlightenment rationalism carried the movement forward, the nineteenth century turned to a more scientific historical-critical method. For example, in 1807 Wilhelm De Wette (1780–1849) proposed that the earliest portions of the Pentateuch (Genesis-Deuteronomy) were to be dated from the period of David (c. 1000 B.C.E.). An influential theologian who taught at Heidelberg, Berlin, and Basel Universities, De Wette believed that separate redactors, drawing from fragmentary sources, had compiled each book. By the later nineteenth century, the German biblical critic Julius Wellhausen (1844–1918) adopted some of the characteristics of the Hegelian school, proposing an evolution of the Pentateuch documents.

Wellhausen posited a Pentateuchal composite of a "Jehovistic" source (J) dated ninth century B.C.E.; an "Elohistic" source (E) from the eighth century B.C.E.; a "Deuteronomic" source (D) from the seventh century B.C.E.; and a "Priestly" source (P) from the fifth century B.C.E. The entire corpus was, he concluded, revised and edited around 200 B.C.E. to form the Pentateuch as it is known today. This JEDP theory occupied a position of authority in the world of biblical criticism analogous to Darwin's in the area of biological science. It demanded reevaluation in philosophical and theological circles concerning the validity of the creation accounts, miracles, historical data in the Bible, and claims to authorship, such as the frequent claim that Moses wrote the Pentateuch.

Indeed, this was the essence of the challenge presented by Englishman Charles Darwin (1809–82). His theory of evolution not only proposed organic development of the species but also evolution of religion itself. His theory was formulated by the 1840s; but his own inner turmoil kept him from publication until 1859, when *Origin of Species by Means of Natural Selection* appeared. Although Darwin originally intended to be a Protestant clergyman, he vacillated between the Protestant faith and agnosticism until his death.

Darwin's inner turmoil was reflected in the Protestant movement itself. In the world gathering of the Evangelical Alliance in New York in 1873, a debate raged over the Evangelical's relationship to Darwinism. Some felt that evolution did not pose a serious threat to the Christian faith, while others insisted that "man" in the book of Genesis could not be "sprung from primeval matter." Even in this alliance, formed in London in 1846 "to confess the unity of the Church of

92

Christ," disarray in the theological spectrum over the relationship between science and Protestantism was evident.

Protestantism faced a predicament. The Bible claimed to be authoritative, and yet some of the miraculous accounts defied a scientific understanding of the universe. Furthermore, the Bible presupposed a three-story universe, that is, earth in the middle, heaven above, and hell below. For the sixteenth-century Reformers this posed no problem, but for modern nineteenth-century intellectuals, scientific discoveries had exploded such a scenario. They questioned whether or not they could retain the Protestant emphasis on the centrality of the Bible and still be biblical scholars of integrity in their modern age. For some, the only choices were to modify the biblical faith, adapting it to the modern world, or to cast it away as outmoded and devise a new faith principle. The choice of Liberal Protestant Evangelicalism was the former — to adapt and modify.

LIBERALISM IN AMERICA

Liberalism did not begin to emerge in the United States until 1850, and its most rapid advance against Protestant orthodoxy began in the last quarter of the nineteenth century. Certainly, the Unitarian revolt and rationalism had made some gains in New England in the early nineteenth century, but these pockets of avant-garde theology were relatively small and scattered. In most seminaries, a conservative New England theology that followed the pattern of Jonathan Edwards was predominant. A moderate Calvinism reigned from Princeton to Andover to Chicago.

It is surprising, therefore, that by the year 1900 Liberalism had made spectacular gains among the American intelligentsia and that it matured in the first three decades of the twentieth century. This reconstruction in the theological world that affected professors and, in turn, ministerial candidates, was not due to rationalistic or irreligious forces. Rather, American Evangelicalism was compelled to develop a living faith that could meet the demands of the modern, scientific world. Liberalism was the attempt of one segment of this movement to adjust the ancient faith to the modern world.

Horace Bushnell (1802–76) set in motion some of the influences that preceded Liberalism with his publication of *Christian Nurture* in 1847. Sometimes called the Father of American Theological

93

Liberalism, he, like Schleiermacher, was influenced by the Romantic movement's stress on feeling and the immanence of God. The writings of Samuel Taylor Coleridge were instrumental in Bushnell's conversion experience; and in *Christian Nurture* Bushnell insisted that steady education and Christian influence were the surest ways to inculcate the Christian faith. In other works, Bushnell stressed that spiritual realities demanded understandable symbolic representations. For instance, the death of Christ was a "symbol" of the sacrifice Christians must make for the human race. This contrasted to such an extent with the message of the revivalists that Bushnell prepared the way for the acceptance of the works of Schleiermacher and Coleridge in America.

In scientific theory, Darwin made little impact on the American scene until after the Civil War. Asa Gray (1810–88) of Harvard held to similar ideas and heartily endorsed *Origin of Species* in the 1860s. Progress, however, was slow. From Unitarians to the staunchest of conservative Evangelicals, theologians had viewed the marvelous design of God in the physical world and had stressed God's benevolent hand as humankind moved toward the kingdom of God on earth. Darwin posed instead a "survival of the fittest" ethic, a bloody struggle for existence. Even Bushnell could not accept such "development theory."

Lyman Abbott

The chasm between postmillennial Protestant theology and Darwin's evolutionary theory was bridged by a creative theological reconstruction. Lyman Abbott (1835–1922), a popular Congregational minister who wrote for *Harper's Magazine* and was the successor to Henry Ward Beecher as pastor of Plymouth Church in Brooklyn, described God in his *The Evolution of Christianity* (1892) as an "Infinite and Eternal Energy from which all things proceed." In contrast to the deist's "Watchmaker," Abbott made God the source of physical evolution as well as spiritual evolution, constantly involved in creation's upward progress.

This theological reconstruction of a beneficent divine design of upward evolutionary progress was not Abbott's creation, but was being proposed as early as the 1870s. Nevertheless, he was a great popularizer of religious Liberalism, and his life is a good illustration of how Liberalism was taking hold in America.

Born in Roxbury, Massachusetts, the son of an ordained Congregational evangelist and writer of children's stories, Lyman Abbott's life spanned a horse-and-buggy era before the telegraph was invented to a period when radio broadcasting began and automobiles were in general use. A conservative Evangelical in theology, he neither danced nor played cards. At his college graduation in 1853, he delivered a commencement oration entitled, "Superstition, the Parent of Science." Serving as a law reporter for the *New York Times*, he passed the bar examination in 1856, and spent the next six years as a lawyer.

Restless in his profession and influenced by Henry Ward Beecher (1813–87) and the nationwide revival in 1858, Abbott felt called to enter the ministry, an aspiration he held as a child. In spite of the opposition of relatives to this career change, he began a course of theological reading under the supervision of Beecher, E. N. Kirk of Boston, and Calvin E. Stowe of Andover Theological Seminary. Kirk told him that the Bible should be his main endeavor of study, while all three insisted he must buy an *Alford's Greek Testament*. He was granted ordination as a Congregationalist in 1860 in spite of the fact that he lacked a seminary education.

His book *Jesus of Nazareth: His Life and Teachings* was published by Harper and Brothers in 1869. It represented conservative Evangelical Protestant theology. In fact, in the preface Abbott asserted, "Believing the Bible to be the inspired Word of God, it has been enough for my purpose to assume that the Gospels are authentic narratives." As a gibe at those who denied the miracles of the Scriptures, Abbott concluded, "Christian faith in the Christian miracles is the truest rationalism." In optimistic fervor that Christ would establish his kingdom, Abbott exclaimed near the end of this work, "The very air is full of the portents of His coming." In the subsequent *Old Testament Shadows of New Testament Truths* (1870), he totally accepted Mosaic authorship of the Pentateuch and the "veritable history" of the Bible.

In 1876, Abbott became coeditor with Beecher of the *Christian Union* (later called the *Outlook*), a journal he edited until his death. As biblical criticism and Darwin's evolutionary theory increasingly invaded the theological sphere, Abbott became perplexed, as did many Protestant preachers and teachers. Reading widely in the literature of this "new theology," he finally accepted the biblical critical approach and soon became a theistic evolutionist, as had his mentor,

95

Beecher. "I became a radical evolutionist," he later explained in *Reminiscences* (1914), "by which I mean I accepted to the full John Fiske's aphorism: 'Evolution is God's way of doing things.' " American John Fiske (1842–1901) had popularized a blend of evolution and idealism in works such as *Outline of Cosmic Philosophy* (1874) and *The Destiny of Man* (1884).

Abbott was quick in his conclusion to *The Theology of An Evolutionist* (1897) to stress that "evolution is not to be identified with Darwinism." For him, it was simply "the doctrine of growth applied to life," not the survival of the fittest and a struggle for existence. Evolution could not be the last word, for there was no "last" word. "Evolution itself," Abbott insisted, "is inconsistent with the idea that there can be any last word. . . . The doctrine of evolution is the doctrine of perpetual growth. . . . "

For Abbott, as for many of the advocates of the "new theology" of Liberalism, Christianity was an evolution, a growth of the revelation of God. The incarnation of the person of Jesus Christ was to bring humans and God together, while strengthening their respective individuality and personality. Most important, Protestantism was neither a creed nor a ceremony, but the very life of God in the soul of man. This life recreated the individual, who, in turn, constituted the church, which in its turn would transform society into the kingdom of God.

Liberalism and Modernism

Both Abbott and Beecher received considerable criticism for their adherence to the "new theology," and the battle over Liberalism raged on Protestant seminary campuses. At Union Theological Seminary in New York City, Professor Charles A. Briggs, who held the chair of biblical theology and was a leading authority on the Hebrew Bible and Presbyterian confessions, was put on trial for heresy by the Presbytery of New York for subscribing to biblical criticism and the "new theology." Because the General Assembly could veto a professor in a Presbyterian seminary since the Union of 1869–70, it exercised this right in 1891. Briggs continued to teach at Union Theological Seminary, however, because the seminary severed its relation with the General Assembly in 1892. He was suspended from the ministry of the Presbyterian church in 1893. Another Presbyterian Old Testament scholar, Preserved Smith of Lane Seminary, was expelled in

1894, while New Testament scholar A. C. McGiffert of Union was forced to resign from the Presbyterian ministry in 1900.

Seminaries such as Union, Harvard, and Yale took up the gauntlet of Liberalism, while Boston University (Methodist) and Crozer (Baptist) soon followed suit. When John D. Rockefeller (1839–1937) generously funded the University of Chicago Divinity School (Baptist), an accomplished faculty was hired, which soon became one of the country's strongest centers of Protestant Liberalism. In an effort to distance themselves from radical skepticism, Chicago theologians emphasized that they were part of the Modernist movement — a movement that they believed was not identical with Liberalism. Modernists adapted religious ideas to modern culture, claiming that God was revealed in the cultural development of the human race.

Shailer Mathews (1863–1941), dean of the University of Chicago Divinity School, asserted in *The Faith of Modernism* (1924) that "Modernists as a class are evangelical Christians. That is, they accept Jesus Christ as the revelation of a Savior God." In contrast to the trend of some Protestant liberals to criticize and repudiate doctrines of Christianity, Mathews declared that the Modernist "like any other investigator has a presumption in favor of the reality of that which he is studying" and "by preference his religious starting point is the inherited orthodoxy of a continuing community of Christians." Therefore, while Modernism embraced biblical criticism, it insisted on a continuous and developing Christianity in which God was immanent in culture. "In brief, then," Mathews explained, "the use of scientific, historical, social method in understanding and applying evangelical Christianity to the needs of living persons, is Modernism." "Confessionalism is the evangelicalism of the dogmatic mind," he concluded. "Modernism is the evangelicalism of the scientific mind."

Congregationalist, Protestant Episcopal, Methodist, Presbyterian, and Baptist churches were heavily affected by Liberalism and its Modernist application, each denomination in crisis over the new challenge. As denominational seminaries graduated liberal ministers, however, the new theology progressively penetrated the grass roots of Protestantism. While the advocates of Liberalism progressively dominated the Protestant educational and intellectual milieu in the early decades of the twentieth century, many unashamedly traced their roots to nineteenth-century Evangelicalism, declaring that they were fulfilling the mandate of that great movement.

SOCIAL CONSCIOUSNESS

Emphasis on the person of Jesus Christ and the model he presented for the modern Christian was a key component in Liberalism. This led some liberals to apply the social principles of Jesus to the ills of their society. Lyman Abbott, for example, soon published the book *Christianity and Social Problems* (1896), which began: "Christ's mission was twofold—individual and social; to make men worthy to be called the children of God, and also to make a state of society on earth worthy to be called the Kingdom of God." He decried the fact that Protestant theology had so often emphasized the former mission to individuals and neglected Christ's mission to society.

Certainly, Friedrich Schleiermacher's advocacy of the "God-consciousness supremely expressed in Jesus Christ" set the stage for such a view. German Protestant theologian Albrecht Ritschl (1822–89) placed even more emphasis on the historical Jesus and the "value-judgments" of the moral and spiritual life of faithful followers. In *The Christian Doctrine of Justification and Reconciliation* (1870–74), Ritschl declared that the central teaching of Jesus was the kingdom of God and the ethic of love through which humanity must be organized. "In Christianity," he affirmed, "we can distinguish between the religious functions which relate to our attitude towards God and the World, and the moral functions which point directly to men, and only indirectly to God, Whose end in the world we fulfill by moral service in the Kingdom of God . . . the highest good which God destines for us. . . . "

In England, Anglican minister and professor Frederick Denison Maurice (1805–72) anticipated the modern ecumenical movement in his book *The Kingdom of Christ* (1838). He interpreted the Bible as a progressive manifestation of the covenant between God and man that reaches beyond the individual to the church and society. "I have endeavoured to prove, that if Christ be really the head of every man, and if He really has taken human flesh, there is ground of a universal fellowship among men," he explained about the theme of the book in a letter to a friend. Discussing the variations of Protestant belief, including Lutheran, Calvinist, and Zwinglian perspectives, Maurice in *The Kingdom of Christ* concluded that as long as the varied Protestant traditions stood for constructive principles, they "served the truth." When they hardened into systems that were exclusive and

98

negative in character, decay was inherent and the kingdom of Christ was deflected from its main purpose. " 'Let all thine enemies perish, O Lord'; all systems, schools, parties which have hindered men from seeing the largeness and freedom, and glory of thy kingdom," he burst out in conclusion to this voluminous work, " 'but let them that love Thee,' in whatever earthly mists they may at present be involved, 'be as the sun when he goeth forth in his strength.' "

With the advance of the factory system in Europe after 1815 and its deplorable working conditions, a humanitarian idealism from the Enlightenment gave rise to small secular utopian socialist movements in France and England. Both the upper and lower ranks of society had criticized industry's evils and proposed reforms. In January, 1848, however, Karl Marx (1818–83) and Friedrich Engels (1820–95) published the famous *Communist Manifesto,* advocating violent revolution. Although Marx was a relatively unknown figure at this time, workers did revolt in France the same year, demanding "the right to work."

Convinced that these secular socialist movements would shake the foundations of Christianity if not "made Christian," Maurice with others formed the Society for Promoting Working Men's Associations in January 1850. He also wrote a series of tracts entitled *Tracts on Christian Socialism* to explain what they were about. Maurice knew that fear of socialism would bring them conflict merely because of the title; but he insisted that the title "would commit them at once to the conflict they must engage in sooner or later, with the unsocial Christians and the un-Christian Socialists."

Maurice was concerned about the social imperatives of the gospel rather than with specific political or economic goals. He saw injustice around him caused by greed and avarice, and he tried to counteract this through workers' cooperatives. As professor of English literature and modern history at King's College, London, and later professor of theology at its new theological college, he sought to challenge his students to the "work of the Kingdom," *not* to make them Socialists. Protesting against communism, anarchy, and the upheavals of 1848, he wanted to show the working classes that law and Christianity were the "protectors of all classes" and not the "agents of capital." Writing to Dr. Jelf, principal at King's College, on December 20, 1851, Maurice explained this, noting: "We believe that Christianity has the power of regenerating whatever it comes in contact with, of making that morally healthful and vigorous which apart from it must be either mischievous or inefficient."

Frederick Denison Maurice's life was embroiled in controversy. Although a fervently committed Anglican, his criticism of the popular view of eternal punishment in his *Theological Essays* (1853) was used as a pretext for his dismissal from King's College. And yet he continued to view himself as a unifier, a proponent of "positive belief." On October 24, 1862, he wrote to Rev. A. P. Stanley that positive belief was necessary then because "the world seems divided between orthodoxy and liberalism, each seeking to stifle everything but itself, each recognizing no enemy except the other."

Appointed Knightbridge Professor of Moral Theology and Moral Philosophy at Cambridge University in 1866, he continued his teaching, writing, and pastoral duties. He has been portrayed as one of the greatest thinkers of Protestantism in Victorian England, a portrayal he might have found curious. "To preach the Gospel of that Kingdom [the kingdom of Heaven that renews the earth]," he once stated at age forty-seven, "the fact that it is among us, and is not to be set up at all, is my calling and business."

AMERICA'S SOCIAL GOSPEL

Nineteenth-century postmillennialism and the new theology combined in a small group of American Protestants to produce one of the most significant contributions of Protestant Liberalism—the Social Gospel movement. Building upon the social consciousness and kingdom of God theologies nurtured in Europe, the Social Gospelers would in due time have a great impact on Protestant theology throughout the world.

Periodic depressions in the United States had served historically to bring the problems of the poor and destitute to the attention of the American public. After fifteen years of increasing prosperity, the summer of 1857 found an epidemic of bank and business failures that spread gloom over the American populace. *Harper's Weekly* (October 10, 1857) noted the deep apprehension on the American scene and reported that "never has the future seemed so incalculable as at this time."

Private and public funds were mustered to meet the emergency, most public funds being aid grants by city governments. As private agencies and private citizens evaluated this public relief effort, they saw the danger of public officials' using the funds for political ends, and the lack of expertise even among those who had good intentions. A debate ensued over which was superior, public or private relief. The general American attitude that prevailed after the Civil War was summed up by the Philadelphia Society for Organized Charity in 1885: "Experience proves that public money voted for such relief is often wasted and sometimes stolen. . . . It directly encourages the idle, the shiftless and degraded to live at the public charge rather than earn their own bread."

In the wake of the depression of the 1870s and this nineteenth-century philosophy of "private" philanthropy, Christian charitable organizations flourished. Evangelical organizations, such as the Young Men's Christian Association and the Salvation Army, reached out to the poor in a variety of services. Local branches of the Y.M.C.A. distributed money, food, and clothing to poor families. They also instituted surveys to establish conditions in their cities, a technique that would be copied by social workers in the last decade of the nineteenth century. In revivalist fashion the Y.M.C.A. during this period put evangelism as a number-one priority, because it believed that the poor had to have a spiritual renewal of their lives to make physical help complete. Nevertheless, its emphasis on relief measures and the social concern manifested in its help in any charitable work in its community made the Y.M.C.A. a reputable and respected organization throughout the United States.

The Salvation Army, an offshoot of William Booth's (1829–1912) successful evangelism and mission in London in the 1870s, spread to the United States by 1880. Its "slum brigade" lived in the inhospitable tenements and both physically and spiritually helped their neighbors, that is, prostitutes, former prisoners, vagrants, unwed mothers, unemployed. These Protestants identified their own interests with the welfare and well-being of their neighbors in the slums. Living next to the unfortunate helped these workers identify more clearly the problems that needed attention and, more importantly, to view these people as human beings. The publication of William Booth's *In Darkest England* in 1890 served to awaken other Americans to the plight of the poor. American Protestantism was growing toward a more sympathetic understanding of the total situation of the poor, an understanding that would characterize the emerging twentieth-century Progressive movement under President Theodore Roosevelt (1901–09).

And yet, even Protestant liberals had much to learn. In spite of the awakening social conscience from 1865 to 1890, it was generally assumed by American Protestantism that the poor had brought their afflictions on themselves. The average nineteenth-century American felt that any man of initiative could work his way from rags to riches, and such a view infected Protestantism as well.

For instance, Lyman Abbott's mentor, Rev. Henry Ward Beecher, who in 1847 declared that he must have freedom to speak out on social issues and used his pulpit in the Plymouth Church to oppose slavery, looked out on New York City from his pulpit in the 1870s and declared: "The general truth will stand, that no man in this land suffers from poverty unless it be more than his fault—unless it be his sin—if men have not enough, it is owing to want of provident care, and foresight, and industry, and frugality, and wise saving. This is the general truth." Thus the poor were blamed for their own circumstances.

The noted social worker and founder of Hull House in Chicago, Jane Addams (1860–1935), was so upset by such statements that in 1897 she castigated the delegates to the National Conference of Charities and Correction for their belief that the people they aided "might not deserve their aid." Ironically, two years later, Washington Gladden (1836–1918), famed pastor of First Congregational Church in Columbus, Ohio, and proponent of social consciousness, addressed the same conference, emphasizing that indeed many in the poorer classes were selfish and did not want to work. He noted that he had declared this many times in the past and that "the business of breeding paupers" must be stopped. Little wonder that Jane Addams's graphic account of her famed settlement house, *Twenty Years at Hull House* (1910), called the decade from 1890 to 1900 "a period of propaganda as over against constructive social effort; the moment for marching and carrying banners, for stating general principles. . . , " instead of providing for laws and organization to solve social ills.

In spite of the complacency, self-satisfaction, and social conservatism of liberal Protestants as they groped their way toward theoretical understanding of the plight of fellow human beings, the prophetic impulse of the Social Gospel grew stronger among their ranks. From 1893 to 1897 depression and despair laid the problem of society's structure and lack of regulation squarely on the Protestant churchgoer's doorstep. Groups of unemployed marched on Washington, D.C. in the spring of 1894, and some clergymen took note.

Washington Gladden's exposure to the plight of the working class in his pastorates at North Adams, Massachusetts and in the industrial city of Springfield, Massachusetts engendered compassion as he determined to aid the coal miners in the Hocking Valley Coal Strike of 1884. Later, his criticism of the American industrialists' abuse, and his demand in print and speech that Protestantism concern itself with social injustice, helped awaken Christians. He became one of the most influential clergy in America, and published thirty-six books.

Others, such as Josiah Strong (1847–1916), pastor of Central Congregational Church in Cincinnati, Ohio, and general secretary of the Evangelical Alliance, convened interdenominational conferences on the urban plight, while professors such as Francis Greenwood Peabody (1847–1936) of Harvard Divinity School instituted courses on social ethics to influence a new generation of Protestant ministers. Through similar courses at Andover Theological Seminary, evangelical liberal professors, such as William Jewett Tucker (1839–1926), inspired the formation of a settlement house in Boston's South End. The "Andover Liberals" turned their "progressive orthodoxy" into a powerful ideological weapon for social justice, while Strong's *Our Country: Its Possible Future and Its Present Crisis* (1885) and Peabody's *Jesus Christ and the Social Question* (1900) became influential books at the turn of the century.

Walter Rauschenbusch

The passionate prophet, however, of what came to be known as the Social Gospel was Walter Rauschenbusch (1861–1918). The son of German immigrants who were pietistic Baptists, Walter was brought up in Rochester, New York, where his father, Karl, taught in the German department of Rochester Theological Seminary. Receiving his early education in Germany and the United States, Walter, in his latter teen years, underwent a conversion experience that had deep meaning for him for the rest of his life. He returned to Germany the same year (1879), spending four years in classical studies and becoming familiar with German biblical criticism. Called to the ministry in 1883, he came back to America and graduated from both the University of Rochester and Rochester Theological Seminary.

A deeply pious man in the Evangelical tradition, he offered himself to the German Baptists for missionary service, but was rejected because some conservative members of the board doubted the orthodoxy of his views concerning biblical criticism of the Old Testament. He was appointed instead to be pastor of the Second German Baptist Church on West 45th Street in New York City, near a poverty-stricken area known as "Hell's Kitchen."

The move was fortuitous, because Rauschenbusch came face to face with the plight of the poor. Malnutrition, disease, despair, unemployment, and crime were brought to his doorstep and soon challenged his theology. As social awareness grew, he became a passionate advocate of social reform. Reinhold Niebuhr (1892–1971) has stated that Rauschenbusch was "the real founder of social Christianity in this country."

During this pastorate Rauschenbusch wrote a monograph entitled *The Righteousness of the Kingdom.* This early work was not published during his lifetime and was discovered in the archives of the American Baptist Historical Society only in the 1960s. The passions of the young pastor explode throughout the volume, giving insights into the profound changes in his life and thought. "Christianity is in its nature revolutionary," he thundered, explaining that the aim of the revolutionary movement inaugurated by Jesus was the "Kingdom of God." Near the end he affirmed that the struggle for the kingdom was a battle, one that neither politics nor education, but only religion, could win. "Let us have no illusions," he concluded. "The world will not evolve into a Kingdom of God by natural processes. It is uphill work. It is a battle. Every inch will have to be fought for . . . the hope of the world therefore lies in religion."

In 1891, due to partial deafness, Rauschenbusch had to resign his pastorate, traveling first to England and then studying in Germany. There he became increasingly aware of the import of the writings of Schleiermacher, Ritschl, Wellhausen, the Christian socialists, and others who had forged biblical criticism and the liberal movement. He became an Evangelical liberal, combining his deep pietism with liberal scholarship.

Called back to teach at Rochester Theological Seminary in 1897, he became professor of church history in 1902. He began to write once again on social issues and his finished product was *Christianity and the Social Crisis*, a thorough success when it appeared in 1907 in the midst of the Progressive movement. Rauschenbusch was inundated with calls to speak and write on the issue.

In his introduction to *Christianity and the Social Crisis*, Rauschenbusch explained that "Western civilization is passing through a social revolution unparalleled in history for scope and power," but this social revolution had been slow in reaching the United States. He indicated again that "the Church, the organized expression of the religious life of the past, is one of the most potent institutions and forces in Western civilization." In the early chapters of the text, he documented the history of social Christianity, from the Hebrew prophets to the message of Jesus to the life of the early church. He maintained that "history is never antiquated, because humanity is always fundamentally the same."

Against this social backdrop, he then asked the question, "Why has Christianity never undertaken the work of social reconstruction?" He answered that the church was in bondage to the world, dominated at first by the state and later by the clergy and their monarchical organization. The Protestant Reformation, in Rauschenbusch's estimation, began a change that broke the power of such a hierarchy, until "those Protestant bodies which constitute the bulk of Protestantism in America and of free churches in England all have the essence of church democracy." Even the Roman Catholic church would not escape the democratic influence.

Since the "intellectual prerequisites" for "social reconstruction" were currently on the scene, Rauschenbusch noted the "profound sense of God's presence and overruling power" in the affairs of mankind. "We are standing at the turning of the ways," he challenged his readers. "We are actors in a great historical drama. It rests upon us to decide if a new era is to dawn in the transformation of the world into the Kingdom of God, or if Western civilization is to descend to the graveyard of dead civilizations and God will have to try once more."

With this prophetic challenge, Rauschenbusch laid "the Present Crisis" at the feet of his readers, moved on to the modern church's responsibility to the social movement, and gave suggestions in a later chapter on how to promote "social evangelization." He concluded that men and women must change their own personality, repenting of the sins of existing society and appropriating "the revolutionary consciousness" of Jesus. Through family, school, and church, cooperative and fraternal organizations, such religious faith and moral strength will "snap the bonds of evil and turn the present unparalleled economic and intellectual resources of humanity to the harmonious development of a true social life. . . . "

In the following work, *Christianizing the Social Order* (1912), Rauschenbusch evaluated the industrial, capitalistic system and proposed reforms that would fully Christianize the "semi-Christian" civilization. A few years later, in *The Social Principles of Jesus* (1916), part of the eight-part College Voluntary Study Courses for the Sunday School Council of Evangelical Denominations, he reiterated the fundamental convictions of Jesus about social and ethical relationships as well as the responsibilities of men and women to practice those convictions.

Significantly, Rauschenbusch's *Theology of the Social Gospel* (1917) appeared at the end of his life. Expanding on his Nathaniel W. Taylor Lectures at Yale School of Religion, the church historian and social prophet turned reluctant systematic theologian. "It is just as orthodox as the Gospel would allow," prefaced the man who had once called the theological enterprise "the esoteric thought of the church." But in the first sentence of his main manuscript he gave his rationale for such a project: "We have a social gospel. We need a systematic theology large enough to match it and vital enough to back it." Rauschenbusch then plunged into topics ranging from the fall of humankind and the nature of evil to the kingdom of Evil and the kingdom of God.

In Walter Rauschenbusch, the social prophet, all of the themes of the Social Gospel came together, that is, that the social principles of Jesus, through dedicated individuals, could bring in the kingdom of God, converting once evil institutions to progressive, divine instruments. His clarity, vision, and passion made him the "soul" of the Social Gospel, a gospel that was propounded by only a small but significant minority of the liberal movement. Modern Protestantism would capture the spirit of Rauschenbusch's message and view it as one of its most precious legacies.

TWENTIETH-CENTURY CHALLENGES

The twentieth century dawned with an air of postmillennial optimism and hope of the kingdom of God. Industrial progress and technology increased, and Christianity seemed to be spreading throughout the world in the wake of colonization and evangelization. Nevertheless, the period of World War I (1914–19) through World War II (1939–45) would catapult Protestantism into an era of new challenges and creative responses.

World War I

World War I almost completely discredited postmillennial eschatology among Protestant theologians and lay people. This view that humanity was "getting better," moving toward an era of peace and prosperity to which the Messiah would return, did not harmonize with the massive, worldwide destruction in which thirty nations were involved. Armed forces numbering sixty-five million were locked in merciless battle, nearly one-seventh of them dying and another one-third maimed. In Europe, large civilian casualties brought the specter even closer to every Protestant home. Technology and science had been used for death and destruction, and the world soon understood that the era of chemical warfare had arrived.

Concepts of the kingdom of God and the manifest destiny to make the world "Christian" had been abused and distorted by all sides in the conflagration to further their respective war aims. Extreme Protestant nationalism in Germany and Britain overshadowed the few pockets of Protestant pacifism that survived. In the aftermath, the horrors of global war would convert many more Protestants to the viewpoint that war was "the greatest evil" and should not be supported or condoned in any way.

In the United States, liberals and conservatives alike called for restraint. America's entry into the war was delayed; yet an anti-German hysteria was built up that provided vast resources of deep hatreds that could be tapped once the U.S. entered the war. The University of Chicago Divinity School, for example, a bastion of postmillennial Liberalism, heralded the idealism of the "Christian crusade," World War I. Shirley Jackson Case, professor of early church history, patriotically declared in his colleague Shailer

Mathews's journal, *The Biblical World* (July 1918), "The American nation is engaged in a gigantic effort to make the world safe for democracy." In his book *The Millennial Hope* (1918), published by the University of Chicago Press, he insisted: "Instead of growing worse, the world is found to be growing constantly better." By viewing a "long perspective" of the ages, the atrocities of World War I seemed to Case to be comparatively few and far off.

Such arguments did not last for long, and Protestant liberals along with some segments of the conservative movement found themselves accepting various positions of *a*millennialism, the view that the thousand-year reign of Christ is symbolic and not literal. In this view, the world was not required to become *progressively* better to facilitate the return of the Messiah, but the church continued to be "the salt of the earth." As will be seen in the next chapter, a premillennialist view dominated the Fundamentalist-Evangelical movement of Protestantism. This view of the future declared that only the return of Jesus could initiate the millennium, and the world was becoming progressively worse, not better.

Theology of Success in America

Although social problems still existed in the United States after the war, the legislation enacted by the Progressive movement, that is, child labor laws (passed but not implemented for many years), women's suffrage, antitrust legislation, and so on, made the average church member feel that much had been done for the poor and the outcasts of society. The "successful" war effort brought a new mentality which slackened the reform impulse in the 1920s. The nation assumed that the task of reform "had been accomplished." Liberals and conservatives alike allowed big business and government to develop close relationships, which appeared to be blossoming into a life of material abundance for the average American. With church attendance up and piety high, Protestants began to succumb to the lure of the American dream. The affluent society posed as deep a challenge for Protestant ethics as the war itself, for American Protestantism faced a theology of success.

A good example of the success-oriented mentality that inaugurated the decade with a baptism of religious fervor was the Interchurch World Movement. Based on organizational techniques learned during the fund-raising drives for the war effort and claiming to be "a cooperative effort of evangelical churches" to ascertain their common tasks and bind together in an immense drive to accomplish those tasks, the I.W.M. sought to unite every benevolent and missionary agency in American Protestantism in one campaign to secure needed money, workers, and religious fervor. Liberal Protestants spurred the drive as world needs were analyzed, broad educational programs in business and management for churches were initiated, and elaborate promotional campaigns were launched. Their bulletin released in April 1920 described "the biggest business of the biggest man in the world":

> Christ was big, was He not? None ever bigger.
> Christ was busy, was He not? None ever busier.
> He was always about His Father's business.
> Christ needs big men for big business.

The I.W.M. fell victim to its elaborate goals and awesome overhead. It was unable to pay its debt and within two years was bankrupt.

In 1922, William Adams Brown (1865–1943) published his monumental book, *The Church in America: A Study of the Present Condition and Future Prospects of American Protestantism.* Roosevelt Professor of Systematic Theology at Union Theological Seminary, Brown was one of Protestant Liberalism's most eminent and influential teachers. He viewed the Interchurch World Movement as "the most signal expression" of the hope that the lessons of war might be learned for all time. Believing in an ideal that Protestantism might "throw aside all pettiness and provinciality," contributing to the "welfare of the whole," Brown insisted that the I.W.M. was the "religious counterpart" to the League of Nations. To Brown, the failure of the I.W.M. occurred because the war had been so "successful" in proving to various denominations that they had first "to set their house in order."

Although he recognized that the war left a psyche of indulgence among the American populace that also contributed to the fall of the I.W.M., Brown upheld business as a philanthropic career opportunity. "Even business is losing its exclusive association with money-getting," he related with pleasure, "and is coming to be regarded in a new light as a form of public service." Optimistically, he concluded that "democracy has a right to expect of the Church a unifying spiritual influence," an influence that promotes the ends of democratic Western culture and produces the new social order of the kingdom of God. H. Richard Niebuhr later criticized this as "culture-Protestantism."

During the Roaring Twenties, the appeal of success and the romanticism of business spread. While President [John] Calvin Coolidge (1923–29) declared, "America's business is business," a number of books on Jesus as the "successful businessman" were published. Advertising executive Bruce Barton's *The Man Nobody Knows: A Discovery of the Real Jesus* (1924) not only depicts Jesus as "the founder of modern business," but also an advertising specialist, a socialite, and an executive. The *New York Times Book Review* called his treatment "reverent," and Barton's following work on the Bible was entitled *The Book Nobody Knows* (1925).

Former lawyer turned Philadelphia Baptist minister, Russell H. Conwell, delivered his address, "Acres of Diamonds," all over the world. To millions of eager listeners he emphasized that wealth lies all around them "awaiting development." Orison Sweet Marden's *Success Magazine* had a circulation of nearly 500,000 in the 1920s; and he published fifty books after his initial *Pushing to the Front: or, Success Under Difficulties* (1894), a book translated into many foreign languages.

The message of the theology of success was much the same no matter who proposed it. Presenting Protestantism with one of its greatest challenges, it in turn provided Protestantism with one of its greatest historical lessons. "Nice" people were said to own homes in the suburbs, and "poor" people were castigated because they did not manage their money properly. "Successful" rich Christians were pointed out by pastors as shining examples of good Christian initiative. Money was important — money was power! Money was *not* the root of evil, only the love of money was. With money, the successful Christians could reach the world for Christ, send out missionaries to the far corners of the earth, and help the needy.

An affluent Protestant middle class wallowed in its theology of success, prodded by ministers with catchy slogans and success-oriented clichés. Multimillion-dollar churches were built; pews were filled. However, the fairyland that comprised the American dream proved to be shallow. Even when the church helped others, it was often accompanied by a smug superiority and self-satisfaction. American

Protestantism was God's chosen; capitalism was God's economy; success was God's way.

Neo-Orthodoxy

Within Liberal Protestantism, a movement arose that not only called to task the theology of success, but also challenged basic tenets of Liberalism. Seeking to recover the principles of Protestantism and its Reformation heritage, these theologians and historians from diverse backgrounds and varying viewpoints were often categorized under the rubric "theology of crisis" or "Neo-Orthodox," a category that they would not necessarily apply to themselves. But they challenged Liberalism's optimistic view of human nature and questioned the possibility of a cultural kingdom of God.

The increasing secularism within Protestantism and the catastrophe of World War I caused Swiss pastor and theologian Karl Barth (1886–1968) to reassess his German liberal training under Adolf von Harnack (1851–1930) in Berlin and to reevaluate the religious socialism he avowed in his Basel community. Like Martin Luther, Barth turned to the biblical Book of Romans, finding that God, not humankind or culture, was the center of true religion. In his subsequent commentary on Romans, *Römerbrief*, published in 1919, he asserted that only God could dispel the despair and contradiction that surrounded humankind, and that God intersected humankind's world like a vertical line in the person of Jesus Christ. God as "Wholly Other" could not be identified with anything in the world; and the individual's encounter with Jesus on the merely human level missed the full revelation of the risen Christ.

As Kierkegaard held nearly a century earlier, Barth reiterated that truth could be perceived only in an "encounter of faith," not by scientific historical analysis or by human manipulation. Finding liberal emphases on the fatherhood of God and brotherhood of man incomplete and inadequate, he stressed that the knowledge of God occurs in the revelation of the Father, through the Son, and by the Holy Spirit. Barth avowed that God revealed himself through the Bible and that all forms of natural theology that attempted to find God by other means were fruitless and "sinful." While still affirming the Christian commitment to justice, Barth no longer associated such emphases with an eschatological kingdom of God.

With the help of others, Barth founded a theological journal, *Zwischen den Zeiten (Between the Times)*, to which both Emil Brunner (1889–1966) and Rudolf Bultmann (1884–1976) contributed. Brunner would soon challenge Liberalism by stressing the priority of divine revelation over human knowledge and reason. In his book *Der Mittler (The Mediator)*, published in 1927, Brunner singled out Liberalism's failure to make Jesus Christ more than a religious genius, thereby providing a powerless Christology. Brunner became internationally known through lecture tours and writing in the 1930s.

Bultmann, professor of New Testament at the University of Marburg, also criticized Liberal Protestantism for believing it had discovered the authentic "historical Jesus," underscoring that the word of God to humankind demanded the response of faith and was not dependent on scientific history. Nevertheless, using extreme biblical criticism, Bultmann believed that the Synoptic Gospels (Matthew, Mark, and Luke) related the theology of the early church rather than the history of Jesus. For Bultmann, the historical Jesus was an enigma of whose life and personality one can know little if anything. The teachings of Jesus, however, were not only knowable but were also relevant for the modern world. Bultmann's "demythologization" of the New Testament would undergo periodic popularity in Protestant Liberalism during the twentieth century.

In America, Reinhold Niebuhr (1892–1971) and his brother, H. Richard Niebuhr (1894–1962) called into question liberal optimism and the complacent theology of success. In the December 13, 1928 issue of *The Christian Century*, Reinhold published "Barth — Apostle of the Absolute," a review of the translation into English of Karl Barth's *The Word of God and the Word of Man*. Niebuhr observed that Barth posed a problem that "liberal religion has sadly neglected." "It is the highest function of religion to create a sense of guilt, to make man conscious of the fact that his inadequacies are more than excusable limitations," he argued, "that they are treason against his better self. . . . [Sin is] treason against God."

Reinhold Niebuhr admitted that the "moral limitation" of such a view would possibly be to preoccupy oneself with sin to such a degree as to "lose interest in specific moral problems and struggles which must be faced day by day." But he questioned his liberal readers: "Is not the doctrine of progress little more than dogma? Is it not true that history is the sorry tale of new imperialisms supplanting old ones; of man's inhumanity to man. . . ? Is it not a monstrous egotism and foolish blindness which we betray when we imagine that this civilization in which commercialism has corrupted every ideal value is in any sense superior to the Middle Ages . . . ?"

As pastor of the Bethel Evangelical Church in Detroit for thirteen years, Reinhold Niebuhr had viewed poverty and the plight of people caught in the industrial complex of the Ford Motor Company, and he had witnessed the failure of the old Liberalism to minister to their needs. Now, as professor of applied Christianity at Union Theological Seminary in New York City, Niebuhr continued his critical focus on church and society, arguing for a balanced view of human nature and humanity's depravity. In *Does Civilization Need Religion?* (1928), he claimed that the liberal remnants of the past decades were helpless to touch the life of modern people or to cope with the technological revolution. In *Moral Man and Immoral Society* (1932), he contended that the kingdom of God is built by God. He was wary of even the clergy's attempt to construct the kingdom.

His brother, H. Richard Niebuhr, acknowledged Reinhold's "constant interest" in his preface to *The Social Sources of Denominationalism* (1929). Like his brother, H. Richard Niebuhr began his first chapter by castigating Christendom for "ignoring the precepts of its founder," and for glorying in "self preservation" and the "gain of power." H. Richard wrote that in dealing with social evils such as slavery, war, and social inequality, the church had "discovered convenient ambiguities" in the Scriptures to allow it "to ally itself with the prestige and power . . . adapting itself to the conditions of a civilization which its founder had bidden it to permeate with the spirit of divine love." Prone to compromise, the church had lost its prophetic role.

As professor of Christian ethics at Yale Divinity School, H. Richard Niebuhr coauthored *The Church Against the World* (1935), in which he asked the church to withdraw from its uncritical alliances with nationalism, capitalism, and humanism. In his scholarly work *The Kingdom of God in America* (1937), he noted that Protestantism is a movement more than an institution or series of institutions, and is dynamic rather than static. While the danger of Puritanism lay in its effort "to attain security by means of faith in divine sovereignty alone" and the danger of Evangelicalism lay in its tendency "to make sufficient the reign of Christ within all," Niebuhr insisted that the danger of Liberalism was "in its idealism and its tendency to deny the presuppositions on which it was based."

"But Protestantism was never liberal in the sense that it made the free man the starting point of its theology or its ethics," H. Richard Niebuhr pointed out in *The Kingdom of God in America,* maintaining that Protestantism from the time of the Reformation rejected "the liberal assumption that man must begin with himself, with his reason, his will, his ideals, his self-possession." To Niebuhr, Liberal Protestantism seemed to be ambiguous and confused in relation to the burning issues of its culture.

The Great Depression

Such a critique was needed because only the Great Depression throughout the world in the 1930s brought "poverty" and the "needy" to the forefront of concern among Protestants. In America, the theology of success had been so effective that Americans would blame themselves for not being able to get a job, for not being able to support their families—for not being "a success." The Depression was viewed as a personal affront, a personal failure.

For example, the first reaction to the Depression was the optimism of the theology of success in the 1920s, that is, "Don't emphasize hard times and everything will be all right." A good attitude and American ingenuity would bring success. This optimism produced a propaganda that hindered effective measures to relate to the needs of the American urban populace during the early Depression. Any hint of crisis was played down in newspapers as the elite of corporate enterprise assured the American public that the economy was sound. One could trust the "good" people of business when they asserted that everything was under control. Incredibly, the headlines on October 30, 1929, the day after the stock market crashed and hundreds of thousands went bankrupt, encouraged the public. The *New York Times* headline read: "Stocks Collapse in 16,410,030-Share Day But Rally at Close Cheers Brokers."

In the midst of such turmoil, few Protestant Liberals were able to reassess their optimistic theology and speak meaningfully to what was happening. One signal exception was Harry Emerson Fosdick (1878–1969), possibly at that time the most influential clergyman in America. "One of the most dangerous evils in the world is the highly prized habit of always looking on the bright side of things," he preached to his Park Avenue Baptist Church in New York and later over NBC's National Vespers, his nationwide radio program. He then pointed out that Christians "ought most poignantly to feel the human consequences" of economic distress and that American society could never be changed "by external adjustments only."

Fosdick had been deeply embroiled in the Fundamentalist-Modernist controversy of the 1920s. He was considered the preacher of Modernism. Throughout these years he had a sensitivity to social concerns and a disdain for the shallow theology of success, a sensitivity that he carried into the Great Depression. In "Beyond Modernism" in *The Christian Century* (December 4, 1935), he wrote that Christians must go beyond modernism, reaffirming the root of Christianity in biblical revelation and challenging modern culture as Christ would have done. In 1936 he declared: "Essential human nature is much the same wherever it is found, and it is as false and dangerous to glorify the proletariat as it is to play sycophant to the privileged. Sin is 'no respecter of persons.' Its demonic, corrupting power runs through all classes. . . . " It is significant to note that as early as 1922 in his book *Christianity and Progress*, Fosdick realistically wrote about the sinfulness of humankind, anticipating the criticism of the Neo-orthodox movement.

In his autobiography, *The Living of These Days* (1956), Fosdick reminisced that he had endeavored to be "an intelligent, modern and a serious Christian." An excellent preacher, devotional writer, radio personality, social reformer, and professor of practical theology at Union Theological Seminary, his alma mater, he sought to convey a practical Christianity to those struggling with the problems of life. As the Great Depression deepened, his critique of Liberalism's false confidence in social progress and excessive preoccupation with intellectualism affected a new generation of liberal Protestant clergy.

The New Paganism

Meanwhile, in the land of the Reformation, where Protestant theology had displayed such creative expression in the nineteenth century, the "demonic, corrupting power" of extreme nationalism and anti-Semitism worked as a cancer on the body politic. The history of this diabolical development holds crucial lessons for the modern meaning of Protestantism.

At the beginning of the nineteenth century the armies of Napoleon were overpowering Europe, crushing the famous Prussian army at the battles of Jena and Auerstedt in October 1806. This was a time of humiliation for the German people; and because Jews gained some freedom under French rule, the Germans accused them of plotting secretly with Napoleon.

This sense of defeat was intensified by the Germans' own emphasis on nationalism and the superiority of their race. Johann Gottlieb Fichte (1762–1814), professor of philosophy at the University of Berlin, delivered "Addresses to the German Nation" in 1807, which stirred the German people to realize their "exceptional heritage" and to believe that only under Germanic peoples could a new era of history blossom. In a period of anti-French feeling, Fichte's view that Latins, especially the French, and Jews were members of decadent mongrel races while the Germans were the purest was particularly encouraging. Fichte maintained that world affairs were determined by humankind's moral purpose and that the German nation-state must be based on moral convictions—convictions best suited to the Germanic peoples. In spite of his respect for the Bible and for some individual Jews, Fichte wrote: "A mighty state stretches across almost all the countries of Europe, hostile in intent and engaged in constant strife with everyone else. . . . This is Jewry." He portrayed the Jews as in direct conflict with the national aspirations of the German people, in direct conflict with the "moral" German state. It is of no minor consequence that Georg Wilhelm Friedrich Hegel succeeded to the same chair of philosophy in Berlin upon Fichte's death, and the influence of Hegel's philosophy on extreme Germanic nationalism has been noted in chapter 6.

After Napoleon's defeat, the Germans took revenge on the Jewish people. Eighteen sixteen was a year of severe famine and unemployment, and Jakob Friedrich Fries (1773–1843), an anti-Semitic philosopher who lectured at both Jena and Heidelberg Universities, led demonstrations of ultranationalistic students against Jews, urging that they be "destroyed root and branch." Christian Friedrich Ruehs (1781–1820), history professor at the University of Berlin, emphasized that Jews should not be citizens of the *Christian* German state, and that allowing Jews to prosper had brought decline and decay. During the same period, the Jewish community was claiming its right to freedoms provided by the Enlightenment, rights that were systematically being taken away from them. In 1819 riots against Jews broke out in

Germany and spread to neighboring countries. Crying 'Hep! Hep! Hep! Death and destruction to all the Jews," mobs smashed windows and looted businesses and homes.

In this environment, a scientific racism began to develop. It is ironic that one of the first contributors to this "science" of racism was a Frenchman who had no particular aversion to Jews. In his *Essay on the Inequality of the Human Races* (1853), Count Joseph Arthur de Gobineau (1816–82) used the word "Aryan," a word linguistic scholars had used only in reference to a number of related languages including German and Latin, to denote a supreme and original white race. Gobineau claimed that race was the determining factor in the rise and fall of civilizations, postulating a hierarchy of humanity ranging from the superior white race to the inferior black race. Racial mixing had brought decline to the Latin and Semitic peoples, whereas Aryan Germans—the western Germanic tribes—held the key to successful human destiny. These powerful people, he said, could be brought down only by the degenerative effect of race mixing.

Composer Richard Wagner (1813–83), an anti-Semite who blamed all his problems on a fantasized Jewish control of the press and theater, and his son-in-law, Houston Stewart Chamberlain (1855–1927), were among those who broadened Gobineau's "Aryan" to include all Germanic peoples, that is, tall, blond, and long-headed peoples. Adolf Hitler noted in his book, *Mein Kampf* (1925), those to be admired: "Side by side with Frederick the Great stands a Martin Luther as well as a Richard Wagner."

Scientific racism was influenced by a number of other pseudoscientific theories promoted after 1850. The most important of these was Social Darwinism. In England, Herbert Spencer (1820–1903) proposed that there was a constant struggle between humans in which the strongest would win. He suggested the existence of two kinds of knowledge: individual knowledge and racial knowledge. Spencer and his disciples believed natural law dictated that the weak and poor of society should *not* be protected. Social Darwinism was subsequently applied on the national level, implying that stronger nations were the best and had a right to rule others.

These ideas had grave consequences not only for the Jewish community but also for Protestantism. Thinkers like Karl Eugen Dühring (1833–1921), a Social Darwinist who taught philosophy and economics at the University of Berlin, shared Wagner's thesis that Christianity was a product of "Hebraic orientalism" and that those who persisted in the Christian tradition could not possibly fight Jews or defend the Aryan spirit. Eventually, a new paganism evolved, a movement to exalt pre-Christian German folk traditions in an effort to bolster nineteenth-century German nationalism. Ironically, at the same time, medieval Christian stereotypes of Jews and religious anti-Semitism were being brought into the modern age.

The consolidation of the German states into the Second Reich (the second German empire) on January 18, 1871 uplifted the whole nation. Many German Protestants felt that God was instrumental in founding this "Christian" state. A civil religion developed, equating "German" with "Christian," accompanied by both religious and racial anti-Semitism. Religious anti-Semitism insisted that Jews could not retain their Jewish identity, and it demanded that they convert and assimilate. Racial anti-Semitism treated the Jew as a parasite, a biological inferior that conversion and assimilation would not cure, a danger to the body politic.

Often, religious anti-Semitism led to a support structure that racial anti-Semitism could utilize. For example, Adolf Stoecker (1835–1909), a Lutheran minister who rose to the exalted position of Court and Cathedral Preacher in Berlin in 1874, launched his own "Christian" party—the Christian Social Workers' Party—in 1878. He began a vigorous campaign against the Jewish people, declaring that they were the most corrupting influence in German society. In party speeches such as "What We Demand of Modern Jewry" (September 19, 1879), he emphasized that the Jews were "a great danger to German national life" and proposed that the "Christian-German spirit" be strengthened. He likened Judaism to a "cancer," and called for legislation to limit Jewish participation as teachers, judges, lawyers, and businesspeople. Elected to the Reichstag (parliament) from 1881–92 and from 1898–1908, Stoecker influenced the Conservative Party's *Tivoli Programme of 1892*, its political platform which included a paragraph that read: "We oppose the many-sided thrustful and disintegrating Jewish influence upon our national life. We desire to have a Christian Government for our Christian people and Christian teachers for our pupils." The *Tivoli Programme* remained in effect until the outbreak of World War I.

It is little wonder that after the humiliating defeat and reparations of World War I, this anti-Semitism and extreme nationalism grew. To their discredit, many German Protestants were responsible for bringing down the struggling democratic government of the Weimar Republic, an act that led not only to the rise of Adolf Hitler but also to his legal election as chancellor on January 30, 1933.

During the mid-1920s, it is estimated that 70 to 80 percent of the Protestant pastors had allied themselves with the right-wing nationalist Protestant German National People's Party. The large majority of Protestant clergy in Germany believed democracy was non-Christian. They also believed that the fatherland had endured a monstrous stab in the back as they looked with nostalgia on the lost glory of "Christian" Imperial Germany. As one pastor asserted: "From our Christian way of looking at life, we seek to act as a breakwater against the democratic waves of the present time. All efforts to make the State democratic are basically designed to dechristianize the *Volk* (common people). We Christians remain reactionaries by God's Grace."

Anti-Semitism became an integral part of the Protestant German National People's Party program through the 1920s. This amalgam of political conservatives, radical nationalists, and anti-Semites claimed to fight "against the Jewish predominance in government and public life." In the 1924 election campaign, party posters called for resistance to Jewish influence on all fronts. One Protestant pastor defined "Christian anti-Semitism" as "genuine Germans and convinced Christians — the best weapon against alien infection." In addition, the principal church weekly publications in the 1920s consistently supported this "Christian" nationalism, preaching Jewish responsibility for the collapse of the "Christian and monarchical order." Jews became scapegoats for everything.

This constant bombardment weakened the moral resistance of many Protestant church members to the initial anti-Semitic measures of the Nazis, blunting basic Christian humanity and outrage at sinful anti-Semitism. William Laible, editor of a Lutheran weekly with the largest circulation in the country, propagated anti-Semitic slanders, and in 1929 he editorialized that, because of the Jews' responsibility for the religious, economic, and moral decline of the nation, readers should welcome "for the sake of the German people . . . every expression of justifiable anti-Semitism."

Nevertheless, a few individual pastors, such as Eduard Lamparter in Stuttgart, courageously stood alone and without compromise against anti-Semitism. In a 1928 booklet entitled *Evangelical Church and the Jews*, Lamparter condemned the expanding anti-Semitism within the church. He wrote that the church ought "to feel it her duty to bear witness against the anti-Semitic violation of Right, Truth and Love." He denounced racial theories, saying they had no authentic scientific foundation. According to this Lutheran pastor, the church must right past wrongs and prevent future injustices; it must explode anti-Semitic stereotypes that "worked like poison" within the Christian. In 1931 the Church of Wurttemberg, where Lamparter was pastor, attempted to get the German Evangelical church to pass an official motion condemning anti-Semitism. The effort failed.

By 1933, it was too late. The large majority of Protestants who thought they knew "God's" political, economic, and ethical system actually supported a regime that was godless, hated the church, and would perpetrate some of the greatest atrocities in the history of humankind. The Nazis appeared as the angels of light and successfully deceived even supposedly knowledgeable Protestants into casting their vote of support for darkness.

Hitler was able to incorporate the church of the Reformation into his political network as "German Christians," in spite of the protests of the Pastors' Emergency Alliance, led by Martin Niemöller (1892–1984), Lutheran pastor of Berlin's Dahlem Church. The Barmen Declaration of May 1934, written under the guidance of Karl Barth, repudiated the false doctrine of the "German Christians" and recalled the German Evangelical church to the central truths of Christianity. It also rejected undivided loyalty to the state and the state's attempt to usurp the role of the Protestant church.

Unfortunately, although Niemöller attacked the laws against non-Aryans in the ministry as a violation of the confessional stance of the Christian church, and although many of these people fought for the rights of their Hebrew Christian pastors, this Confessing church failed to cry out against the violation of the civil and religious rights of the Jewish people. Dietrich Bonhoeffer (1906–45), who realized in 1933 that the critical issue was the Nazi treatment of the Jews, was an exception. Niemöller, Barth, and other Protestant theologians and clergy admitted later to fighting inadequately for the Jewish cause. Protesters were treated like members of any resistance movement.

120

Niemöller was reproached by the Nazi hierarchy and fellow pastors. Arrested on July 1, 1937, he was tried in 1938 and sent to the Sachsenhausen concentration camp and transferred to Dachau in 1941. A worldwide effort was launched to free him, but to no avail. Barth was dismissed on June 22, 1935, from his position as professor of theology at the University of Bonn. He spent the rest of his life in Switzerland as professor of theology at the University of Basel. Bonhoeffer joined the German underground. Implicated in a plot to kill Hitler, he was arrested on April 5, 1943, and executed on April 9, 1945 — only three weeks before Hitler committed suicide. His book, *The Cost of Discipleship* (1937), however, lives on, illustrating the significance of Jesus' Sermon on the Mount for contemporary living. A number of less celebrated German Protestants also maintained their integrity in opposing the Nazis.

Some Protestant leaders would learn from this experience and would seek to teach a new generation the pitfalls of a fascination with the "Christian" or "Protestant" state. They would present the awesome potential of "man's inhumanity to man" even in a civilized society and the dire consequences for those who do not protect the rights of other racial or religious groups.

The Holocaust, the extermination by the Nazis and their compatriots of six million Jews and five million Gentiles, would be a starting point for more intense Jewish/Christian dialogue and relationships, and in the last two decades has figured more prominently in the Protestant theological enterprise. Nevertheless, it was a costly lesson for Protestantism. Two-thirds of European Jewry, one-third of the Jewish world population, were killed by "Christians." Those comparatively few Protestants who sacrificially gave of themselves to help the Jewish people stand today as beacon lights toward a more modern meaning of Protestantism — a meaning that incorporates Jesus the Jew.

LIBERALISM AND PROTESTANTISM

One of the refugees from Nazi Germany was the eminent philosophical theologian, Paul Tillich (1886–1965). H. Richard Niebuhr had translated his book *The Religious Situation* (1926) into English in 1932, and as the Nazis rose in power, there was a great fear for Tillich's life. Tillich had warned his compatriots in print against giving their loyalty to the Nazis, emphasizing that Protestant principles demanded a protest against such idolatry. Hated for his words as much as for his Christian socialism, Tillich was amazed that his theologically liberal colleagues succumbed in such numbers to Nazi pressures and became social conservatives.

Reinhold Niebuhr and Union Theological Seminary president, Henry Sloane Coffin (1877–1954), provided a haven for Tillich. Niebuhr had written against the Nazis and had visited Germany in the summer of 1933. He immediately realized the hopelessness of the situation and the danger Tillich was in. Tillich was persuaded to bring his wife, Hannah, and seven-year-old daughter, Erdmuthe, to the United States in October. He began teaching at Union and Columbia in February 1934, the Union faculty contributing part of their salaries as well as household items to make his stay possible. Through distinguished refugees from Germany who visited Tillich, the Union faculty and students became more aware of the surrender of German Protestantism to the new paganism of the Nazis.

Tillich became a synthesizer between Liberalism and Neo-orthodoxy. Like Karl Barth, he rejected Liberalism's culture-Protestantism. He provided an alternative to Barth by trying to mediate the split between the religious and the secular realms. His attempt centered around the fact that "the Word became flesh" (John 1:14) — that Jesus entered cultural as well as human reality. To Tillich, "For God so loved the *world* that He sent His only begotten son" (John 3:16) meant that divine grace could heal the *totality* of the world. Unlike the Neo-orthodox movement, he was neither willing to leave the secular culture to its own devices nor even to treat as accidental the meeting of God and humankind. For Tillich, humans and culture discover their true identity in God, the "Ground of Being"; and he called their mutual relatedness "ultimate concern." Tillich was a master at relating the center of the Christian faith to the various structures of the secular sphere, relentlessly seeking the meaning of humanity and life itself. Even the many liberal Protestants who disagreed with him would respectfully take into account his system of ethics, "symbol" and "myth" categorizations, views on Protestant principles, and his "crisis and renewal" view of history.

Although Tillich had no intention of abandoning classic Protestant doctrines, he, like many other modern Protestant theologians, rejected a literal interpretation of the Bible. Liberalism's tradition,

122

therefore, of rethinking the Bible, theology, and history in an effort to ascertain truth in a modern culture remained intact. Even that critic of Protestant Liberalism, Reinhold Niebuhr, would recognize this important contribution of the movement in a 1956 essay entitled "Literalism, Individualism, and Billy Graham." He wrote in *The Christian Century* (May 23, 1956) that the "end of the First World War represented the effective end of the 'liberal' world view," particularly the conceptions of "the perfectibility of man and of historical progress." Niebuhr also recognized that Liberal Protestantism had failed because it had not included the "Christ of the Bible" in its modern schemes of redemption and had "departed from the classical and Biblical Christology." For Niebuhr, it was this "scandal" of eliminating the heart of the gospel that led to Protestant Liberalism's misrepresentation of human nature and history.

Nonetheless, Niebuhr worried that the return to "orthodoxy" had brought the "danger of sacrificing one of the great achievements of 'liberal' theology — namely, the absolute honesty with which it encouraged the Church to examine the Scriptural foundations of its faith," that is, loyalty to the truth and fidelity to the intellectual standards of the modern world. Niebuhr also underscored the fact that the Social Gospel and its love of justice arose in the great stream of Protestant Liberalism; and he complained that evangelist Billy Graham's "framework of pietistic moralism" presented Christian salvation as a magic panacea to temptations that continued to affect devoted Christians. Niebuhr's keen analysis both described Liberalism's ongoing contribution and indicated its areas of weakness.

Since in 1956 Billy Graham represented the center of the stream of Fundamentalist-Evangelical Protestantism that flowed from nineteenth-century Evangelicalism, it is important to analyze this other great movement that contributes to the dynamic of modern Protestantism.

SUGGESTED READING

Hutchinson, William R. *The Modernist Impulse in American Protestantism.* Cambridge, Mass.: Harvard Univ. Press, 1982.

Marty, Martin E. *The Irony of It All: 1893–1919.* Chicago: Univ. of Chicago Press, 1986.

Mathews, Shailer. *The Faith of Modernism.* New York: Macmillan Co., 1924.

Miller, William R., ed. *Contemporary American Protestant Thought, 1900–1970.* Indianapolis: Bobbs-Merrill, 1973.

Niebuhr, H. Richard. *The Kingdom of God in America.* New York: Harper & Brothers, 1937.

Reardon, Bernard M. *Liberalism and Tradition.* New York: Cambridge Univ. Press, 1975.

Rochester, Stuart I. *American Liberal Disillusionment in the Wake of World War I.* College Park, Pa.: Pennsylvania State Univ. Press, 1977.

Rupp, George. *Culture-Protestantism: German Liberal Theology at the Turn of the Twentieth Century.* American Academy of Religion, Studies in Religion, no. 15, 1977.

Welch, Claude. *Protestant Thought in the Nineteenth Century: Vol. 2, 1870–1914.* New Haven, Conn.: Yale Univ. Press, 1986.

8

FUNDAMENTALISM

Like American Liberal Protestantism, American Fundamentalism came to prominence in the latter decades of the nineteenth century in reaction to the challenge of biblical criticism and Darwin's theory of evolution. This eary Fundamentalist Protestantism is a complex entity for the historian to define because, like the Puritan movement, its leadership, periodicals, and meetings are extremely visible, but difficult to classify and categorize.

Episcopalians, Methodists, Congregationalists, Presbyterians, Baptists, and other denominations joined the ranks of Fundamentalism — making a denominational classification irrational if not impossible. Theologians from a multitude of diverse educational institutions collaborated on its theology — making an educational classification impractical. Lay people with varied backgrounds and skills entered its ranks — making a vocational classification implausible. Participants from different classes and ethnic groups subscribed to its tenets — making a class distinction unattainable. Because most of its members belonged to a major American Protestant denomination, the early Fundamentalist movement developed into a church within the church.

While historians disagree on the major roots of the movement, two essential doctrinal stances appear to be integral to the early Fundamentalist movement. The first was an emphasis that the Bible was the literal Word of God and that it must be taken in context as the supreme rule of faith and practice. This position was directly related to the Conservative Evangelicalism that dominated most of nineteenth-century Protestantism. Thus, Fundamentalism would arise as a stream within the conservative Evangelical movement.

The second essential doctrinal stance was an emphasis on

premillennial eschatology, that is, the view that only the return of Jesus Christ could properly order the world and institute a millennium of peace and prosperity. As has been shown, this viewpoint contrasted completely with the prevalent eschatology of the nineteenth century, Protestant postmillennialism, which taught that cultural progress through the church and conversion would initiate the millennium.

One notes the systematizing of these doctrinal attitudes into a decisive foundation in the latter decades of the nineteenth century. Since these teachings received great emphasis and detailed analysis in the Fundamentalist-Evangelical movement of the twentieth century and are woven into the fabric of modern Protestantism, each must be considered.

BIBLICAL LITERALISM

As biblical criticism became more vocal in the nineteenth century, a number of books defending the infallibility of the Bible were published. One that would become very popular in the early Fundamentalist movement was written by a Swiss Reformed pastor and founder of an independent evangelical seminary in Geneva, François Samuel Robert Louis Gaussen (1790–1863). Entitled *Theopneustia: The Plenary Inspiration of the Holy Scriptures deduced from Internal Evidence, and the Testimonies of Nature, History and Science*, it was published in French in 1841, but soon was translated into English and distributed throughout Britain and the United States. Over a century later, Moody Bible Institute's Fundamentalist-Evangelical publishing company, Moody Press, issued a new edition under the title *The Inspiration of the Holy Scriptures* (1949).

Even at the end of the nineteenth century, Fundamentalists had been worried that the original title used in the text would "repel ordinary readers." Throughout the text, "plenary inspiration," "divine inspiration," and "verbal inspiration" were substituted for the author's *theopneustia*, a term derived from the Koine Greek word *theopneustos*, used in 2 Tim. 3:16, that is, "All scripture is given by *inspiration of God, and is profitable for doctrine, for reproof, for correction, for instruction in righteousness.*" Gaussen explained at the beginning of his monograph: "This term is used for the mysterious power which the Divine Spirit put forth on the authors of the scriptures of the Old and New Testament, in order to their composing these as they have been received by the Church of God at their hands."

Using internal proofs from statements in the Bible, Gaussen insisted that the inspiration of the Bible was asserted throughout, but never "precisely defined." He castigated critics, such as Schleiermacher, De Wette, "and many other German divines," for rejecting the miraculous in Scripture; and he decried English scholars for assigning "degrees of divine inspiration." "To our mind," Gaussen noted, "these are all fantastic distinctions; the Bible has not authorized them; the Church of the first eight centuries of the Christian era knew nothing of them; and we believe them [the critics] to be erroneous in themselves, and deplorable in their results."

"Scripture is then from God; it is everywhere from God, and everywhere it is entirely from God," Gaussen concluded, after answering critics from the testimony of Scripture and the history of the church. "That is our thesis; and this is what we have done to establish it; this we could only do by Scripture." He summarized that "there are in the Christian world but two schools, or two religions: that which puts the Bible above every thing, and that which puts something above the Bible." There was no doubt that Gaussen was of the former.

The great English Baptist preacher and prolific writer, Charles Haddon Spurgeon (1834–92), praised Gaussen's *Theopneustia* as "the turning point of the battle between those who hold 'the faith once delivered to the saints,' and their opponents." Spurgeon added, "If we have in the Word of God no infallible standard of truth, we are at sea without a compass, and no danger from rough weather without can be equal to this loss within."

Such European defense of the Bible was augmented by developments in America at Princeton Theological Seminary. The "Princeton Theology," as outsiders referred to it, became the bastion of nineteenth-century Reformed theology and the defender within Conservative Evangelicalism of the inspiration of the Bible. Fundamentalist-Evangelicals would join forces with these Reformed theologians in an effort to impede the spread of biblical criticism.

In his three-volume *Systematic Theology* (1872–73), Charles Hodge (1797–1878), professor of exegetical and didactic theology at Princeton Theological Seminary, maintained that the Bible was "the Protestant Rule of Faith." "All Protestants agree in teaching that 'the word of God, as contained in the Scriptures of the Old and New Testaments, is the only infallible rule of faith and practice.' " He substantiated his claim by quoting Lutheran, Reformed, and Anglican confessions of faith.

Hodge went on to defend the "plenary inspiration of the Bible," affirming that all of the books of the Protestant canon were "fully inspired." "This of course does not imply that the sacred writers were infallible except for the special purpose for which they were employed," he explained. "As to all matters of science, philosophy, and history, they stood on the same level with their contemporaries. They were infallible only as teachers, and when acting as the spokesmen of God."

Hodge admitted that "the Scriptures do contain, in a few instances, discrepancies which with our present means of knowledge, we are unable satisfactorily to explain," but affirmed that "they furnish no rational ground for denying their infallibility." Hodge's student, Benjamin Breckinridge Warfield (1851–1921), spent a considerable amount of time taking "alleged errors" in the Scriptures and demonstrating how the discrepancies could be resolved. So scholarly was his treatment in his article "Inspiration" that appeared in the *Presbyterian Review* (April 1881), that the early Fundamentalist leader, James Hall Brookes (1830–97), editor of *The Truth or Testimony for Christ,* thought that Warfield was presenting a "lower view" of inspiration. Upon further explanation by Warfield, however, Brookes admitted that he had misjudged the theologian, and Warfield became a respected ally of the early Fundamentalists with regard to the inerrancy debate. Warfield's insistence that the words of the Bible were inspired "without error" in the "original autographs" would become the standard argument of the Fundamentalist-Evangelical movement.

As a conservative evangelical product of the nineteenth century, Warfield could never reconcile premillennial eschatology with his postmillennial viewpoint. As a staunch "old-school" Calvinist, he also opposed revivalism and the free will movements in Protestantism, believing they were subjective aberrations of biblical doctrine. He found himself increasingly isolated in his latter years, and Princeton Seminary's New Testament scholar, John Gresham Machen (1881–1937), would take his place as spokesperson for Conservative Evangelicalism.

PREMILLENNIALISM

One of the founding fathers of the early Fundamentalist movement, Nathaniel West (1826–1906), was a Presbyterian minister as well as a theological professor at Danville Theological Seminary from 1869 to 1875. He had emigrated from England as a boy and graduated from the University of Michigan in 1846. A principal catalyst of the First International Prophetic Conference held in New York October 30 to November 1, 1878, West was a key theologian of the premillennialist movement and his writings were often referred to by later premillennialists.

The object of the 1878 conference was to stress the premillennial advent of Jesus Christ and to gather those of like mind in discussions on related topics. West delivered a lecture entitled "History of the Pre-Millennial Doctrine," and subsequently enlarged it in his edited monograph of the conference, *Premillennial Essays* (1879). From this lecture the attitude and thought process of premillennialists in the early Fundamentalist movement becomes clear.

Protesting against a postmillennialism that held to an unbroken evolution toward an absolutely perfect kingdom of God and denigrating an amillennialism that was a "vapid idealism which volatilizes the perfect kingdom into a spiritual abstraction, apart from the regenesis of the earth," West insisted that Jesus must return *before* the millennium. For West an inerrant Bible was essential, because premillennial doctrine was grounded on the visions of Daniel as subsequently completed in the visions of John recorded in the Book of Revelation. "On such foundations, supported by instruction from our Lord and His Apostles," West declared, "did the Church of the Apostolic Age rear its doctrine of the Millennial Kingdom, and the Pre-Millennial Advent of Christ to inaugurate the same."

West believed that the Book of Daniel was the "sacred calendar of the future." Through its representation of four successive gentile empires "closing with the overthrow of the Beast and Little Horn, and the erection of Daniel's fifth and everlasting Kingdom as an external polity, upon the extinct polities of all nations," the scope of the earth's history was unfolded. The second coming of Jesus Christ would inaugurate the millennial kingdom of God, the fifth and last kingdom in Daniel's scheme. Confidently, West underscored the point that "with such a view it was impossible for the early Church not to be Pre-Millenarian, for the visions of Daniel (Chapter 7) and of John (Revelation, Chapters 4–22) were one."

West described in elaborate detail the support premillennialism received in the early church. Beginning with the apostles themselves and through the early church fathers, he sought to prove that the premillennial view of the future was "the common inheritance of both Jewish and Gentile Christians, and passed from the Jewish Christian to the Gentile Christian Church precisely in the way the Gospel passed." This doctrine, West asserted, was crushed by the union of church and state under Constantine, and the Roman Catholic church "spiritualized" the doctrine to apply to itself. According to West, Protestant Reformers such as Luther and Calvin did not spend time in detailed analysis of the future, although pockets of premillennial adherents following the doctrine of the early church had always existed.

Documenting the gain in followers during the nineteenth century, West declared that this century "promised to be the triumphal century" for premillennialist doctrine. Jubilantly, he proclaimed: "As we look back upon three quarters of the nineteenth century, now passed, and mark the progress of the Premillennial doctrine, by what a galaxy of illustrious names it is adorned, by what piety commended, and by what unquestioned orthodoxy and scholarship supported. . . ." West listed three and one-half pages of names of those nineteenth-century personalities who supported premillennialism, noting in sorrow at the outset: "It is simply impossible to catalogue all the names. . . . I can mention but a few."

Indeed, the premillennial view of the future had been growing in small cell groups and within larger church denominations in both Britain and America throughout the nineteenth century. A number of diverse scenarios for the future had evolved in the process, and even West explained that he did not know "every detail." He, like all Fundamentalist-Evangelicals, disassociated himself from New York Baptist minister and founder of the Adventist movement, William Miller (1782–1849). Calculating from Scripture, Miller had set the date of the second coming of Christ precisely on October 22, 1844. Many followers of Miller were disappointed and left the movement, an illustration that Fundamentalist-Evangelicals used under the rubric "no man knows the day or hour" of Christ's return. Jesus was to come as "a thief in the night."

One of the most popular premillennialist schemes of the future among Fundamentalists was systematized by John Nelson Darby (1800–1882), the British leader of the Plymouth Brethren movement. Known as Dispensationalism, it divided history into separate eras or dispensations in which God worked the redemptive plan for humankind in differing manners, progressively revealing God's will. The world was viewed as a household administered by God, where men and women were responsible to respond to the revelation God had given them during their particular era. God's program for the church was viewed as separate from God's program for Old Testament Israel. Thus, the church could not claim the promises made to the Jewish people or usurp their status as the "chosen people." This theological system also taught that there would be a "secret rapture" of believers before a period of horrendous tribulation.

Darby spread dispensational views through seven lecture tours to the United States and Canada between 1862 and 1877. He proselytized in Europe and New Zealand as well. Dispensational premillennialism has been propagated throughout the twentieth century by the *Scofield Reference Bible* with its extensive notes and King James Version text.

Begun in 1902 by Cyrus I. Scofield (1843–1921), a well-respected pastor and Bible conference teacher, and incorporating suggestions from other early Fundamentalist leaders, such as James M. Gray (1851–1935) and Arno C. Gaebelein (1861–1945), the first edition of the *Scofield Reference Bible* was published by Oxford University Press in 1909. When Gaebelein wrote *The History of the Scofield Reference Bible* in 1943, it had sold nearly two million copies. The version has been lauded by its premillennialist friends, viciously attacked by its foes. Nevertheless, it has been an extremely influential Bible in the Fundamentalist-Evangelical movement, and *The New Scofield Reference Bible* edited by modern dispensational premillennialists was released by Oxford University Press in 1967.

PROPHECY CONFERENCES AND THE JEW

Through biblical literalism applied to "prophetic" passages in books such as Daniel and Revelation, premillennial Fundamentalists had a unique world view and a fresh perspective toward the Jewish

131

people. They claimed that the world was headed for a period of "great tribulation" lasting seven years and culminating in the Battle of Armageddon. The focus was on the Middle East, particularly Palestine, where the early Fundamentalists believed the Jewish people would be reinstated in the promised land and be blessed of God in that land.

However, a world political leader, called the antichrist, would rise up and take control of the world under the guise of a program of peace. At first he would befriend the Jewish people, but would later turn against them and persecute them ruthlessly. His religious leader, the false prophet, would ask the Jewish people, as well as the rest of the world, to worship the antichrist. Only the return of Jesus Christ would save the world and the Jewish people from the antichrist's destruction. At this time, Christ would be accepted as Savior of the world and the Messiah of the Jewish people. The millennial kingdom, the kingdom of God on earth, would be instituted with its main headquarters at Jerusalem. Early Fundamentalists underscored that this was not a fantasy view, but was literally prophesied in the Bible and held by the apostles and early church. They claimed that it was not pessimistic, but rather realistic in light of the Bible and humanity's depraved nature.

In contrast to the Puritans and many postmillennialists, this premillennial view of the future maintained that the church had no right to usurp triumphalistically God's promises to the Jewish people, nor should Christians claim that their nation was becoming the kingdom of God. In addition, Fundamentalist-Evangelicals were Zionists, in that they proclaimed that God had given the holy land to the Jewish people and that those who fought against the return of the Jews to the land were literally fighting God. Through periodicals and conferences, this message was promulgated from the latter decades of the nineteenth century through the present period.

In fact, the premillennial view of the future has been proclaimed, reassessed, and strengthened through a unique institution that was a vital part of the early Fundamentalist movement and is clearly visible in the Fundamentalist-Evangelical movement today: the prophecy conference. An offshoot of the nineteenth-century Bible conference where the doctrine of inerrancy of the Bible was affirmed and where an in-depth study of biblical passages and topics was pursued, the prophetic conference aimed specifically at defending and proclaiming the doctrine of Christ's second coming through special speakers, discussion, and publicity.

The size of the prophecy conferences has varied throughout the nineteenth and twentieth centuries from assemblies that filled Carnegie Hall and enlisted a battery of illustrious speakers to the small sanctuary of a Fundamentalist church where one or two speakers would spend a weekend on prophecy. In essence, the large conferences became transdenominational associations, bringing together ministers, theologians, and lay people of different denominational backgrounds and uniting them around the central belief in premillennial eschatology. In the smaller meetings, a particular church body was educated in premillennial doctrine and bolstered in the fervency of the belief that Jesus would soon return. Sometimes the publicity surrounding the special speaker would draw people outside the membership of the smaller church and at least draw the attention of the surrounding community. Indeed, the resiliency of the prophecy conference in the twentieth century supports the fact that these meetings were important institutional vehicles for Fundamentalism.

There was an aspect of camaraderie and fellowship within the meetings that bound together those of different social classes, different educational backgrounds, and even different countries. The feeling that they held mutual citizenship in heaven and that they agreed on the imminent second coming of Jesus Christ produced a close kinship among the participants in the conference that made their time together a spiritually uplifting experience. Those who had felt at one time or another that they were nearly alone in their premillennial faith learned of the many who interpreted the Bible as they did. Those who were groping for greater understanding of the Bible's map to the future were instructed, challenged, and encouraged from the platform. Among the leadership there was a further interaction that developed strong friendships and joint projects.

It is not easy to categorize the prophecy conference with respect to speakers, audience, attendance, and format in either the early or modern period. There were certain elements in general, however, that appear to be apparent: a spirit of prayer and worship as the participants approached the deeper truths of the Word of God; a joyous singing of a hymn or two that expressed the theme of the Bible's importance and the certainty of the second coming; and an unusual crowding of the particular meeting place with people dressed in their Sunday best, listening intently to the speaker and jotting down as many points as they could. Often speakers would relate their message to the current events of the time, never trying precisely to date the second coming, but only emphasizing the signs that may have pointed to the imminence of that event.

The interest in the future and the Bible's predictions of that future were incredible ingredients for an extremely popular conference topic. The prophecy conference has prospered and has produced a group of respected leaders within Fundamentalism who are loved by the members of the movement for their expertise on the Bible and their spiritual qualities. While many of these leaders have devoted their lives to teaching and preaching on a multitude of biblical topics, their stand on the premillennial prophetic interpretation is important to the Fundamentalist — a crucial prerequisite to "rightly dividing the Word of Truth."

Choosing the key conferences of the early period of Fundamentalist-Evangelicalism is not as difficult as one might think because early Fundamentalist leaders banded together to produce a series of international prophetic conferences that would attract worldwide attention. In his welcoming address to the delegates of the Prophetic Bible Conference held at Moody Bible Institute in February 1914, Dr. James M. Gray, Dean of M.B.I., explained that this conference was the fifth in the series of "special" prophetic conferences. He informed delegates that the first was held in 1878 in New York, the second in Chicago in 1886, the third in Allegheny, Pennsylvania, in 1895, and the fourth in Boston in 1901. Concerning their gathering at M.B.I. for the fifth, Gray explained, "Many brethren felt that the time had now come for another testimony to the doctrine of our Lord's second coming, hence the invitation to which you have now responded."

Since the Holy Land and the Jewish people were the central elements in premillennial eschatology, the prophecy conference always made reference to them. Speakers continually seemed to be in awe of "God's Chosen People." For example, during the First International Prophetic Conference held in New York City in 1878, Bishop William R. Nicholson (1822–1901) of the Reformed Episcopal Church in Philadelphia exclaimed: "Can the world show anything like it [the miraculous preservation of the Jewish people]? Twice eighteen hundred years old, they saw the proud Egyptian perish in the waters of the Red Sea; they heard the fall of great Babylon's power; they witnessed the ruins of the Syro-Macedonian conquests. And now they have outlived the Caesars, and outlived the dark ages. . . . Earth's men of destiny, before the venerableness of whose pedigree the proudest scutcheons of mankind are but as trifles of yesterday." Such an attitude was in distinct contrast to the New York Bar Association, which had the year before blackballed a Jewish lawyer; and to the Grand Union Hotel in Saratoga Springs, New York, which had refused lodging to Jewish businessman Joseph Seligman and his family because of race.

Bishop Nicholson, a premillennialist, explained to those assembled in the Church of the Holy Trinity that he found himself "in the midst of an embarrassment of riches" when it came to proving biblically the restoration of the Jewish people to Palestine. He insisted that "the regathering of Israel" spoken of in passages such as Ezek. 36:22–36 "can possibly refer only to the literal Israel, and to their restoration to Palestine. . . . It is yet in the future."

During the Second International Prophetic Conference held in Farwell Hall in Chicago in 1886, Professor Ernst F. Stroeter of Wesleyan University in Warrenton, Missouri, linked anti-Semitism to the triumphalism in the prevalent Protestant world views. He gently castigated the commentators who "are very ready to simply spiritualize away all that is prophesied to the political Israel and to the geographical Palestine of restitution and rehabilitation . . . and to appropriate quietly to the Gentile Church all there is predicted of BLESSING TO ISRAEL." To Stroeter, anti-Semitism was linked to this spiritualization of the word "Israel" in Scripture to mean the "Christian Church." "Without the equally literal fulfillment of this aspect of Israel's hope — to which Jesus himself and His disciples likewise stand committed — Israel's glory among the nations is lost forever. . . . The name of Israel will continue a reproach forever among the nations."

Stroeter, a German Methodist, would later become a professor at the University of Denver. In 1894, he joined Arno C. Gaebelein's "Hope of Israel Movement," editing the first issues of Gaebelein's

Fundamentalist-Evangelical periodical, *Our Hope* (published 1894–1957, absorbed by *Eternity* magazine). In the August 1894 issue, he declared that "the apathy, and even antipathy, toward the Jew, into which the church has fallen, must be removed, and a better feeling awakened in her toward God's age-lasting people. . . . In *Our Hope* we preach to the Gentile church *in behalf* of the Jew."

In the latter 1890s, Stroeter emigrated to Germany and traveled throughout Europe lecturing and writing on behalf of the Jewish people and in defense of "biblical Christianity." He even toured southern Russia "on Israel's behalf," finally making Düsseldorf, Germany, his home base and fighting against the rising tide of German anti-Semitism.

D. L. MOODY

Dwight Lyman Moody (1837–99) was unable to be present at the 1886 Prophetic Bible Conference because of "binding engagements," but sent a letter expressing "for the purpose of the conference the greatest sympathy." Moody was by the 1880s a familiar figure busily preaching in many parts of the world. Even Lyman Abbott in *Reminiscences* (1915) would write without hesitation: "The greatest evangelist of my time was Dwight L. Moody; the monuments which he built and which will long preserve his memory are the school for girls at Northfield and the school for boys at Mount Hermon."

Moody had been raised in Northfield, Massachusetts, and was baptized in the local Unitarian church at the age of five. His education was minimal both in religion and in academics, and it was not until he moved to Boston to seek his fortune at the age of seventeen that he had a "conversion experience." He had become a sales clerk in his uncle's shoe store in Boston and had begun attending the Mount Vernon Congregational Church. It was in this church that his Sunday school teacher, Edward Kimball, asked him to commit his life to Jesus Christ. In a quiet, solemn response Moody accepted, although he knew little of the teachings of Protestantism. For example, when Kimball had asked the class to turn to the Gospel of John during Moody's first class period, Moody began thumbing through Genesis looking for the text. For a year, Moody was refused membership in the church because of his ignorance of church doctrine. Even when he was famous, Moody's evangelistic campaigns were not highly emotional and were never rigorously academic. He conducted himself with dignity and in an orderly fashion.

Moody always considered that it was only by the grace of God that he had been used to touch the lives of millons. Moving to Chicago, he had built up a respectable shoe business, but gave it up to work full time as a Y.M.C.A. evangelist. He organized his own Sunday school for poor immigrant children and worked with soldiers during the Civil War. Because his Sunday school was so successful, parents began attending. Soon they outgrew the facilities, built a large building, and became the Illinois Street Church at the end of 1864. Moody in the meantime had become a prominent speaker in the Chicago religious community, known for his homey anecdotes, personal illustrations, and fervent appeals. In 1866 he was voted president of the Chicago Y.M.C.A.; and in 1870 he addressed the national Y.M.C.A. meeting in Indianapolis.

With his music associate, Ira D. Sankey (1840–1908), Moody sailed for the British Isles in 1873. He had limited success in Northern England, but was greeted by large crowds in Scotland. Returning to London for a four-month period, Moody spoke to even larger crowds, his total attendance at meetings reaching more than two and a half million. Two years later he returned to the United States a successful, world-famous evangelist with high-level contacts among British clergy and academics. Through well-planned campaigns in the United States, he spoke to an estimated 100 million people by the end of his life and traveled more than a million miles. In fact, the illness that contributed to his death was contracted during an evangelistic campaign he held in Kansas City.

Moody was a premillennialist and, in contrast to earlier evangelist Charles Finney, thought of evangelism as spreading the gospel message wherever and whenever possible, rather than converting the world and establishing the kingdom. In the 1870s he preached at least once in each of his major revival campaigns on the second coming of Jesus Christ. As a Fundamentalist-Evangelical, he also held firmly to the literal interpretation of the Bible. For instance, in his book, *Heaven: Where It Is, Its Inhabitants, and How to Get There* (1880), he began by quoting 2 Tim. 3:16–17, and declared: "What the Bible says about heaven is just as true as what it says about everything else.

137

The Bible is inspired. What we are taught about heaven could not have come to us in any other way than by inspiration. No one knew anything about it but God, and so if we want to find anything about it we have to turn to His Word. Dr. Hodge, of Princeton, says that the best evidence of the Bible being the Word of God is to be found between its own two covers. It proves itself."

Moody was alarmed by higher criticism of the Bible and Darwin's theory of evolution. He had little patience with the liberal view of the Bible as being figurative, and he often referred angrily to those who "just figure away everything." "I notice if a man goes to cut up the Bible," Moody asserted, " . . . when he begins to doubt portions of the Word of God he soon doubts it all."

In his book *Pleasure and Profit in Bible Study* (1895) Moody termed this "Clipping the Bible." "Now, if I have a right to cut out a certain portion of the Bible, I don't know why one of my friends has not a right to cut out another. . . . You would have a queer kind of Bible if everybody cut out what he wanted to."

And yet, in the preface of this volume, Moody wrote: "I think I would rather preach about the Word of God than anything else except the Love of God; because I believe it is the best thing in this world." Moody deplored the rancor and division that were occurring within Evangelical Protestantism, between Liberals and Conservatives; Modernists and Fundamentalists. He believed that such feuding was impeding the message of the gospel.

Ironically, after his death in 1899, his son Paul would lean toward Liberalism, while his other son, William, remained a Conservative Evangelical. Paul Moody wrote in *The Christian Century* (August 2, 1923) that if his father were alive in the 1920s, he would be "more in sympathy with the men who, like Fosdick, are preaching what he loved to spread—the love of God and the power of Christ—than with those who are attempting to persecute them because they will not subscribe to certain shibboleths."

In the article and letter war in a number of Protestant periodicals that followed Paul Moody's remarks, both Fundamentalists and Modernists claimed D. L. Moody. These constituted a tribute to the universal respect enjoyed by this nineteenth-century giant; yet it shed little light on the man himself. Liberals pointed to his catholicity of spirit and his love, neglecting his staunch Fundamentalist-

Evangelical theology. Fundamentalists pointed to his theology, downplaying his catholicity of spirit. Both groups needed to learn from Dwight Lyman Moody's total message and committed life.

THE FUNDAMENTALIST-MODERNIST CONTROVERSY

Moody had expressed his desire for an educational institution in Chicago, the city where he rose to fame, that would stress biblical literalism and train men and women to teach the Bible. With Moody's support, Fundamentalist-Evangelicals in Chicago organized a series of trial training sessions in 1886 and incorporated on February 12, 1887, as the Chicago Evangelization Society. Moody convinced many well-known Bible teachers of the time to spend a few weeks at "the institute," and soon it was known informally as "Moody's School." After his death, the school became Moody Bible Institute and was considered by many Fundamentalist-Evangelicals the West Point of their movement. Certainly, it was the prototype of a network of Bible institutes and Bible colleges that educated a new generation of Fundamentalist-Evangelical missionaries, teachers, and pastors.

It is little wonder, then, that the faculty of the great bastion of liberal Protestantism in Chicago, the University of Chicago Divinity School, would monitor with special alarm the growth of the premillennialist Institute and indeed the Fundamentalist movement itself. Although Moody Bible Institute's very first graduate, William Evans (diploma, 1892), would subsequently earn his B.D. (1900) and Ph.D. (1906) at the University of Chicago Divinity School, the controversy between the two groups intensified.

Shirley Jackson Case (1872–1947), professor of early church history and New Testament interpretation at the University of Chicago Divinity School, recognized the potency of premillennial eschatology and tried desperately to curtail the influence of this challenge to the prevalent postmillennial world view. While his methods were not laudable and would later be viewed as scandalous for a "liberal" theologian, Case exemplified the struggle of the postmillennial liberal Protestant to cling to a view of progressive world peace in the midst of a horrendous world war. He would later become the respected dean of the Divinity School; but his vitriolic statements during World War I would at least partially precipitate the Fundamentalist/Modernist controversies of the 1920s.

In *The Millennial Hope* (1918), Case argued that apocalyptic movements, such as premillennialism, grew dramatically in times of political and economic crisis. He portrayed premillennialists as "pessimists" and their theology as "fairy stories." In *The Revelation of John* (1919), he denigrated the premillennial biblical interpretation of the last book of the Bible as a prophetic document that discussed the future. Instead, Case insisted that *Revelation* referred to the social environment of the Roman Empire around 90 C.E. Nevertheless, both of these books were within the pale of scholarly standards of literary presentation and balanced temper.

In "The Premillennial Menace," however, published in *The Biblical World* (July 1918), Case went far beyond the bounds of restraint. "Under ordinary circumstances one might excusably pass over Premillenarianism as a wild and relatively harmless fancy," he wrote, "but in the present time of testing it would be almost traitorous negligence to ignore the detrimental character of the Premillennial propaganda." Defending World War I as a "gigantic effort to make the world safe for democracy," Case accused premillennialist teaching of being "fundamentally antagonistic to our present national ideal" and "a serious menace to our democracy." In addition to referring to the premillennial movement as "suspiciously Teutonic" and implying that "enemy gold" may be financing this Fundamentalist theology, Case even added a "red scare" suggestion that the "principles of Premillennialism readily lend themselves to the purpose" of the socialist International Workers of the World. "Concretely our special task is that of defending the sacred rights of democracy, and helping to make this ideal supreme in all international relationships," he summarized.

While the New Paganism blamed Jews for both capitalism and socialism, Case showed some of the same attitudes in his diatribe against premillennialists. "This type of thinking was especially popular within certain Palestinian Jewish circles, where it was offered as a means of escape from sufferings experienced during the first and second centuries B.C. and the first century A.D.," the liberal Protestant scholar of early Christian origins explained, continuing, "From Judaism this elusive hope passed over to Christianity, where it was linked with the expectation of an early return of Christ in visible form to rescue his disciples from their unhappy position in a hostile pagan world." As biblical literalists, evangelical premillennialists may have welcomed Case's backhanded compliment to the first-century origins of their views, but they were furious over his distorted portrayal and vicious innuendos about their movement. And Shirley Jackson Case was not above repeating the same polemic to the Chicago newspapers.

Case's reference to premillennialism as a "spiritual virus" sounded more fascist than liberal, and future generations of liberal Protestants would bitterly regret his attacks. In *The Roots of Fundamentalism*, a book copyrighted by the University of Chicago Press in 1970, the late Ernest R. Sandeen, a Ph.D. from the University of Chicago, sadly commented on Case's diatribe: "The Fundamentalist apparently never cornered the market on invective. . . . Rancor had existed in previous decades, but the spirit of open hostility, so characteristic of the twenties, seemed to find food for its soul in the First World War."

Fundamentalist-Evangelicals, for their part, enjoyed the problems the postmillennialists faced with Case's biblical interpretation. At the Sixth International Prophetic Conference held in Carnegie Hall in New York City in November of 1918, there was a substantial discussion of the "error of Postmillennialism." Otho F. Bartholow, pastor of the First Methodist Episcopal Church of Mount Vernon, New York, explained how he was educated in a Methodist seminary in "post-millennial theory" but that "by reading the Bible instead of commentaries" he became a premillennialist rather than the enemy he had been. "A few months ago I got into a conference where there were eight men who were Post-millennarians arguing against one pre-millennarian; eight to one," he gloated to the overflow crowd. "Well, it takes eight of them to overcome one of us; then they cannot do it." To the Fundamentalist-Evangelical, World War I had confirmed that the world was not getting better; and the Balfour Declaration (1917) attested to the fact that the "chosen" Jewish people were finally going to get their land.

Such was the setting for the Fundamentalist/Modernist controversies of the 1920s. Contrary to high school and college textbooks that portray American Fundamentalism as a redneck agrarian phenomenon of the rural South and point to the 1925 Scopes Trial about teaching evolution as an example of Fundamentalist mentality, the

Fundamentalist-Evangelical movement was in fact the product of highly educated Northerners from an urban environment. Many of the characteristics of this movement were molded before 1920, including a conservative life style that exemplified the culture of the 1920s — a culture in which even the main Protestant denominations, including the Federal Council of Churches, supported the Prohibition Amendment.

Liberalism and Fundamentalism would clash in the 1920s, however, as never before. In 1922 Harry Emerson Fosdick (1878–1969) preached the sermon "Shall the Fundamentalists Win?" which was later published in *The Christian Century*. Fosdick criticized the Fundamentalists' emphasis on inerrancy of Scripture and the second coming of Christ. He also castigated their effort to exclude the teaching of evolution in public schools. Clarence E. Macartney (1879–1957), conservative pastor of Arch Street Presbyterian Church in Philadelphia, responded with the article "Shall Unbelief Win: An Answer To Dr. Fosdick" (*The Presbyterian*, July 13, 1922), accusing Fosdick of diverging from traditional Christianity. In the subsequent battle, Baptist Fosdick was forced out of his pulpit at First Presbyterian Church in New York City.

Macartney would not label himself a "Fundamentalist" because he was not a premillennialist. But he was the prototype of conservative Evangelicals who many times led Fundamentalists in the conflict within Protestantism. In like manner, J. Gresham Machen (1881–1937), whose *Christianity and Liberalism* (1923) was a centerpiece for Fundamentalist biblical orthodoxy in the twentieth century, never considered himself a Fundamentalist because he, too, was not premillennialist. Machen resigned from Princeton Theological Seminary in protest over Liberalism's triumph there and was integral in the formation of conservative evangelical Westminster Theological Seminary in Philadelphia in 1929. He was also instrumental in the founding of a new Presbyterian denomination, the Orthodox Presbyterian church. The rancor and battles of conservatives and liberals that split churches, denominations, and seminaries within Protestantism in America in the 1920s and 1930s are too numerous to detail; but many of the basic conflicts are still evident today.

The 1920s would also witness a flowering of Holiness and Pentecostal movements that often absorbed both the biblical theology and eschatology of Fundamentalist-Evangelical Protestantism.

While Fundamentalist-Evangelicals often questioned the Holiness view of a "second blessing" through the Holy Spirit and clearly resented the Pentecostal emphasis on the necessity of "speaking in tongues" as the evidence of the "Baptism of the Spirit," all three groups would participate in the formation of the National Association of Evangelicals in 1942. As will be seen in chapter 10, the emerging modern charismatic movement has forced Fundamentalists to come to grips with their revivalist holiness heritage.

PREMILLENNIALISM AND SOCIAL CONCERN

Premillennialism, a view of the future professing that world conditions will get worse until the messiah comes to institute the millennium, has often been accused of lacking social concern. It is said that inherent within this eschatology is a pessimism that precludes one from helping others, because help would only be wasted on a disintegrating society. Nevertheless, the historian who analyzes the history of premillennialism finds an active social concern similar to the prevalent postmillennialism of the nineteenth century or the amillennialism of the twentieth century.

For example, premillennial rescue mission leaders, like Jerry McAuley, were often products of slum areas and returned upon conversion to live and help among the poverty-stricken and destitute. McAuley was an Irish immigrant who had served a prison term in Sing Sing. After his conversion, he founded the Water Street Mission in New York City in 1872 and influenced the founding of more than a hundred other missions thereafter.

Pacific Garden Mission, the second oldest, was founded in 1877 by a premillennial couple in Chicago who abandoned a position of high social standing and wealth to work among drunkards, prostitutes, and outcasts. Sarah Clarke had begun a visitation program among the poor before she married Colonel Clarke in 1873. Both were convinced of the need to help the destitute in an area of the Chicago Loop which had been destroyed by fire in 1871. After the Great Fire, while Chicago churches scattered to the outskirts of the city, saloons, brothels, and gambling halls moved in. The Clarkes squeezed their tiny mission into Whiskey Row on South Clark Street, and it has remained open ever since.

It was at the Pacific Garden Mission that Billy Sunday (1862–1935), a nationally known baseball player, dedicated his life to Jesus Christ and became one of the most famous Protestant evangelists at the turn of the century. Mel Trotter was about to commit suicide when he dropped into the mission, and he later joined Jerry McAuley in a ministry to rescue missions across the United States. Premillennialists have overwhelmingly continued to staff rescue missions, many living side by side with the derelicts of society.

The premillennialists' emphasis on evangelism of the destitute could be taken to the extreme in overlooking the social needs of the poor or the cries of labor. Postmillennial Evangelicalism was certainly guilty of the same bias. But there is also a viable historical social consciousness in premillennial Fundamentalist-Evangelicalism which had the capacity to reach out to the destitute. A zealousness to "save souls" drove the Fundamentalist-Evangelical social worker to the scene of the most deplorable social problems in the country. A belief that men and women were worthwhile in God's sight, that Jesus Christ died for every person, that salvation could change any individual, and that sin was the real root of humankind's problems gave the Fundamentalist-Evangelical social worker the distinct advantage of not blaming the poor for their own problems and of exuding an indomitable optimism.

However, Fundamentalist-Evangelicalism could also be charged with concern about the soul to the exclusion of the body. *The Christian Herald,* a popular evangelical weekly that by 1910 had become one of the most widely circulated religious magazines in the world (250,000), castigated conservative Protestantism in 1895 for changing the parable of the good Samaritan into an evangelistic topic. While admitting that Protestantism had given freely to charity and was probably responsible for most of the great hospitals, orphanages, and charitable organizations, *The Christian Herald* deplored the fact that the Christian church had failed with regard to social welfare. "The Church of the past century has been giving tracts and preaching when it should have given the oil and wine of life," the evangelical magazine declared. "This it ought to have done and not left the other undone." *The Christian Herald* believed that there must be a balance between evangelism and social projects. "Christ was never indifferent to the hungry, or to the physical suffering of those around him. He sought to save men altogether—body, soul, and spirit."

There is no doubt that the rising tide of socialism and the Social

Gospel helped to turn the Fundamentalist-Evangelical toward social welfare. It is a mistake, however, to assume that the premillennial Evangelical accepted such views as viable philosophies. To the premillennialist, the Social Gospel was "another gospel" that turned people away from their need for a redeemer to change their lives. Environmental change was not sufficient to cure the ills of society.

The premillennial evangelical attitude can be found in *The Fundamentals*, a series of twelve books intended to reaffirm the "fundamentals" of Christianity. Published from 1910 to 1915, these volumes contained articles by leaders in the Fundamentalist-Evangelical movement, and included such conservative evangelical stalwarts as Benjamin B. Warfield in areas other than prophecy. In fact, sixty-four different authors wrote ninety articles on a wide range of doctrinal issues, including twenty-nine articles devoted to defending an inerrant Bible.

The brainchild of a Fundamentalist-Evangelical oil magnate, Lyman Stewart, the volumes were originally planned to be published every two or three months and to be distributed free "to every pastor, evangelist, missionary, theological professor, theological student, Sunday school superintendent, Y.M.C.A. and Y.W.C.A. secretary in the English speaking world, so far as the addresses of all these can be obtained." Many lay people as well as ministers became interested in the volumes and over 250,000 earlier issues had to be reprinted. So strenuous became the task that only three volumes were printed in 1910, three in 1911, and three in 1912. The last three were spread over a three-year period ending in 1915 with volume twelve. By this time, nearly three million copies had been distributed and the mailing list of Christian workers numbered 100,000.

It is interesting that on the cover of every volume of *The Fundamentals* was printed "Compliments of Two Christian Laymen." Lyman Stewart was shy and wanted no credit or applause for the gift. The other "layman" was Lyman's brother, Milton, who helped monetarily to support the project at Lyman's request. However, he seemed to give little active support to the organization of the volumes and correspondence with the editors. The Stewarts were successful in the Union Oil Company, but they believed that Christian stewardship was their main duty to God. They were featured in 1924 in *Missionary Review of the World* as the epitome of Christian stewardship.

In the last volume of *The Fundamentals*, Charles R. Erdman

145

(1866–1960), a premillennial evangelical professor at Princeton Theological Seminary, discussed the sudden rise of socialism and its influence on the church. It is important to deal with his essay because it characterized the premillennial approach. "Socialism, strictly defined," he wrote, "is *an economic theory* which proposes the abolition of private capital and the substitution of collective ownership in carrying on the industrial work of the world." He cautioned his readers that socialism must be distinguished from communism. Communism advocated the "collective ownership of all wealth," while socialism "does not deny the right of private property, but of private capital." One could own a house under socialism, but would not be allowed to rent it out for gain. This collective ownership would be administered by the extension of government to regulate the life and labor of every individual.

Erdman suggested that it was impossible to identify Jesus as a socialist. "He rebuked social sins, injustice, and selfishness; but when asked to divide a possession on a certain occasion He asked, 'Who made Me a judge or a divider over you?' " Erdman explained. As for socialism in the early church, Erdman noted that "it was practiced only in Jerusalem, no one was compelled to divide or sell his property; not all adopted the practice . . . it was never admitted or established as an abiding principle of Church life."

Erdman proposed that the church should never be "identified with socialism," although socialists may adopt Christian principles and Christians may decide to be socialists. "Most Christians admit the wisdom of many socialistic proposals, but feel that they are at liberty to act without the interference of the Church." Nevertheless, Erdman insisted that "socialism is a *serious protest against the social wrongs* and cruelties of the age, against the defects of the present economic system, against prevalent poverty, and hunger, and despair."

In conclusion, Erdman felt that socialism was a challenge to the church "to proclaim more insistently *the social principles of Christ.*" "This does not mean the adoption of a so-called 'social gospel' which discards the fundamental doctrines of Christianity and substitutes a religion of good works," he explained, "but a true Gospel of grace is inseparable from a Gospel of good works. Christian doctrines and Christian duties cannot be divorced."

Evangelism was not to be lost in such an interpretation, and in some cases the theology and missionary zeal of the Fundamentalist-

Evangelical seemed to be a definite asset in accepting the destitute. P. W. Philpott, premillennialist pastor of Moody Memorial Church with an active roll of 3,750 in 1929 and located in an urban slum of Chicago, confirmed: "The advantages of an evangelistic ministry are manifold. In the first place, it *amalgamates*. It brings unity among believers as nothing else can. No better solvent can there be for differences of race, social standing, and denominational peculiarity, than the earnest, persistent effort to bring men and women to a saving knowledge of the Lord Jesus Christ. Faced with an open Bible and a seeking soul, no sincere Christian can successfully harbor bitterness or long engender strife."

In addition, some Fundamentalist-Evangelicals felt that churches were pouring too much money into their building projects in the 1920s, and they often regretted the millions spent for building construction. Premillennialist G. A. Griswold lamented in *Our Hope* in 1930 that the congregations of "false Protestantism," misguided in their zeal, were "seeking to out-do each other in the building program of cathedral-like Churches."

As with liberal Protestants, the Depression made premillennialists reevaluate the economic system. While their conclusions would not eliminate the profit-making motive from the economic order, they believed that it was the Christian's responsibility to see that the economic system functioned properly. The Fundamentalist-Evangelical periodical, *Moody Bible Institute Monthly*, went so far as to publish an article in 1933 by Rev. F. W. Haberer of Richmond, Virginia, "proving" that socialism came closer to first-century Christianity than capitalism. An editorial note pointed out, however, that "capitalism is bad enough, but socialism may be only out of the frying pan into the fire." The editor (possibly James M. Gray, editor in chief at that time) concluded: "Let us keep out of politics, capitalistic or socialistic, and endeavor, like Paul, by all means to save some (1 Cor. 9:22). Socialism in itself is no more Christian than capitalism, nor can it be except as the hearts of its votaries are cleansed through the blood of Christ. And when that is true of the capitalist, he is as good a citizen as the socialist, and vice versa."

One notes the same theological emphasis that is found in Erdman's discussion in *The Fundamentals*. The premillennialist could agree with the Christian's responsibility toward the poor in the same wording as the Social Gospeler, but could not accept the assumption, which they attributed to the Social Gospelers, that humankind is basically good and the world is basically Christian. For example, an editor of *Moody Bible Institute Monthly* (July 1933) agreed totally with the following statement of the Special Committee for the Department of Research and Education of the Federal Council of the Churches of Christ in America whose leaders were Social Gospelers:

> It remains as always, a fundamental task of Christianity to develop the kind of personality and character that can work social plans, use social tools and bring ideals into actuality. Without sustained purpose and discipline in the life of the individual, all social planning is useless and all worthwhile goals are impossible of realization.

However, the editor was quick to note that the Federal Council of Churches' earlier statement that "the Christian religion is at heart hostile to any system founded on the private interest of the individual" was contrary to the above statement with which he agreed.

The Social Gospeler's statements posed a dilemma for the premillennialists who cared about the poor, but believed that poverty could never be totally abolished by human efforts. In the midst of the Great Depression, they considered what their responsibility was as Fundamentalist-Evangelicals and what God required of them. As the *Moody Bible Institute Monthly* editor stated earlier: "One dare not lightly pass over such proposals [by the Federal Council of Churches], or speak lightly of the thoughtful and earnest men and women who present them for the consideration of the public."

In October 1933, *Moody Bible Institute Monthly* supported the National Industrial Recovery Act and in 1936 decried the "depersonalization" found in governments based on collectivism, that is, fascism in Italy, nazism in Germany,, and communism in Russia. According to the Fundamentalist-Evangelical periodical, the church had lost sight of the individual as well. It declared: "The Church is impersonal in its message. The so-called social gospel is collective in its appeal. The reformation of society is its goal. But its calls to society to reform are unproductive. Society is an abstraction. The only concrete thing in the whole matter is the gospel of the individual. It begins in the man and works out to his environment."

As one analyzes the period 1865–1940, there is an ardent premillennial Protestant social concern and vital ministry to the destitute that refutes the idea of the "social impotence of premillennialism." In addition, there is a fervent liberal Protestant Social Gospel movement that innovated and led churches into social work. These Social Gospelers believed that the change of environment (or society) would change the individuals in society. In contrast, the premillennialists believed that the change must begin with the individual, and work its way out to the environment. It must be noted that both groups have theorists; both groups work at changing the environment.

Americans as a whole were socially conservative during this time. There was a lack of concentrated effort by the whole of Protestantism to help the needy. In spite of all the talk, Protestantism did not fulfill its potential for reform or social consciousness. Consequently, as has been shown in the last two chapters, it is false to assume that theological liberals were "reform" oriented while theological conservatives opposed reform. Ironically, some of the most socially conservative groups in America were theological liberals and vice versa. By World War II, a very large percentage of "faith" missions in the inner city and around the world were staffed by theological conservatives. Premillennialists were *no less active* than their postmillennial or amillennial counterparts.

Finally, it seems that those Protestants who were in closest contact with the poor in society, whether theologically conservative or liberal, were the ones with the best chance not only of understanding the destitute, but also of truly helping them. If they lived, had lived, or daily rubbed shoulders with the poverty-stricken, it often took them from a theoretical pseudohelp to a heartfelt contractual obligation. It appears that evangelistic theology, which Fundamentalist-Evangelicalism grew to dominate, had an especially effective impulse for initiating and sustaining contact with the poor when it was balanced with social understanding and concern. Thus the ministries of both the Y.M.C.A. and the Salvation Army during this period serve as a challenge to today's Protestantism.

COMMUNISM, FASCISM, AND CONSPIRACY THEORY

The premillennial eschatology of Fundamentalist-Evangelical leaders kept them alert to world events. One of the most respected Bible and prophecy teachers in the movement was Arno C. Gaebelein, the editor of *Our Hope*. In the 1920s, he foresaw serious

dangers in the communist movement and, much like Aleksandr Sol-
zhenitsyn or Anatoly Shcharansky today, alerted Protestants to the
gravity of the persecution of Jews and Christians under the Soviet
regime. Upon the rise of Adolf Hitler, Gaebelein labeled him in 1930
"an outspoken enemy of the Jews . . . one of the most fanatical anti-
Semites of Europe."

An avid reader with contacts around the world, including Germany and Russia, Gaebelein underscored the growing power of fascism in Europe in the 1920s and in *Our Hope* (August 1932)
remarked: "Especially threatening is it in Germany. Adolf Hitler, the
clever fascist leader who is winning out in Germany and holds the
power in his hands, is a rabid anti-Semite." When Hitler became
chancellor in 1933, Gaebelein saw this as a serious "setback" for the
German people, and he detailed Nazi boycotts of Jewish department
stores and limitation of Jewish rights. To Gaebelein, fascism meant
"the political conditions of the entire world are breaking up." It
appeared as though the Great Tribulation was near.

And yet Gaebelein had no patience with those who tried to pin-
point or date prophetic events or who would try to guess who the
antichrist might be. His philosophy was well illustrated when he
wrote in *Our Hope* (November 1933): "The Editor has no use for day-
and-year-setters, nor has he any use for figuring out the duration of
the times of the Gentiles, nor has he any sympathy with men who
prophesy that Mussolini, Hitler, Feisal, or any other person is the
Antichrist. It is a morbid condition which seems to suit certain
minds."

Gaebelein continued to write about atrocities against the Jewish
people and the rise of German Teutonic paganism. An article on the
Nazis in February 1936 was entitled "The Devil Marches On in Germany." When Adolf Hitler used the 1936 Olympic Games as a great
propaganda ploy and tried to hide the persecution of the Jewish
people from journalists, tourists, and government officials, Gaebelein
was appalled that even David Lloyd George (1863–1945), the British
statesman, was misled.

Unfortunately, some evangelical officials were also deceived.
Fundamentalist-Evangelicals today generally assume that "true,
Bible-believing Christians" in Germany never supported Adolf Hitler
and that Nazism arose in a truly liberal Protestant country ruled by
higher criticism of the Bible and Darwinian theory. Nevertheless, one

of their own evangelical statesmen, Oswald J. Smith (1889–1986), testified otherwise.

Smith was pastor of the missionary-minded Peoples Church in Toronto, Canada. He was the author of nearly thirty books, a radio preacher, and missionary statesman, and was highly regarded in Fundamentalist-Evangelical circles. Billy Graham, recounting how Smith's books touched his life, stated: "The name, Oswald J. Smith, symbolizes worldwide evangelization." Yet, Smith's article, "My Visit To Germany," shows how effective Adolf Hitler was in his Olympic cleanup campaign and in his brainwashing of good, decent Protestants. The forty-six-year-old Smith was taken in by the fervent testimony of "true Christians" he visited in Germany during the Olympic Games. "What, you ask, is the real attitude of the German people toward Hitler?" Smith wrote. "There is but one answer. They love him. . . . Every true Christian is for Hitler."

Smith added that German Protestants did not like all the "Little Hitlers" serving under Hitler. They felt these men did not have their leader's spirit. But the people rationalized, saying that Hitler could not "personally attend to everything" and "must of necessity leave much to those under him." They also impressed upon Smith that "the Bolsheviks were prepared to take over the country" and that "Hitler has saved Germany." Smith listened "spellbound" to the contented, happy Protestants, joyously writing that "all girls are trained to be mothers," makeup and lipstick had been eliminated, and mass immorality was being eradicated.

"Before Hitler's days, Spiritism flourished," Smith rejoiced. "Now occultism of every description is banned." In addition, Smith was more than thrilled that Russellism (Jehovah's Witnesses) was banned as dangerous to the nation. He suggested that the "United States and Canada could learn a valuable lesson in this regard." In actuality, both Smith and the German Protestants were to learn that when one person's religious freedom is violated, all religious freedom is on the chopping block.

Smith's experience underscored the Protestant danger of believing in conspiracy theories, a danger that premillennialists also constantly faced in their quest for the antichrist's machinations. By emphasizing a "communist plot" that ostensibly had marked even Protestant pastors for death, the Nazis had manipulated the German people, and Hitler appeared as a knight in shining armor. "The Bolsheviks were preparing to take over the country . . . Germany was doomed," Smith related. "Then came Hitler, and just in time. Two days later and communism would have been in complete control." Smith believed that it now was "German freedom instead of Soviet slavery. Hitler has saved Germany." According to Smith, Jewish communists had caused the "God-fearing Jews" to suffer evil, "betrayed by their renegade brethren."

Smith was so completely deceived by the propaganda that he referred to the "spiritual awakening that is coming to the German people." The Dom Cathedral in Berlin was full, with a minister who "preaches the old-fashioned Gospel. He spares no one. And none interferes with him. He deals openly with sin and salvation." The "true Christian" Protestants of Germany had convinced Smith that they were on the brink of religious revival. "France I do not trust. France is Red, immoral and godless," Smith concluded. "Germany is Protestant. It was from Germany that Luther came."

Smith's article was published by Gerald Winrod (1900–1957) in his *Defender* magazine, and his references to Martin Luther indicate that he was not aware of Luther's about-face concerning the Jewish people. Ironically, Winrod himself would do an "about-face" because of his association with anti-Semites such as Colonel Eugene H. Sanctuary, and his immersion in conspiracy theory texts. Although from a more Holiness and Pentecostal orientation, Winrod was nevertheless a staunch Dispensationalist. In the 1920s, he defended Jews against anti-Semitic distortions such as the blood libel, and early in the 1930s he compared Nazi anti-Semitism with the horrifying communist pogroms. But by 1935, he began uncritically to accept Nazi anti-Semitism as justifiable and believed unequivocally in a worldwide Jewish plot. Although Gaebelein and other Fundamentalist-Evangelicals would soon label Winrod "a secret follower of Hitler," the fact that he had twisted a pro-Jewish Dispensationalism into a severe attack on the Jewish people was sobering.

Smith himself was unaware of Winrod's stance when he wrote the article for the *Defender*. Fundamentalist-Evangelicals, such as Gaebelein, who had toyed with the idea that *The Protocols of the Learned Elders of Zion* might have been written by "apostate Jews" plotting a world revolution from a communist base, were shocked to learn that the documents had been deliberately used by Winrod and others against the "Chosen People." Gaebelein, Harry Ironside, Keith

Brooks, and many other Fundamentalist-Evangelicals signed Donald G. Barnhouse's petition repudiating the *Protocols* as an anti-Semitic forgery.

During Hitler's "final solution" to the Jewish problem, Fundamentalist-Evangelicals believed that the Jewish people were being exterminated by the millions, while more liberal Christians and periodicals, such as *The Christian Century*, were labeling the reports atrocity propaganda. Gaebelein's *Our Hope* magazine gave factual reports of atrocities against the Jewish people during the 1930s and 1940s. The Fundamentalist-Evangelical world view lent itself very well to such convictions, even when they seemed beyond the realm of belief and left the premillennialist in shock. However, Fundamentalist-Evangelicals found that they too could be manipulated by fraudulent moral pretensions and by the suggestion of conspiracy. Being human, they were also subject to blandishments and misleading philosophical arguments. Balance would prove crucial for an effective Protestant ethic for both conservatives and liberals.

MODERN FUNDAMENTALIST-EVANGELICALISM

From the 1920s to the 1940s, a "militant" Fundamentalism emerged, a separatistic movement much more volatile than the more intellectually based Fundamentalism of the later nineteenth century. Members of this militant faction seized the name "Fundamentalist" and used it as a battle cry against what they considered "apostasy" in every major Protestant denomination. They called for separation from the cultural milieu of Protestantism and increasingly made life style an important ingredient of Fundamentalist belief.

Some Fundamentalist-Evangelicals saw that the media were publicizing this connection, watching their beloved word "Fundamentalist" or "holding to the fundamentals" take on the connotation of narrow, divisive, anti-intellectual, bigoted, uncaring, unloving, antisocial. Unwilling to be categorized in such a way, by the 1940s they began to call themselves "Evangelicals." Some even used the word "neo-evangelical" for a time; but it seemed too close to the term "Neo-Orthodox" to be comfortable.

The label "Evangelical" seemed more appropriate for the Fundamentalist-Evangelical during the 1940s, because those within American Liberalism no longer used the term to identify themselves.

In addition, the massive immigration at the turn of the century had made the nation much more pluralistic, and the United States no longer considered itself Evangelical. Premillennialist evangelist Billy Graham, one of the best-known evangelists in the world, would be in the trend of the historic Fundamentalist-Evangelical movement flowing from the nineteenth century to the present. Jerry Falwell would be in the line of the separatist Fundamentalist movement, a small group that grew in the 1960s through what they called "super-churches." Both men hold in common biblical literalism and a premillennial eschatology, and the current Fundamentalist movement is the right wing of Fundamentalist-Evangelicalism.

There is debate today over the use of "Evangelical" as an accurate label, and the Fundamentalist-Evangelical is lost in the vast number of perhaps sixty million Evangelicals in the United States. When the National Association of Evangelicals was founded in 1942, it contained a high percentage of premillennialists. That percentage is significantly lower today. However, many Evangelicals, Fundamentalists, Pentecostals, Holiness churches, and other similar groups, will always be categorized as "fundamentalists" because of their biblical literalism and world view.

Fundamentalist-Evangelical Protestantism provided a counterbalance to the extreme Liberalism that strongly influenced European and American Protestantism. It endeavored to bring men and women back to a more stable Word of God and a more satisfying Christian experience. The movement also provided an alternative world view that affects tens of millions of Protestants today, including a large body outside the United States. It is a comfort and solace to its growing constituency, a continuing challenge to those who disagree with its precepts. No matter how one evaluates what we have termed "a complex entity," Fundamentalist-Evangelicalism is an indispensable part of the mosaic of modern Protestantism.

SUGGESTED READING

Ahlstrom, Sydney E. *A Religious History of the American People.* New Haven, Conn.: Yale Univ. Press, 1975.

Hudson, Winthrop S. *Religion in America.* 3d. ed. New York: Charles Scribner's Sons, 1981.

Marsden, George F. *Fundamentalism and American Culture.* New York: Oxford Univ. Press, 1980.

Nawyn, William. *American Protestantism's Response to Germany's Jews and Refugees, 1933–1941.* Ann Arbor, Mich.: UMI Research Press, 1981.

Rausch, David A. *Zionism Within Early American Fundamentalism, 1878–1918.* Lewiston, N.Y.: Edwin Mellen Press, 1980.

Ribuffo, Leo. *The Old Christian Right: The Protestant Far Right from the Great Depression to the Cold War.* Philadelphia, Pa.: Temple Univ. Press, 1983.

Ruether, Rosemary R., and Rosemary S. Keller. *Women and Religion in America: Volume 3, 1900–1968.* New York: Harper & Row, 1986.

Russell, C. Allyn. *Voices of American Fundamentalism.* Philadelphia: Westminster Press, 1976.

Sandeen, Ernest R. *The Roots of Fundamentalism.* Chicago: Univ. of Chicago Press, 1970.

9

RELIGION IN
THE BLACK COMMUNITY

"Protestantism, by its policies and practices, far from helping to integrate the Negro in American life, is actually contributing to the segregation of Negro Americans," wrote Frank S. Loescher in *The Protestant Church and the Negro*. Published in 1948 by the Y.M.C.A.'s Association Press, the book was not meant to be pleasant reading. Its thesis was that, in spite of increased sensitivity toward America's race problem following World War I, Protestantism through congregational practices, educational institutions, and denominational guidelines had maintained a caste system with regard to black Protestants. Through interviews, denominational policy statements, and detailed statistical analysis, Loescher thoroughly substantiated his case. He found both liberal and conservative Protestants guilty of segregation and ethical stagnation. "If one were to write a history of Protestantism's relation to Negroes," Loescher summarized, "the balance sheet would be heavily on the debit side."

THE SLAVE TRADE

Slavery is an ancient institution that invaded the northern countries of East Africa during the early centuries of the Christian church. With the rise of Islam, Arab traders moved the slave trade south and west, establishing a significant commercial enterprise by the time European exploration began. The Portuguese brought the first Africans to Europe in 1442; and Catholic explorers such as Christopher Columbus (1451–1506), Hernando de Soto (1500?–1542), and Hernando Cortes (1485–1547) took blacks with them to the New World. Enslavement of the African blacks soon replaced bondage of the native American Indian.

Portugal was the first European nation to charter companies to deal in African gold and slaves from West Africa. In 1516, a year before Martin Luther posted the Ninety-five Theses, Charles V granted a Flemish trader permission to transport four thousand slaves annually from Africa to the West Indies. The slave trade grew so rapidly that soon the major nation-states of Europe were involved. The Atlantic slave trade was at its peak from 1701 to 1810 and extended from Northern Europe to Latin America, from North America to India and China. Approximately ten million black African slaves were exported to the New World.

COLONIAL AMERICA

In 1619 twenty blacks were sold as "indentured servants" to settlers in Jamestown, Virginia by the captain of a Dutch man-of-war. Five years later, a black child was baptized as a Protestant Christian. Although blacks in general began to accept the Protestant faith, colonial Englishmen progressively degraded them through legal enactments. Around 1659 a reference to "negro slaves" appeared in the statutes of the Virginia Assembly and in 1667 an assembly act declared that the baptism of children "that are slaves by birth" did not "alter the condition of the person as to his bondage." This act claimed that such a ruling permitted masters to "more carefully endeavor the propagation of Christianity."

In 1680 the same assembly judged that "frequent meeting of considerable numbers of negroe slaves" was "of dangerous consequence," and declared that a slave who presumed "to lift up his hand in opposition against any Christian" was to receive "thirty lashes on his bare back well laid on." Throughout the colonies, fear of slave revolts grew as the slave population increased, and added restrictions bordered on the ludicrous. Freedom of movement was restricted, civil rights were annulled, and severe penalties were inflicted for even minor offenses. Any attempted or perceived "insurrection" was savagely suppressed by the white Protestants.

In the Massachusetts Bay Colony, where the Puritans' holy experiment was in process, merchants began to engage in the slave trade at an early date. At first they sold captive male Pequod Indians to the West Indies, while making slaves at home of the tribe's women and children. Soon, Massachusetts took the lead in supplying black labor to the sugar plantations in the Caribbean. In 1644 Boston traders went directly to Africa for additional slaves, and by the mid-1670s were bringing slaves from the distant island of Madagascar. Boston traders then began supplying the other colonies, making large profits as slave transporters. While there were little more than a thousand actual slaves in all of New England at the beginning of the eighteenth century, the Puritan colonies became the lucrative commercial hub of the famous triangle between Africa and the West Indies. Even during the Great Awakening, New England was the greatest slave-trading section in America, slave merchants advertising their wares in the same newspapers that carried information on George Whitefield.

Some strange twists occurred as the biblical law of Massachusetts Bay interacted with the immorality of the slave trade. Property was a sacred right, and the Bible explicitly stated that "man-stealing" was a criminal offense. When the General Court of the Massachusetts Bay Colony learned that two of its slave merchants had participated in a 1645 Sunday attack on an African village, killing approximately a hundred persons and bringing at least two back as slaves, it registered "indignation" at the sin of man-stealing. Massachusetts law stated that "he that stealeth a man, and selleth him" should be put to death. Had the slave merchants lawfully purchased the slaves from other slave traders they would have "legally" and "biblically" been innocent according to Massachusetts law. The Puritan establishment seemed to be more concerned, however, that their slave traders had desecrated Sunday, the Sabbath. Over a century later, the same colony protested to England about the Sugar Act of 1764, claiming that the duty would directly destroy the slave trade and disrupt its economy. Blacks had indeed become chattel, and human decency had been sacrificed to the "Christian" economy.

And yet, because the Puritans had adopted the Old Testament slave code, their own New England slaves fared better than those in other colonies. Slaves had the dual status of both property and persons. Most punishment was limited to whipping, whereas Southern colonies practiced branding and maiming. New England slaves could be inherited and bought or sold as property, but masters were forbidden by law to kill them. New England slaves could not strike a white, could not be on the streets after 9:00 P.M., and could not buy liquor; but they were allowed to testify against a white in court and could own property. Such legal rights prepared the way for emancipation, as a number of blacks sued for their freedom in the 1760s. Although this was an expensive process, the gradual outgrowth of freedom ensued from it. In the Quok Walker Case of 1783, the Massachusetts Supreme Court ruled slavery unconstitutional.

THE RISE OF BLACK PROTESTANTISM

The white community and the black community lived in two different worlds, and the suffering of the black slaves should never be minimized. Even in Puritan New England, taskmasters could be unmercifully brutal. Nevertheless, in matters of faith and polity, the black church soon reflected the structure and doctrinal stance of the emerging Evangelical Protestantism. Black Protestants added, however, a powerful creative synthesis to the mosaic of Protestantism, a depth of feeling, faith, and pride that only oppression could cultivate.

Before the Civil War, there was no single entity that could be called "the black church." Religion in the black community was determined by the environment in which the blacks found themselves, that is, plantation or urban, North or South, slave or free. In the South, blacks were either made second-class members of a white congregation or were formed into a black congregation under the supervision of whites. Often blacks were segregated to the gallery or back pews of white congregations.

Missionaries began an intensive and systematic effort to convert and "Christianize" blacks during the eighteenth century. In the Church of England, the Society for the Propagation of the Gospel in Foreign Parts was founded in London in 1701 to work among the inhabitants of the North American colonies. Its first responsibility was to Anglican members, but it specified that it would also "minister" to Indians and black slaves. The first missionary sent by this society to South Carolina, Rev. Francis Le Jau (a 1706–17 tenure), was met with hostility by native American Indians and thus spent most of his time among the slaves. Stationed at the Goose Creek parish near Charleston, he notified the secretary of the society in 1709 that he had a congregation of approximately 100 persons. "On Sunday next I design God willing to baptise two very sensible and honest Negro Men whom I have kept upon tryal these two years," Le Jau reported (October 20, 1709). "Several others have spoken to me also; I do nothing too hastily in that respect."

Le Jau assured the society that he obtained permission from "their Masters" and part of the slave's confession of faith included the following: "You declare in the Presence of God and before this Congregation that you do not ask for the holy baptism out of any design to free yourself from the Duty and Obedience you owe to your Master while you live, but merely for the good of Your Soul and to partake of the Graces and Blessings promised to the Members of the Church of Jesus Christ."

The experience of the Great Awakening led Methodists and Baptists as well as some Presbyterians to proselytize blacks. Spreading from New England to the South and West, the warmth and message of revivalist preaching appealed to the black slaves. Revivalist Protestantism taught that God's love extended to all human beings, and that in Jesus Christ there was neither slave nor free. To some slaves, the fact that God had delivered the Hebrews from the bondage of Egypt meant that God recognized the plight of black children and would hear their cries. Furthermore, their trials on earth would reap glory in heaven.

As blacks were converted, fears grew among slave owners. Legislative acts were written to work against black congregations. In 1715, for example, North Carolina passed a law fining white persons who permitted blacks to build a house of worship; in 1770 Georgia forbade slaves "to assemble on pretense of [religious] feasting," allowing those who did so to be whipped "bare back twenty-five stripes" without trial. In spite of these regulations, black Protestants persisted in the practice of their faith. In Savannah, Georgia, a black, Andrew Bryan (1737–1812), became pastor of the First African Baptist Church although he and his followers had been forbidden to hold religious services. Whipped publicly and imprisoned several times, Bryan proclaimed that he would continue "to preach Christ crucified." Shamed, his critics and persecutors were soon silenced by other white Protestants. Bryan's congregation had 850 members in 1802 and spawned other congregations as well, predating the rise of independent black denominations in the North.

In Methodism, Harry Hosier (d. 1806), known as "Black Harry," traveled with Francis Asbury (1745–1816), the "Father of American

Methodism," and Thomas Coke (1747–1814) as one of their favorite missionaries to the black community. Both Asbury and Coke felt that Hosier was a better preacher than they, and the Oxford-trained Coke wrote about the "amazing power" that accompanied Hosier's preaching. Coke remarked in his journal that although Hosier could not read, "I really believe he is one of the best preachers in the world. . . . " Indeed, after hearing Hosier, Benjamin Rush (1745–1813), surgeon-general in the Continental Army and a signer of the Declaration of Independence, exclaimed that Hosier was "the greatest orator in America." Hosier even preached to white congregations, a practice that would be frowned upon in later decades. In 1786, for example, he accompanied Asbury to New York and preached in the John Street Church for several weeks.

That same year, Jupiter Hammon (1720–1806?), the first black in America to write and publish poetry, delivered an address to the African Society in New York, insisting: "Now whether it is right, and lawful, in the sight of God, for them to make slaves of us or not, I am certain that while we are slaves, it is our duty to obey our masters, in all their lawful commands, and mind them unless we are bid to do that which we know to be sin, or forbidden in God's word." Hammon then quoted the apostle Paul in Eph. 6:5: "Servants be obedient to them that are your masters. . . . "

THE GROWTH OF THE
INDEPENDENT BLACK CHURCH

Hammon was greatly affected by the Wesleyan revivalist movement, and yet his views on slavery were quite conservative in comparison to some other black leaders affected by the evangelical egalitarianism of the time. Nevertheless, he admitted that freedom was "a great thing" and "worth seeking," and he hoped for gradual emancipation of black slaves. The need for ecclesiastical emancipation among black Protestants also became glaringly evident in Philadelphia in the 1780s when, traditionally, Richard Allen (1760–1831) and Absalom Jones (1746–1818) mistakenly sat in a section other than that reserved for Negroes. While they were on their knees praying in the St. George Methodist Episcopal Church, the two black Methodist leaders and another member of the congregation were pulled to their feet and led from the sanctuary.

This discriminatory act by trustees of St. George pointed to the increasing segregation occurring even in the North. That it occurred among Methodists, a group that had had many integrated meetings and where white and black together "broke bread" and "testified openly," indicated the inflexible social system that was pressuring Protestantism, including the Southern church's success in lobbying against being "too permissive" to blacks. In spite of the pressure, the General Conference of the Methodist Episcopal church in 1800 permitted the ordination of black preachers as deacons and by 1812 had authorized their ordination as elders. Even so, the regulation was not printed in the Methodist *Discipline* for fear of Southern opposition. The cotton gin, new varieties of cotton, and westward expansion were smothering black religious freedoms in the South at a time when Northern blacks were forming independent ecclesiastical systems.

After being humiliated by the St. George Church, Richard Allen and Absalom Jones organized the Free African Society in 1787, an organization intended to improve the condition of black people. A slave converted by Methodist Evangelicals in 1777 and freed by a Delaware planter who became convinced that slavery was wrong, Allen intended to remain a Methodist; but Jones was increasingly drawn to the Episcopal church. Jones organized the African Protestant Church of St. Thomas, which was received in the communion of the Protestant Episcopal church in 1784 with Jones as its first deacon. Other independent Methodist and Baptist churches, such as Zion Methodist Church in New York City (1796) and Joy Street Baptist Church in Boston (1807), followed his lead. First African Presbyterian Church of Philadelphia was formed in 1807, the first black Presbyterian group.

Allen organized the Bethel Church in 1794, the building itself dedicated by none other than Bishop Francis Asbury. Asbury also ordained Allen a deacon (he later became an elder) in the Methodist Episcopal church. In much the same manner as Wesley's "societies" within the Church of England, Richard Allen's "African Methodist" churches spread to other cities, becoming a separate denomination, the African Methodist Episcopal church, in 1816. Allen was elected bishop, and the A.M.E. patterned itself in rules and articles of faith after the Methodists. By the 1830s, the African Methodist Episcopal Zion, the Negro Baptist conferences, and several smaller denominations had organized as well, preferring their own setting free from the humiliation of white racial discrimination and segregation.

In the South, churches for blacks existed according to the whim of the authorities. The scattered independent black churches in the antebellum period were mainly urban and formed by free slaves who constituted one in ten blacks in America in 1800. Most blacks who worshiped were provided special sections in white churches and heard a message that called for unquestioning obedience to their masters. Only after the Civil War would blacks have the same opportunity for independent black organizations as their Northern counterparts.

During the Century of the Evangelical, black Protestants displayed the same missionary impulse as white evangelicals. Their biblical rationale was the same: Jesus commanded in Matt. 28:19–20, "Go ye therefore, and teach all nations." Interested in home missions, denominations such as the A.M.E. sought to establish churches in the North and the West. Caught up in the postmillennial enthusiasm for the kingdom of God on earth, Northern black evangelical missionaries soon were going to Africa, the Caribbean Islands, and black settlements in Canada. They felt a special spiritual and cultural tie to Africa, and there was a major wave of black nationalist and black emigrationist sentiment among Northern blacks in the 1840s and 1850s. This was not an escapist movement, but rather an effort to strengthen and protect Africa from further harm. Reverend Nathaniel Paul of the African Baptist Society of Albany, New York declared in 1827 that the day would come when "the sons and daughters of Africa" would spread the gospel of Jesus Christ in the land of their fathers.

In his book *The Future of Africa* (1862), black Episcopalian minister Rev. Alexander Crummell (1819–98) called upon free blacks to aid Africa through Christian conversion and economic development. He challenged blacks to save the continent from ruin and to destroy "the power of the devil in his strongholds, and to usher therein light, knowledge, and blessedness, inspiring hope, holy faith and abiding glory."

Black Evangelicalism stressed moral and spiritual improvement, rebuking those who continued to live in sin and immorality. Blaming slavery for its negative effects on the black community, black reform advocates stressed the power God provides every true Christian to live a disciplined life. As part of the "benevolent empire," black denominations supported the temperance movement, built educational institutions, participated in the Sunday school movement, and organized mutual aid societies in every Northern state. During the 1830s, for instance, Philadelphia had more than forty black benevolent and charitable organizations that believed it "to be the duty of every person to contribute" toward alleviating the misery of the less fortunate. In *The Future of Africa*, Rev. Crummell would proudly point to the African Methodist Episcopal church as a vibrant example of what "tens of thousands of the sons of Africa" had done and could do.

THE ANTISLAVERY MOVEMENT

The participation of over five thousand black soldiers in the War of Independence against the British strengthened the growing Protestant opposition to slavery that had existed from colonial times. No doubt, the struggle of the American colonies for freedom from "English tyranny" led some patriots to realize that they must not hold black men, women, and children in bondage. After the war, masters from many states released hundreds of black soldiers and their families; and in the next two decades legal slavery in the United States was gradually ended. In 1777 Vermont became the first state to abolish slavery; and by 1804, Massachusetts (1780), New Hampshire (1780), Connecticut (1784), Rhode Island (1784), Pennsylvania (1780), New York (1799), and New Jersey (1804), had approved legislation to abolish slavery. Ohio (1802), Indiana (1816), and Illinois (1818) outlawed slavery through their constitutions. In 1808 the United States abolished the slave trade. By 1820, there were approximately 100,000 free blacks in the Northern states.

The first antislavery society was founded by a group of Philadelphia Quakers in 1775. This certainly was fitting since a group of Quakers in Germantown, Pennsylvania had issued the first public denunciation in America against slavery. In 1776 Quaker Anthony Benezet convinced the Society of Friends to expel members who were slaveowners, and Quaker Benjamin Lundy (1789–1839) convinced Baptist temperance leader William Lloyd Garrison (1805–79) to join the antislavery forces.

In the Christmas Conference (1784), in which the Methodist Episcopal Church of America became a separate denomination, American Methodism banned slaveholding among its members. Many Baptists and Presbyterians initially took a stance against slaveholding. Ironically, in an effort to reach slaveholders and Southerners with the gospel, Methodists, Baptists, and Presbyterians soon watered down their opposition; and it is estimated that by the 1840s over one thousand Methodist ministers and evangelists owned slaves. Finally, after years of equivocation, the Methodist General Conference in 1844 condemned its bishop over Georgia for holding slaves. The denomination split the following year into North and South. Baptists and Presbyterians experienced similar divisions before the Civil War.

As evangelical William Wilberforce (1759–1833) led the antislavery forces in England (see chap. 6), American evangelical philanthropists, such as Lewis and Arthur Tappan, financed a crusade against slavery in America. Evangelist Charles Finney (1792–1875) and Oberlin College (founded 1832) were helped by the Tappans in both their evangelistic and antislavery campaigns, while Finney's convert, Theodore Dwight Weld (1803–95), fearlessly converted slaveholders and seminary students to the abolitionist cause. The American Antislavery Society, founded in Philadelphia in 1833 as a national movement and partially funded by the Tappans, employed the services of Weld as an organizer and traveling agent. It distributed millions of pieces of literature, organizing conferences and lectures during the 1830s to galvanize the reform.

In the South, where slavery had become crucial to the economy, evangelical Protestant ministers formulated elaborate defenses "from Scripture" to prove that slavery was of divine origin and therefore a divine institution. Using some of the European arguments of the new paganism that stressed the "inferiority of Jews and other non-whites," these Southern clergy argued that the Bible taught that God intended "a variety in human status," that the slaves had inherited Noah's curse on Ham, that blacks should be subservient, obedient, and in humble regard for their white masters. Evangelical Southerners even claimed that slavery had profited blacks, snatching them from pagan Africa and advancing the gospel. Unfortunately, such arguments still persist in right-wing extremist groups today, and Protestantism faces the challenge of combating such heresy.

While the South often is accused of such racism, one must note that Northern "free" blacks also faced prejudice and racial discrimination. Anti-black sentiment was strong in the North, and the rights and privileges of blacks were severely restricted. In the Midwest, all seven states had laws that barred blacks from voting. In the North, as well as the South, blacks were barred from public schools, public conveyances, and public amusement. Northern blacks faced economic restrictions and discrimination in housing. Black ministers in New York issued a letter in 1837 decrying such "prejudice against color," explaining that "it meets us everywhere to hedge up the way—at the school, at the workshop, and even in the house of God."

Slave revolts in the South, led by such figures as Gabriel Prosser (in 1800), Denmark Vesey (in 1822), and Nat Turner (in 1831), used biblical themes of justice and deliverance in the attempt to alleviate their plight and bolster their crusade. In the North, however, opposition by whites to the employment of blacks provoked riots in numerous cities, including Cincinnati (1829), Providence (1824 and 1831), and Philadelphia (1834). Frederick Douglass (1817–95), the great black abolitionist, writer, and orator who had lived under both urban and plantation slavery, in 1853 listed the "combined evils" of poverty, ignorance, and degradation as "the social disease of the free colored people in the United States."

The independent black churches and denominations were constantly fighting against the sanctions and hatred directed at blacks in the North as well as the cruelty of the slavery system in the South. To their credit, some black and white evangelicals combined forces in the "Underground Railroad" to bring Southern slaves to freedom, even as they fought discrimination and perfidy in the North. Southerners claimed that by 1850 approximately 100,000 slaves with an economic value of $30 million, had escaped. A courageous exslave, Harriet Tubman (c. 1821–1913), personally led more than three hundred slaves to freedom. Impressing audiences with her deep faith in God, Tubman, like Frederick Douglass, was a member of the A.M.E. Zion church.

"EMANCIPATION"

On the eve of the Civil War, the population of the United States was nearly 32 million; 4.4 million were blacks, 6 out of 7 of whom were still enslaved. From 1861 to 1865, evangelical Protestants in the North and South died believing they were fighting for "God's cause." Chaplains and ministers on both sides prayed for victory, as Protestant clergy and church leaders played leading roles in diametrically opposite sectional movements. One hundred and eighty-six thousand black troops took part in 198 battles and skirmishes, and twenty-two won the Medal of Honor for their heroism. Of these over 68,000 blacks — more than one-third — died.

President Abraham Lincoln (1809–65) issued the Emancipation Proclamation on January 1, 1863, which declared that "all persons held as slaves . . . henceforward shall be, free." After the war, the Thirteenth Amendment to the Constitution was put into effect on December 18, 1865: "Neither slavery nor involuntary servitude, except as a punishment for crime whereof the party shall have been duly convicted, shall exist within the United States or any place subject to their jurisdiction."

The South was finally opened to Northern independent black denominations, and many blacks took the opportunity to exercise their religious freedom. From 1860 to 1870, for example, membership in the A.M.E. Zion church grew from 21,000 to 200,000, an increase due mainly to freed slaves. In December 1870, the Colored Methodist Episcopal church (the Christian Methodists of today) was formed. In 1880, the African Methodist Episcopal church had approximately 400,000 members. The two largest black Baptist denominations, the National Baptist Convention, U.S.A. and the National Baptist Convention of America, were formed in 1895 and 1916 respectively.

Most of the independent black denominations, outside of schisms and mission work, were founded before 1906; and the census of that year indicated that there were 36,770 black church organizations with a membership of 3,685,097. Baptists and Methodists had 96 percent of the total number of communicants in 1906, and 86 percent belonged to independent denominations, that is, the National Baptist Convention (the largest and a fusion of rival groups in 1895), the A.M.E., the A.M.E. Zion, and the Colored Methodist Episcopal church, in that order. The Protestant faith was a central element in the black religious experience in America, and through black mission boards this experience had reached out to many other parts of the world.

In 1840, Rev. Charles B. Ray (b. 1807), pastor of the Bethesda Congregational Church in New York City and the last editor of *The Colored American*, had written for that paper the article entitled "Colored Churches in This City" (March 28, 1840). He declared, "We are convinced that the greatest amount of the prejudice in our country, which exists against our people, has its foundation in wrong views of them, and that such views are predicated upon ignorance." He believed that the white population needed to know what was "meritorious" and "virtuous" in the black community, and maintained "that contact by our people, in every possible way, will be a very efficient method to change the views and the feelings of the public." Ray, like other black leaders, tried desperately to change the racist attitudes of both Northerners and Southerners. Unfortunately, "wrong views" and "ignorance" persisted after the Civil War, and black Protestantism had to contend with racial injustice and discrimination even from fellow Protestants.

Despite progress, the black community was not really "emancipated." By 1900, nine out of ten blacks still lived in the South and were plagued with a tenant farming system that kept them enslaved. As sharecroppers, they did not own their land, and the landlords kept the accounts, insisting that all supplies be purchased from them at their prices. Southern whites blamed the blacks for the atrocities of the Civil War, and unleashed venomous attacks of racial discrimination. Using the Thirteenth Amendment phrase "except as a punishment for crime" as a ploy to convict blacks of "crimes," the South formed labor gangs of black convicts that worked off long sentences for minor offenses. The Ku Klux Klan was formed the same month the amendment was implemented, and through the violence perpetrated by its growing membership, terrorized and beat blacks into submission. "Black Codes" were developed in the Southern states that restricted blacks once again, and legal chicanery took both the vote and education from the black population.

In 1896, a conservative Supreme Court ruled in *Plessy* v. *Ferguson* that "separate but equal" facilities did not conflict with the thirteenth or fourteenth amendments of the Constitution. The Fourteenth Amendment had been added in 1868 to assure the constitutionality of the Civil Rights Act of 1866. In an era of Black Codes, this amendment pronounced in part that "No State shall make or enforce any law which shall abridge the privileges or immunities of citizens" nor should they "deprive any person of life, liberty, or property," or "equal protection" under the law. The Supreme Court decision in *Plessy* v. *Ferguson* upheld a Louisiana statute that required railroads to provide separate coaches for white and black passengers. Plessy, who was one-eighth black and seven-eighths white, had been arrested because he insisted on sitting in the coach reserved for whites. The Supreme Court's infamous decison noted that the Fourteenth Amendment "could not have been intended to abolish distinctions based upon color" and laws of separation "do not necessarily imply the inferiority of either race to the other."

Blacks were kept separate but were never equal. The North continued to enforce its brand of separation as well, and as blacks moved to the urban areas of Northern cities they were confined to ghettoes. During World War I, blacks were allowed to serve only as messboys in the Navy and were barred from the Marines. The Army attempted to bar them as officers, and the Y.M.C.A. recreation units made no provisions for blacks.

Black Protestant ministers led the black community in protesting such "legal" enslavement and discrimination. Reverend Reverdy C. Ransom (1861–1959), pastor of the Charles Street A.M.E. Church in Boston, delivered a blistering indictment of both white Protestantism and American Christian practice in his address "The Race Problem in a Christian State, 1906." Speaking to the Park Street Church in Boston in the era of the Social Gospel, he expounded: "There should be no Race problem in the Christian State. . . . A Christian State is one founded upon the teachings of Jesus; . . ." and said Jesus had "founded Christianity in the midst of the most bitter and intense antagonisms of race and class," treating all men and women the same. Believing that America had the right "to call itself a Christian nation" because it was "born with the Bible in its hands," Ransom admitted that the "Negro Question" had been with the nation from its governmental foundation.

"The Race Problem in this country is not only still with us an unsolved problem," Ransom warned, "but it constitutes perhaps the most serious problem in our country today." In the midst of a Protestantism which asserted that the world was progressively getting better, Ransom asserted that "compromises" had ended in failure and he proclaimed: "American Christianity will un-christ itself if it refuses to strive on, until this Race Problem is not only settled, but settled right; and until this is done, however much men may temporize and seek to compromise, and cry 'peace! peace!' there will be no peace until this is done."

In the pattern of so many black pastors, politicians, educators, and activists before and after him, Ransom directed his challenge squarely at the door of white Protestantism: "The white millions of this nation can never lift themselves up in Christianity and civilization by beating back and trampling under foot the simple rights and aspirations of ten million blacks." Ransom would see black soldiers being segregated into separate units during World War II, and he would fight against discriminatory laws for the rest of his life. But he would also relish black accomplishment in the arts, science, literature, sports, the political arena, philosophy, education, and religion. The pride and determination of the black community never ceased to amaze him, and his heart cried out for the plight of his people. Retired in 1952, he lived another seven years, long enough to see the budding of the Civil Rights movement.

Protestantism, in general, had failed to answer Ransom's challenge; it had neglected to heed his warning. When Bishop William Scarlett of the Episcopal Diocese of Missouri wrote the foreword to Loescher's *The Protestant Church and the Negro* in 1948, he emphasized that in spite of notable exceptions, "the Church has acquiesced in the pattern of segregation." Maintaining that "on purely religious grounds there is no defense for segregation within the Church" and "in the presence of God the divisions of race are transcended," Bishop Scarlett affirmed that the "tide" against segregation would "gather momentum." "The Protestant Church is not an authoritarian organization. It proceeds by the democratic process, which means that leadership must carry the people with it," he explained. "The process may be somewhat slow. But there has been ample opportunity for the education of our people; the time for action is now at hand."

MARTIN LUTHER KING, JR.

Religion in the black community has never forgotten its historic background of slavery and segregation. In Protestantism, it has combined a gospel of hope with a theology of suffering that was woven in the fabric of the black experience. Black religion grasped the evangelical message of a future world, where evil could not prosper and the justice of God would prevail. And yet, black religion was not otherworldly, but rather a protest movement for social justice against societal structures of evil.

Negro spirituals underscored black religion's themes of protest and

171

hope. In its first verse, "When Israel Was in Egypt's Land" begins in protest:

> When Israel was in Egypt's land,
>   Let my people go,
> Oppressed so hard they could not stand,
>   Let my people go.

Within a few verses, however, the spiritual rings out with hope:

> No more shall they in bondage toil,
>   Let my people go,
> Let them come out with Egypt's spoil,
>   Let my people go.

Heaven itself was captured in the Negro spiritual as an affirmation of black humanity in the midst of societal structures that steadily tried to dehumanize the black community. "Swing Low, Sweet Chariot" reflects this emphasis as does the later "Oh Freedom!":

> Oh Freedom! Oh Freedom!
> Oh Freedom! I love thee!
> And before I'll be a slave,
> I'll be buried in my grave,
> And go home to my Lord and be free.

Blacks would differ in theology and polity as widely as the religious heritage the majority of black Americans chose: Protestantism. But the biblical principles above would be common to the community.

In spite of persecution, religion in the black community presented a theology of reconciliation that was rarely bitter and always a testimony of Christ's love. It distilled through the personal experience of suffering and injustice basic principles of Protestantism and returned those principles of social justice, brotherhood, faith, hope, love, individual conscience, and freedom as refined gold to imperfect Protestants who needed the object lesson.

These aspects of religion in the black community were abundantly evident in Martin Luther King, Jr. (1929–1968), a man who not only illustrated the power of the Civil Rights movement but also was firmly rooted in the black tradition and experience. That many claim him today as one of their own—from socialists to capitalists, from liberal theologians to fundamentalists, from black theology advocates to pentecostal evangelicals—underscores his impact on both the black and white communities in America and, indeed, throughout many parts of the world. As time passes, his contributions to Protestantism seem to multiply as historians and theologians analyze his life.

Dr. King was raised in the tradition of protest coupled with hope and love. In *Stride Toward Freedom: The Montgomery Story* (1958), he related a trip with his father to the local shoe store in the South:

> We had sat down in the first empty seats at the front of the store. A young white clerk came up and murmured politely: "I'll be happy to wait on you if you'll just move to those seats in the rear." My father answered, "There's nothing wrong with these seats. We're quite comfortable here." "Sorry," said the clerk, "but you'll have to move." "We'll either buy shoes sitting here," my father retorted, "or we won't buy shoes at all." Whereupon he took me by the hand and walked out of the store. This was the first time I had ever seen my father so angry. I still remember walking down the street beside him as he muttered, "I don't care how long I have to live with this system, I will never accept it." And he never has.

Pastor of the Ebenezer Baptist Church in Atlanta, Martin Luther King, Sr., had refused to ride the buses for as far back as his son could remember, because he had witnessed a brutal attack on a busload of black passengers. It was only fitting that his son would lead the Montgomery, Alabama bus boycott (1955–56). Martin Luther King, Jr.'s Protestant theology was dynamic because his black tradition was dynamic.

Martin Luther King, Jr.'s twelve-year public career was phenomenal (Montgomery boycott; Birmingham, 1963; Selma, 1965; Poor People's March on Washington, D.C., 1968 are only some highlights); but it coalesced with a civil rights movement well in progress. The black church had long puzzled sociologists because, even with a conservative theological orientation, local congregants approved of their pastors and their churches speaking out on social and political questions. Furthermore, the black community favored the extension of civil rights to all groups, and was not as parochial with its concerns as were white Protestants. As a pastor and social reform advocate, Dr. King would move in this stream in public ministry, speaking out against white poverty as well as black poverty, decrying the Vietnam War, etc.

Since its founding in 1909, the National Association for the Advancement of Colored People (NAACP) had lobbied for changes and won a number of court battles. In 1943, the Marines were forced to break their 167-year tradition and accept black applicants. New York became the first state to enact a fair employment practice law (March 12, 1945). In 1946, Jackie Robinson (1919–72) broke baseball's "color line," and in 1948 President Harry Truman (1945–53) ordered the desegregation of the armed forces. The NAACP registered black voters in increasing numbers in the South despite intense opposition.

The Supreme Court handed down a number of decisions that countered Southern segregation. For example, in *Morgan* v. *Virginia* (1946), the Supreme Court declared invalid a Virginia statute that required a black interstate bus traveler to move to a back seat in order to make room for a white passenger. The landmark decision, however, occurred in 1954 when the United States Supreme Court struck down the 1896 *Plessy* v. *Ferguson* "separate but equal" doctrine with the celebrated *Brown* v. *Topeka Board of Education* decision. Stating that it could not turn back the clock, but must consider public education in the light of modern America, this decision affirmed that segregation did deprive minority children of equal educational opportunities. The court recognized that the implications of this decision went far beyond education.

Martin Luther King, Jr., entered this movement for civil rights with his nonviolent activism and theology of redemptive suffering. His heritage was that of a Baptist black preacher, and he said on more than one occasion, "The Church is my life and I have given my life to the church." His "I Have a Dream" sermon during the great march on Washington in August 1963, illustrated his eloquence, caught the imagination of the nation, and mobilized support for the Civil Rights Act of 1964. He won the Nobel Peace Prize the same year, traveling to Oslo, Norway on December 4, 1964. Two months later he was in a Selma, Alabama jail, arrested for leading another nonviolent protest.

Dr. King confessed that his favorite dream, a dream that he had not only shared in Washington, but also with a number of other audiences, had at times turned into a nightmare. In a Christmas Eve sermon at the Ebenezer Baptist Church in 1967, he admitted that he was "the victim of deferred dreams, of blasted hopes" because of incidents that had followed in the wake of his 1963 Washington sermon. And yet, Dr. King continued to work, to hope, to struggle, with the same tough and rugged faith that his forefathers had. He died by an assassin's bullet at the age of thirty-nine, but his oft-repeated words to white audiences across the United States express the power of his person and the quality of his tradition:

> We will match your capacity to inflict suffering with our capacity to endure suffering. We will meet your physical force with soul force. We will not hate you, but we cannot in all good conscience obey your unjust laws. Do to us what you will and we will still love you. Bomb our homes and threaten our children; send your hooded perpetrators of violence into our communities and drag us out on some wayside road, beating us and leaving us half dead, and we will still love you. But we will soon wear you down by our capacity to suffer. And in winning our freedom we will so appeal to your heart and conscience that we will win you in the process.

In a meeting called by the mayor during the Montgomery boycott, one of the most outspoken segregationists in the Methodist church explained to Dr. King why blacks were wrong in boycotting the buses. He contended that a minister's job was to lead the souls of people to God, rather than getting tangled up in social problems. Moving on to a discussion of the "Christmas story" and the "Christmas season" that was upon them, he indicated that the black ministers should have their minds and hearts turned toward "the babe of Bethlehem."

Dr. King replied in part that the black ministers assembled had also had an experience with Jesus, and they saw "no conflict between our devotion to Jesus Christ and our present action." "In fact," Dr. King stated, "I see a necessary relationship. . . . The gospel is social as well as personal."

Perhaps another Baptist pastor, Howard Thurman (1900–1981), the dean of Marsh Chapel and professor of Spiritual Resources and Disciplines at Boston University, had both the Christmas story mentioned by the segregationist and the black Protestant tradition in mind when he wrote:

> When the song of the angel is stilled
> When the star in the sky is gone
> When the kings and princes are home
> When the shepherds are back with their flock
> The work of Christmas begins:
> To find the lost
> To heal the broken

To feed the hungry
To release the prisoner
To rebuild the nations
To bring peace among brothers
To make music in the heart.

SUGGESTED READING

Bailey, David T. *Shadow on the Church: Southwestern Evangelical Religion and the Issue of Slavery, 1783–1860.* Ithaca, N.Y.: Cornell Univ. Press, 1985.

Franklin, John Hope, and August Meier, eds. *Black Leaders of the Twentieth Century.* Urbana: Univ. of Illinois Press, 1982.

Frazier, E. Franklin, and C. Eric Lincoln. *The Negro Church in America and the Black Church since Frazier.* New York: Schocken Books, 1974.

Irwin, Graham W., ed. *Africans Abroad: A Documentary History of the Black Diaspora in Asia, Latin America, and the Caribbean During the Age of Slavery.* New York: Columbia Univ. Press, 1977.

Jordan, Winthrop D. *White over Black: American Attitudes toward the Negro, 1550–1812.* Chapel Hill, N.C.: Univ. of North Carolina Press, 1968.

Raboteau, Albert J. *Slave Religion.* New York and London: Oxford Univ. Press, 1978.

Roberts, J. Deotis. *Roots of a Black Future: Family and Church.* Philadelphia: Westminster Press, 1980.

Rose, Willie Lee, ed. *A Documentary History of Slavery in North America.* New York and London: Oxford Univ. Press, 1976.

Simpson, George. *Black Religions in the New World.* New York: Columbia Univ. Press, 1978.

Washington, Joseph R., Jr. *Black Religion.* Boston: Beacon Press, 1964.

Williams, Walter L. *Black Americans and the Evangelization of Africa, 1877–1900.* Madison, Wisc.: Univ. of Wisconsin Press, 1982.

10

NEW RELIGIOUS MOVEMENTS

The nineteenth and twentieth centuries have given rise to a plethora of religious movements. Some of these have continued to impact upon Protestantism, while others are fading relics, testimonials to the creativity of the human religious impulse. Although refraining from prophesying which of the modern religious movements mentioned below will have lasting influence on Protestantism, this chapter will survey some of the movements that Protestants are encountering as the twenty-first century approaches.

OTHER PERSUASIONS

While not strictly speaking Protestant by affiliation nor by derivation, such groups as the Mormons, Christian Scientists, and Jehovah's Witnesses have had a constantly growing influence in modern times. Mormon membership is approximately four million worldwide, while Jehovah's Witnesses claim three million members. Much smaller in membership, the Church of Christ, Scientist, has made a remarkable contribution to the world through its fine newspaper, *The Christian Science Monitor,* and portends to have even greater impress through a global shortwave news network.

During the revivalism of the early nineteenth century, Joseph Smith (1805–44) was converted in Palmyra, New York. As a young Christian, Smith viewed with disdain the growing controversies in Protestantism over biblical interpretation, and at one point retired to a woods to seek wisdom from God. As he later testified, the Father and the Son appeared to him and commanded him to separate himself from all Protestant denominations. They promised him a special ministry, a task directed from heaven itself.

After a period of much testing and further revelations, Smith claimed that the angel Moroni guided him to golden plates that had been buried long before. These plates told the story of the descendants of a lost tribe of Israel, the Nephites and Lamanites, who inhabited America before the Indians. In fact, the Lamanites were the progenitors of the American Indians, and Christ himself had established the proper church order among them and the Nephites. The Lamanites, however, were said to have "apostatized" and killed all of the Nephites except faithful Mormon and his son, Moroni. Through "translating spectacles" which enabled him to decipher the golden plates' "reformed Egyptian hieroglyphics," Smith published the *Book of Mormon* in 1830. His Church of Jesus Christ of Latter-day Saints was founded the same year.

The Book of Mormon not only portrayed America as the promised land but also "solved" every problem that divided American Protestant denominations in the early nineteenth century, from infant baptism to church government. Continuing revelations provided *The Doctrine and Covenants* (1835), a basic systematic theology for the movement which is coupled with the King James Version of the Bible. Smith's contention that God had approved the practice of polygyny led to further recrimination from Protestant leaders and, ultimately, to Smith's death in 1844 at the hands of an Illinois mob.

Brigham Young (1801–77), who had joined the Mormons in 1832 and had become "chief of the Twelve Apostles" in 1838, led the church to Utah, the "Zion in the Wilderness." In 1850, Young became governor of the Territory of Utah, and the Mormon Temple in Salt Lake City remains the center of the Church of Jesus Christ of Latter-day Saints (over three million members). The largest splinter group, the Reorganized Church of Jesus Christ of Latter-day Saints (about 600,000) is headquartered in Independence, Missouri. Although they claim to be the only true church, Mormons have been heralded for their high moral standards and social welfare programs. Their concept of progressive revelation has helped to bridge the cultural gap between centuries. For example, their "priesthood" was denied to blacks until 1978, at which time their president received a new "revelation" to admit blacks to the priesthood.

While Mormonism reflected the popular early nineteenth-century view of the upward progression of humankind (even asserting that gods were once men and men could become gods), Christian Science reflected a post-Civil War interest in hypnotism and mental healing. A devout Congregationalist, Mary Baker Eddy (1821–1910) was plagued with ill health and nervous disorders through three marriages. Embarking on a quest for healing and attempting to restore the early church's emphasis on healing, Mary Baker Eddy alleged that she was taught the "divine science" of healing by God, who dictated to her *Science and Health with Key to the Scriptures* (1875). The book became the foundation stone of her Christian Scientists Association (1876) and her Church of Christ, Scientist (1879). She married Asa Gilbert Eddy in 1877, a man she had cured.

Science and Health maintains that sickness is an illusion, for disease is caused by erroneous thought. Because the Eternal Mind is the source of all being, matter is nonexistent; sin, sickness, and death are not real. Even the virgin Mary conceived Jesus Christ only as a "spiritual idea," and he did not possess a body or die on a cross. Heaven and hell are represented in *Science and Health* as present states of mind.

Christian Science began to prosper when Mary Baker Eddy moved to Boston, reorganizing the "Mother Church," The First Church of Christ, Scientist of Boston, in 1892. Other churches are considered branches of this Mother church, and today over two thousand of them remain active in the United States, with hundreds more scattered throughout the world. These churches have no preachers or sermons, but two elected readers quote selections from *Science and Health* without comment. By the time of her death, Mary Baker Eddy led nearly 100,000 practitioners. Today, she remains the final word through the noninterpretive reading of *Science and Health with Key to the Scriptures*.

Nineteenth-century millennial thought combined with evangelical unitarian doctrine in the inception and growth of the modern Jehovah's Witnesses. Founded in the 1870s by a drapery shop entrepreneur, Charles Taze Russell (1852–1916), the Jehovah's Witnesses began as a Bible class in Pittsburgh, Pennsylvania, with Russell soon becoming "pastor." In 1879 Russell began *Zion's Watchtower* magazine, and in 1884 the group was organized as Zion's Watchtower Tract Society. Russell opposed the traditional doctrine of the Trinity as "three gods" and ridiculed an eternal hell as ludicrous. He believed instead that evil ones would be annihilated after the judgment.

Moving the headquarters to its present location in Brooklyn, New

York, in 1908, Russell predicted that the kingdom of God would be fully established in 1914. His successor, "Judge" Joseph Franklin Rutherford (1869–1942), was able to rally discouraged followers by emphasizing in the 1920s that Christ had returned "invisibly" in 1914 and was overthrowing the world order of Satan. He also "received" from God the name "Jehovah's Witnesses" in 1931 and through an intense publication effort shaped the theology of the current movement. Today, each issue of *The Watchtower* magazine has a circulation of over twelve million in 103 languages, and the Jehovah's Witnesses have an extensive missionary network throughout the world. Their local Kingdom Halls teach an anti-trinitarian doctrine which asserts that Jesus became a divine spirit after his resurrection and that his ransom to God Jehovah removed the effects of sin from Adam's fall. This ransom enables men and women to save themselves through good works and to use these works to accomplish the downfall of Satan's world order. All churches and religious organizations are viewed as the "tools" Satan uses in his world order. Jehovah's Witnesses, therefore, reject a professional clergy, are pacifists, and will not participate in politics or oaths of allegiance. They believe a select group of 144,000 from their number will reign in heaven with Christ after the Battle of Armageddon.

ECUMENISM

Lutheran Georg Calixtus (1586–1656; see chap. 4) proposed a reconciliation of the factions of the Christian church by gathering them around the "fundamentals" of the Christian faith, while Frederick Denison Maurice (1805–72; see chap. 7) concluded that varied Protestant traditions must work together for the kingdom of Christ or they would hinder it. Both are just a sampling of the forerunners of the modern ecumenical movement.

In the midst of the increasing separatism among denominations in the nineteenth century, kindred-minded individuals from over fifty American and British denominations had formed the Evangelical Alliance in 1846 to unify the churches in a cooperative body. At the turn of the century, Social Gospel advocates initiated interdenominational social efforts, such as the Open and Institutional Church League (1894) and the National Federation of Churches and Christian Workers (c. 1895). In 1908, the Federal Council of Churches of

Christ in America was formed in Philadelphia by delegates from more than thirty denominations, vowing their "essential oneness" in applying the principles of the Social Gospel. These too were precursors of the modern ecumenical effort.

The movement traces its inception to the Edinburgh Missionary Conference of 1910. A multidenominational conference with international participation, it was spearheaded by American Methodist John R. Mott (1865–1955), who presided at most of the sessions over more than one thousand delegates. A former general secretary of the Student Y.M.C.A. and chair of the Student Volunteer Movement for Foreign Missions for thirty years, Mott was influenced by D. L. Moody and was thoroughly dedicated to the cause of world missions. A fervent Evangelical, he believed that Christian ecumenism was essential to support effectively the Christian missionary enterprise and to make an impact upon the world. "The end of the Conference is the beginning of the Conquest," Mott declared to the assembled delegates on the last day. "The end of the Planning is the beginning of the Doing."

Through an executive position on the committee delegated by the conference to continue coordinating cooperative missionary efforts, Mott saw his ecumenical movement begin to blossom. As chair of both the International Missionary Council (1921) and the Life and Work Conference at Oxford (1937), Mott spearheaded the drive for a thoroughly ecumenical body. The Life and Work Conference issued a call for a World Council of Churches, and it was joined by the Conference on Faith and Order led by the archbishop of York, William Temple (1881–1944), who in 1942 became archbishop of Canterbury.

In 1938 Mott became vice-chair of the provisional committee of the World Council of Churches and was elected copresident (honorary chair) of the WCC when it was finally established in 1948. Three hundred and fifty-one delegates representing 147 denominations from forty-four countries gathered in Amsterdam to form this international agency of Christian cooperation. At New Delhi, India, in 1961 the Russian Orthodox church joined the WCC and the International Missionary Council merged with the WCC as its Division of World Mission and Evangelism. This gave the ecumenical body more direct contact with the Third World. The adopted 1961 confession stated, "the World Council of Churches is a fellowship of Churches which confess the Lord Jesus Christ as God and Savior according to the Scriptures, and therefore seek to fulfill together their common calling to the glory of one God, Father, Son and Holy Spirit."

In spite of such general bases upon which to work, the road to doctrinal agreement is a long and difficult one. The World Council of Churches' Commission on Faith and Order will hold its Fifth World Conference on Faith and Order in March 1989. The 120-member commission includes a dozen Vatican-named theologians and other representatives of nonmember churches. In 1985, the commission issued the precedent-shattering statement, "Baptism, Eucharist and Ministry," a comprehensive effort to restate these three doctrines of the Christian faith. One of the tasks of the 1989 conference is to evaluate the responses to the hundreds of thousands of distributed copies of that statement. Two other studies deal with church unity and social action, and with the apostolic faith.

Rapprochement discussions are occurring between Anglican officials and Vatican officials and, today, regional ecumenical dialogue is a common phenomenon. German Reformed historian and immigrant Philip Schaff (1819–93), the founder of the American Society of Church History (1888), wrote in *The Principle of Protestantism* (1845) that the nineteenth-century United States was a fruitful ground for such ecumenical enterprises. "As the distractions of Protestantism have been most painfully experienced here," he acknowledged, "so here also may the glorious work of bringing all the scattered members of Christ's Body into catholic union be carried forward with the greatest zeal and soonest crowned with the great festival of reconciliation, transmitting its blessing in grateful love to the world we honor and love as our general fatherland." Schaff's hope was for the reunion of the denominations and sects of Protestantism with Roman Catholicism in a renewed evangelical Catholicism. A century and a half later, the process of ecumenism seems not only more distant, but much more complicated.

SECULARISM

As science and technology sparked a rapid transformation of the social and economic realm, Christianity was challenged once again by a broad range of secular philosophical theories and ideas of progress. Count Claude Henri de Saint-Simon (1760–1825), French social philosopher, insisted that science and technology could replace Christianity as it had been known and would point the way to social recon-struction. Such socialization would strip Christianity of its super-natural base while maintaining some of its ethics to ensure the solidarity of the new society.

His disciple, Auguste Comte (1798–1857), one of the founders of modern sociology, proposed a "religion of humanity" that would sub-stitute "positive" science for traditional Christianity. According to Comte, social theory was the new gospel to replace the old, and in his utopian society social guidance was supplied by philosophical sociologists, while the barons of industry would handle the adminis-trative aspects. Comte called this scientific world view "positivism," and positivism called for the elimination of the supernatural (God, heaven, hell, miracles, etc.). This attempt to transform religious insti-tutions into secular nonsupernatural socialized emotive forces for civ-ilization has had great impact on philosophic thought to this day.

Moving much further toward "liberation" from traditional beliefs, the son of a Lutheran minister, Friedrich Nietzsche (1844–1900), who had once studied for the ministry and was influenced by evolutionary theory, attacked Christianity and its God, asserting that it had been overthrown and that even its ethics were of no use. He called for the abolition of "herd morality" and "slave values" found in the Christian values of kindness, gentleness, humility, and pity. In *Thus Spake Zarathustra* (1883), Nietzsche proclaimed: "Before God! Now how-ever this God has died! Ye higher men, this God was your greatest danger. Only since he lay in the grave have ye again arisen."

To Nietzsche, God and the supernatural were only a projection of a weakling society's ideals, and he idealized a "superman" who exer-cised the genuine governing factor in all human relationships: *might.* Such thought led to uncertainty and frustration, giving rise to twentieth-century nihilism. For some Protestants, their concepts of the transcendence of God and traditional Christian thought were completely eroded. During the 1960s, "radical theology" or the "death of God" proponents exploited Nietzsche's phrase to draw attention to the bankruptcy of most theological endeavors and the vast gulf between what Christians supposedly believed and how they actually lived.

In 1933, a group of liberal thinkers who believed that traditional theism was an outmoded and unproved faith formulated the *Humanist Manifesto,* which stated that humankind and human culture were products of the evolutionary process — a process that had no relation to supernaturalism. It asked men and women to reject all supernaturalism and replace the unworldly tenets with a concrete commitment to human values. The *Humanist Manifesto* maintained that the proper goal of human beings should be the fulfillment of life in the here and now. The hope of salvation, a reward of heaven, and even a God who loves, cares, and hears prayers are false hopes which divert people from loftier attainment and harm the human venture.

Forty years later, a *Humanist Manifesto II* (1973) was issued by 275 intellectuals, claiming that the earlier statement seemed "far too optimistic." "Nazism has shown the depths of brutality of which humanity is capable," the preface declared. "Other totalitarian regimes have suppressed human rights without ending poverty. Science has sometimes brought evil as well as good." Nevertheless, it asserted that "humanism offers an alternative that can serve present-day needs and guide humankind toward the future" and emphasized that "the next century can be and should be the humanistic century."

In relation to religion, the *Humanist Manifesto II* reaffirmed the secular view of the former decades. "As nontheists, we begin with humans not God, nature not deity," the signers affirmed. Although they recognized that some humanists wanted to reinterpret traditional religions and appropriate them to the modern world, they felt that such redefinitions "often perpetuate old dependences and escapisms; they easily became obscurantist, impeding the free use of the intellect." "We need, instead, radically new human purposes and goals," they avowed. "No deity will save us; we must save ourselves."

Thus, articles twelve through seventeen of the *Humanist Manifesto II* call for "the building of a world community in which all sectors of the human family can participate." This world community would transcend national boundaries, develop a system of world law and world order, renounce war and weapons, and use planetary resources for the good of all humankind. "Humanism thus interpreted is a moral force that has time on its side," the document concluded. "We believe that humankind has the potential intelligence, good will, and cooperative skill to implement this commitment in the decades ahead."

Such secular humanism has been portrayed as "sophomoric," "juvenile," and "utopian" by liberal Protestants. Fundamentalist Protestants have attacked its "lack of moral framework" and its "contribution to the decay of moral values in modern society." For their part, secular humanists such as Paul Kurtz have responded with surprise at their "alleged influence in American society and the world."

In his book *In Defense of Secular Humanism* (1983) Kurtz relates the moral and ethical framework of secular humanism while clarifying the humanist position. While he believes that humanism has "become the scapegoat of the fundamentalist right," he nevertheless insists that "the criticisms made by the Moral Majority have some validity." "We cannot simply reject the Moral Majority and say that nothing they claim is meaningful," Kurtz asserts. "Although much of what they say is basically mistaken, it seems to me that they are concerned about many things that we should be concerned about: for example, the breakdown of the family in American life. Many humanists consider the family an important human institution." Underscoring the fact that "humanists believe in freedom, not license or licentiousness," Kurtz deplores "the recent excesses in American life," such as use of drugs, pornography, and promiscuity.

Protestant theologians and philosophers have been forced to grapple with secularism in its many forms and facets. Because Protestant principles advocate the important part Christians must play in the world about them, the relationship between the sacred and the secular is always in delicate balance. Defenders of secularism who refuse to be caricatured and misinterpreted can only sharpen Protestantism's ethical heritage and substantial contribution to humanity and culture.

THEOLOGIES OF LIBERATION

In an effort to define God and the theological enterprise in the face of secularism, scientific advance, totalitarianism, and genocide, twentieth-century Protestant theologians and philosophers joined those of other religious persuasions in the 1960s and 1970s to debate and defend the relevance of religion in secular society. Process theologians, building upon the philosophical analyses of Alfred North Whitehead (1861–1947) and Charles Hartshorne (b. 1897), argued that God was integrally involved in the endless process of world events, even growing in knowledge and experience through God's social relatedness to every creature. Empirical theorist Henry Nelson

Wieman (1884–1975), professor of the philosophy of religion at the University of Chicago Divinity School and author of such books as *Religious Experience and Scientific Method* (1926), for a half-century continually reinterpreted process theology and influenced many young theologians to embrace it.

German theology of hope advocates, such as Jürgen Moltmann and Wolfhart Pannenberg, argue that God understands the world and will make "all things new." As a God of the future, God is known presently in promises, with Christ's resurrection being the assurance of the promises yet to come. As a people of hope and vision, the church is to confront society and break down the barriers that separate peoples and the evil structures that oppress.

In the 1970s American theologians formed a study group under the auspices of the Institute for Ecumenical and Cultural Research to clarify how the Christian church was to meet the challenges of the modern world. The group of approximately twenty-five included Lutheran theology of hope advocate Carl Braaten, and process theology advocates John B. Cobb and Schubert Ogden. Catholic scholar David Tracy was also active in the deliberations. In the ensuing *Christian Theology: An Introduction to Its Traditions and Tasks* (1982), the study group attempted a "constructive theology" that would analyze the factors in the modern world that have eroded traditional dogma and that would reformulate those historic doctrines of the Christian church in ways congruent with modern times.

Similar reconstructions are occurring within the feminist movement and among some black theologians. Presbyterian theologian Letty M. Russell joined Roman Catholic theologian Rosemary R. Ruether in questioning and correcting "male-dominated theology." Mary Daly in her 1968 treatise *The Church and the Second Sex* denounced sexist attitudes, but remained optimistic that they could be corrected. By 1973, she had become much more negative about traditional Christianity and its ability to be corrected. In her *Beyond God the Father: Toward A Philosophy of Women's Liberation* (1973), Daly used the classical Christian outline of systematic theology (i.e., God, Creation, Fall, etc.,) to assert that as long as God is perceived as male, then "the male is God." In a sermon in 1971 at Harvard Memorial Church, Daly portrayed the women's movement as an "exodus community," and concluded that women could not "belong to institutional religion as it exists," a point she supported by noting that she was the first woman in 336 years to preach at a Sunday service in that church.

Black Protestant theologian James H. Cone has called for a radical approach that takes the suffering of black people seriously. He believes this can be accomplished only through a black theology of liberation. In 1969, Cone caused a stir when he wrote in his *Black Theology and Black Power*, "The problem with white society is that it wants to assume that everything is basically all right. . . . In this sense reconciliation would mean admitting that white values are the values of God. . . . But according to Black Theology, it is the other way around. Reconciliation does not transcend color, thus making us all white. . . . God's Word of reconciliation means that we can only be justified by becoming black."

Such theologies of liberation challenge Protestantism today from within and without. Nowhere on earth is Christianity growing faster than in the Third World, and Protestantism is currently making vast inroads. At the same time, Africans, Latin Americans, and other Third World Christians are engaging the theological enterprise to foster social justice. This diverse Liberation Theology emphasizes that social justice is not a secondary matter in the Christian faith, but is inseparable from the spiritual realm. The key to Liberation Theology is the reality of social misery and the goal of that theology is the liberation of the oppressed. The Hebrew exodus is a paradigm of God's action in history on behalf of the poor, the enslaved, and the oppressed. In the Exodus, liberation took place *in* history *as* history. Jesus Christ as liberator took up this theme in Matt. 25:40, when he stated: "As you did it to one of the least of these my brethren, you did it to me."

Liberation Theology does not claim that the poor are God's only people, but it garners substantial biblical evidence that they are very dear to God. It also views salvation in terms of both physical (political) and spiritual liberation. It hearkens back to the Social Gospel in that it finds liberation in Jesus' proclamation of the coming kingdom of God as well as in the actions of Christ's total life. Since "liberation" is the opposite of "domination," African, Latin American, and other Third World entities are pondering their theological premises within the context of their history of persecution and of their present reality, that is, in terms of imperialism, colonialism, economic domination, enslavement, etc.

Marxist social analysis concerning class struggle and a socialist society of more even equality is often used by liberation theologians. They would claim, however, that this occurs to no greater extent than Thomas Aquinas's use of the Greek philosophical system of Aristotle. Whatever the case, through such social analysis, the struggle between the "dominator" and the "dominated" is portrayed. It is from this struggle that the oppressed or "dominated" must liberate themselves. The act of liberation must be initiated by the oppressed because the oppressor is too entangled in injustice to initiate liberation. Ironically, in the process of liberation, the oppressor or dominator is also "liberated" from his evil ways to discover a more humane way of existence.

Theory and practice work together in Liberation Theology, biblical interpretation and hermeneutical evaluation becoming a thoroughly active process. The question, How does what I believe fit with what I do? is intrinsic to the movement, and it has continually brought before Protestantism the fact that following Jesus has social and political responsibilities. Liberation Theology accentuates the point that inhumanity to others is a sin, to be judged by God and resisted by Christians. Its plea for "costly discipleship" encompasses a compassion for the poor with the ethical responsibility that Christians should not remain indifferent to the plight of the oppressed.

Critics have pointed out that Marxism often has turned from a tool of social analysis to a rigid political structure in the Third World and that violence has accompanied such "liberation." Volatile reactions to the liberation movement have engendered oversimplification and caricaturization. Protestantism, however, must understand that an important part of the world is trying to tell it something, something about our tainted history and something about the potential of our Protestant principles. Although they are in the infancy of their theological process, it is their process. As Enrique Dussel has explained in *History and Theology of Liberation* (1976): "Europeans [the first world] are down to splitting hairs [about theology], while we must find out whether we even possess a head of hair; if we do, we must find out how to help it grow."

PENTECOSTAL AND CHARISMATIC MOVEMENTS

The belief in the baptism of the Holy Spirit as evidenced by speaking in other tongues coupled with the teaching of the imminent return of Jesus Christ increasingly influenced pockets of Protestant communities during the nineteenth century. Edward Irving (1792–1834), a Church of Scotland minister, was only one of the many who had seen the glossolalia phenomenon manifested.

Called to minister in 1822 at Caledonian Chapel in London, Irving's popular preaching drew so many hundreds that a new church had to be built in Regent Square five years later. Stressing the charismatic power of the Holy Spirit, Irving declared that there would be a "latter-rain outpouring of the Spirit" just before Christ returned. In 1830 it was reported that speaking in tongues had occurred spontaneously in assemblies in Scotland, and the next year Irving's Regent Square Church experienced the same manifestations. However, opposition to such "excesses" came swiftly, and the presbytery barred Irving from his pulpit. He and most of his followers joined what became known as the Catholic Apostolic Church, a new community that put great emphasis on the work of the Holy Spirit and on millennial expectation.

In spite of intense opposition, such episodes of glossolalia sporadically occurred. "Mother" Ann Lee (1736–84) and her Shaker communal society experienced the speaking of tongues in services in the eighteenth century as did some of Joseph Smith's Mormon followers in the nineteenth. As the twentieth century dawned, Charles Fox Parham challenged his students at Bethel Bible School in Topeka, Kansas to search the Scriptures for a "definite evidence" of the baptism of the Holy Spirit. All forty students surprised him by concluding that speaking in other tongues was the "initial evidence" of a Christian having received the baptism of the Holy Spirit. As Parham and his students began seeking this "gift," Agnes N. Ozman experienced the phenomenon on January 1, 1901. In the next few days, other students, many ministers and teachers, and Parham himself shared in the glossolalia "evidence."

Parham formulated the basic Pentecostal doctrine that the phenomenon of speaking in other tongues as experienced by the 120 followers of Jesus on the day of Pentecost (Acts 2) was normal and necessary for a Christian. Through this same experience, the power of the Holy Spirit was meant to be released in a Christian believer's life. Parham spread this teaching through Kansas, Missouri, and Texas. In 1906, the Azusa Street Revival burst forth in Los Angeles under the leadership of black Holiness preacher, William J. Seymour, a student of Parham's. Holding services every day and evening of the week, Seymour's revival with the accompanying glossolalia experience lasted for three years, drawing thousands of converts, ministers, and missionaries to the movement and eventually building Pentecostalism into a global influence.

Rejected by the Holiness movement to which it owed so much spiritual nurture and vehemently opposed by the Fundamentalist-Evangelical movement from which it garnered its view of the Bible and of the future, Pentecostalism spread by means of independent churches and denominations. The Assemblies of God, for example, were formed in 1914; while the greatest female evangelist and preacher of the early twentieth century, Aimee Semple McPherson (1890–1944), founded the International Church of the Foursquare Gospel in 1927. By the 1920s, worldwide missionary efforts had extended the Pentecostal movement to such diverse areas as Britain, Scandinavia, Europe, Russia, Latin America, China, and Africa. Today, there are over fifty million Pentecostals in more than one hundred nations around the globe. Such spiritual fervor has reduced the charges of "demon possession" leveled at adherents by conservative evangelical opponents of the movement.

The "neo-pentecostalism" of the modern Charismatic renewal movement has brought the pentecostal gifts of tongues, healing, miracles, and prophecy to traditional Protestant and Roman Catholic churches. The glossolalia experience began to penetrate mainline Protestant denominations in the United States in the latter years of the 1950s, when ministers of conventional Protestant bodies were "baptized" with the power of the Holy Spirit. Episcopalian, Methodist, Lutheran, and Presbyterian congregations began actively seeking the phenomenon, sometimes splitting local congregations in the process. In 1967, the baptism of the Holy Spirit fell upon some faculty and students at Duquesne University in Pittsburgh, and the phenomenon quickly spread to Notre Dame, Fordham, and other university centers. Notre Dame soon became the center for the fledgling Roman Catholic Charismatic movement, and in 1970 instituted a yearly National Conference on Charismatic Renewal in the Catholic church. Attracting only thirteen hundred in 1970, this conference now attracts tens of thousands each year, an indication of the Charismatic movement's influence in Roman Catholic circles. In the early

1970s, the movement even spread among Eastern Orthodox congregations.

Worldwide, the Charismatic renewal has gained nearly twelve million adherents in major denominational groups. The basic difference between "older" Pentecostals and these "new" Pentecostal-Charismatics is that older Pentecostalism tended to emphasize that there was *no* baptism of the Holy Spirit without the "initial evidence" of the speaking in other tongues. The Charismatic renewal movement, however, took a milder and less divisive position that there can be no speaking in tongues without prior baptism of the Holy Spirit. This allowed for a Christian to have the power of the Spirit in spite of the fact that tongues were not in evidence. Initially, "older" Pentecostals took a dim view of what they considered "the watered-down doctrine of the Charismatics," but both groups have been increasingly drawn into a closer fellowship through organizations such as the Full Gospel Business Men's association (founded in 1948).

The Charismatic movement's interaction with other conservative Protestant phenomena, such as the Electronic Church and Political Fundamentalism, is viewed most strikingly in the rise of television evangelist Marion Gordon "Pat" Robertson. Born into a political family, Robertson obtained his law degree from Yale and was building a business career when he felt called into the ministry. After theological studies, the Charismatic premillennialist Baptist raised $37,000 in 1959 to purchase a defunct television station. Today, his Christian Broadcasting Network based in Virginia Beach is a $230 million enterprise with tens of millions of viewers.

On his "700 Club" program, Robertson has unashamedly talked about the baptism of the Holy Spirit, prayed for the miraculous healing of those who are sick, and interpreted from the Bible events in the Middle East, positing the early return of Jesus Christ to the earth. His graduate school, CBN University, not only teaches the latest communications techniques with the most modern equipment but also includes courses on the Bible.

Pat Robertson's interest in the 1988 presidential race is only the most recent development in a conservative evangelical foray into the political arena. In the early 1970s Fundamentalists such as Jerry Falwell began feeling increasingly helpless and dispossessed as the federal government and the Supreme Court appeared to them to be leveling dictums against their ideals. No longer shunning politics, conservative groups began banding together, and the Political Fundamentalist movement began to gain a hearing on the national political scene, especially in the Republican Party. The movement blamed secular humanism for eroding the values of America, and enlisted conservative voters to lobby for conservative programs and to back "acceptable" political candidates.

A Democrat most of his life, Robertson has switched to the Republican Party and has fit well into the base of the Political Fundamentalist political agenda, for he has a long history of anticommunist and antihumanist rhetoric. Like Falwell, he has made eloquent pleas for freedom of religion and individual conscience. Nevertheless, other groups far less respectful of religious pluralism in the United States have tried to use such people and organizations to further their own hidden agendas and to wield political power. Whether or not the backlash from such endeavors will swing the pendulum far away from Political Fundamentalism remains to be seen. In spite of the fact that many Fundamentalist-Evangelicals and Charismatic Protestants are questioning such political aspirations and machinations, Pat Robertson remains Charismatic Protestantism's most recent political power broker — adding conservative politics and "traditional values" to the global power of the Spirit.

The new religious movements are a reflection of the constant development and dynamism of the religious enterprise as men and women search for truth. Some of these movements are within the Protestant sphere while others challenge its very foundation. Protestantism must be cognizant of their premises, alert to their values and dangers, and attentive to their proposals for a better world.

SUGGESTED READING

Arrington, Leonard, and Davis Bitton. *The Mormon Experience*. New York: Alfred A. Knopf, 1979.

Beckford, James A. *The Trumpet of Prophecy: A Sociological Study of Jehovah's Witnesses*. New York: Halsted Press, 1975.

Brown, Robert McAfee. *The Ecumenical Revolution*. Garden City, N.Y.: Doubleday & Co., 1967.

Cooper, John Charles. *Radical Christianity and Its Sources.* Philadelphia: Westminster Press, 1968.

Gottschalk, Stephen. *The Emergence of Christian Science in American Religious Life.* Berkeley and Los Angeles: Univ. of Calif. Press, 1973.

Needleman, Jacob. *The New Religions.* Garden City, N.Y.: Doubleday & Co., 1970.

Rouse, Ruth, and Stephen Neill, eds. *A History of the Ecumenical Movement, 1517–1948.* Philadelphia: Westminster Press, 1968.

Selvidge, Marla J., ed. *Fundamentalism Today: What Makes It So Attractive?* Elgin, Ill.: Brethren Press, 1984.

Sochen, June. *Movers and Shakers: American Women Thinkers and Activists, 1900–1970.* New York: Quadrangle Books, 1973.

Stavrianos, L. S. *Global Rift: The Third World Comes of Age.* New York: William Morrow, 1981.

Welch, Sharon D. *Communities of Resistance and Solidarity: A Feminist Theology of Liberation.* Maryknoll, N.Y.: Orbis Books, 1985.

11

PROTESTANTISM—
ITS MODERN MEANING

Protestantism began as a struggling movement that emphasized freedom of religion and individual conscience. As is apparent throughout its history, these emphases have been constantly reinforced in the Protestant heritage, often by groups and movements that questioned the growing authoritarianism, permissiveness, or biblical interpretation of the dominant Christian culture. Thus, Protestantism today has a vitality and creativity matched only by its diversity. This vitality is not a vacuous creative energy, but a thirst for truth and justice that is intrinsic to the principles and ideals of historic and modern Protestantism.

PROTECTOR OF RIGHTS

And yet the history of the Protestant movement attests to the fact that a weak Protestant group which seeks its own freedom and individual conscience may, once in power, restrict or attempt to abolish the freedom and individual conscience of others. From such historic blunders, modern Protestants have the opportunity to learn and to adjust, for the modern meaning of Protestantism must hearken back to its biblical foundation to protect the rights of others, especially the weaker nationality, race, denomination, church, brother, sister, child. The modern meaning of Protestantism underscores the principle that when one group's rights and religious freedom are violated, all religious freedom is imperiled. A Protestant is never safe when he or she is a persecutor of others.

This has been most evident in the corrupting power of civil religion relied upon by extreme nationalism. From fascism to communism, the history of this diabolical development holds crucial lessons for the modern meaning of Protestantism. Acting as a cancer on the body politic, such intolerance corrupts the very principles of the Protestant faith, rendering a vibrant belief system and heritage impotent and a tool for evil. To such corrosive forces intellect, liberalism, and traditionalism have succumbed in the past.

Slavery, the segregation system, and the Holocaust serve as prime case studies in helping the modern Protestant to recognize structures of evil and to act with a Christ-like opposition, even when one's society, denomination, or local church supports such structures. The modern Protestant learns that words are not enough, even when couched in acceptable liberal or conservative platitudes; and that the historic Protestant attitude that "all human institutions fall short of perfection" applies today as it did in yesteryear.

PERPETUAL REFORMER

To avoid spiritual stagnation and institutional dictatorship, the modern Protestant must recognize that the church needs to be reformed in every generation and must respect the rights of those who seek to pursue a differing religious pattern of polity and worship. History has shown that were Protestantism to be so unified as to be uniform, so devoid of differences within its belief system as to be an unbroken continuum of creed and law, the uniqueness of Protestantism would be vitiated, perhaps even drained, and thus utterly destroyed. From the global demands on Protestantism today, to attempt another course is a folly that is certain to end in disaster.

It is comforting, however, that the intrinsic principles of Protestantism have not yielded to narrow interpretations and bigoted ideals. The forces that burst forth from the church in the decades and centuries following the first protests of the reformers were so vibrant with strength that they could not be contained, so alive with a new mode of thinking, praying, and believing that the development of Protestantism in all of its variety could not be stopped. Whenever a group or faction sought to contain this dynamic movement within narrow channels, the currents were so strong and irresistible, so creative and unconquerable, that they surged forth in new and unexpected ways. When the dynamic current of Protestantism was dammed in any part of the world for even a historical instant, the smug self-righteousness and self-centeredness that followed resulted in scholastic stagnation.

FAITHFUL WITNESS

On the other hand, Protestantism was a channel of belief and witness. It had a historic tie to a gracious God who loved the human race and reached out to it through Jesus Christ. The Bible was the absolute norm of the Protestant tradition, a fact recognized by both Liberalism and Fundamentalism. From this wellspring for the human soul, liberal and conservative Protestants, Pentecostals and orthodox Calvinists, high and low church advocates, have exercised their freedom and individual conscience to develop rules of faith and standards of life. Never has a theology, however, encompassed all of Protestant church life, and Protestantism transcends its many confessions. Those who attempted to open the channels of the Protestant faith so wide as to amalgamate or eliminate its belief and witness ended with a stagnant pond that reflected little of the Protestant ethic or identity. And those who attempted to destroy religion altogether met the intrinsic power of surging faith. Indeed repression only makes Protestants stronger.

One example of this today is in Romania, where Communist leaders for forty years have tried to create Lenin's religion-free society. In spite of arrests, evictions, and forced emigration of Christian believers, Protestant denominations have experienced phenomenal growth. Over 200,000 Baptists continue to meet and worship in Romania, smuggling in Bibles and drawing a contingent of dedicated young people. When evangelist Billy Graham traveled to Romania to preach in 1985, he was met by crowds numbering tens of thousands. This was an indication of the phenomenal and growing strength of Protestantism since Graham's itinerary was passed only by word of mouth. There is every indication that the Romanian government will be forced to compromise with the intransigent Protestants, just as East Germany was forced to do with the Lutherans in the 1970s.

PURVEYOR OF JUSTICE

The dignity and worth of all human beings is an intrinsic principle of Protestantism. Within this history, Protestant liberals and conservatives have both experienced an intense social concern. In spite of a prevalent social atmosphere that hindered the reform process, Protestants of the right and the left in the past century have initiated vibrant ministries to the poor and destitute. In doing so, they have upheld the biblical truth of the sanctity of human life and the inherent worth of every "child of God." Both theologically liberal and conservative Protestants maintained close contact with the poverty-stricken and questioned the social structures that worked economically and politically to entangle the lower-class citizen in a web of misery and despair.

Nevertheless, Protestantism has not yet fulfilled its role as a purveyor of justice. As more conservative and liberal Protestants are now studying the problems and being made aware of the world situation in this regard, however, there is great hope for the twenty-first century. Protestantism is beginning to alert a new generation to the pitfalls of the old, not only instilling a new sense of economic responsibility, but also crossing the barriers of racial and religious prejudice that have often hindered the young.

As the world becomes smaller, social justice concerns are more difficult to ignore. The growth of the Third World Protestant movement continues to rise. Protestant church leaders and lay people seem ready to work jointly in a concentrated effort for social justice — to translate social theory into concrete efforts. Today, the intense interest in the family among the baby-boomers has reached out toward the homeless and the indigent, the orphan and the abused. The increasing Hispanic and black populations in America have directed more thought to relevant education and individual potential. American senior citizens and their significance have drawn Protestants to reflect on the responsibility and respect due to them. Technological advances, such as genetic engineering, have posed ethical challenges to Protestantism, while euthanasia advocates have forced a broad spectrum of Protestants to band together in adamant opposition.

BALANCE

Protestantism is a broad movement that is extremely diversified but most passionate in individual beliefs. One cannot expect Liberalism, for example, to be indifferent to the dangers it perceives in Political Fundamentalism. Nor can one expect Fundamentalist-

Evangelicals to sit back quietly when they believe a minority of "secular humanists" are gaining undue political and social power. Nevertheless, Protestantism is at a stage and in a world that are conducive to a balanced approach. The modern meaning of Protestantism connotes a dire need for a full understanding of Protestants of other denominations and perspectives. Congregations will learn to reach out to their brothers and sisters of differing heritages as individuals practice the matchless love of Christ. Modern Protestants must learn that respect and love for one's fellow (indeed, fellow Protestant) does not annul a strong support for one's own heritage: in fact, it only enhances the vitality of that heritage.

Furthermore, Protestantism need no longer be ignorant of, nor intolerant of, other traditions and other faiths. In general, Protestants are quite ignorant of their Jewish heritage and the dynamics of Judaism that inspired Jesus the Jew. Research into first-century Judaism is now beginning to filter down to the average church member, and dialogue between Protestant groups and the modern Jewish community is opening new avenues of understanding. Since the 1970s, a productive Evangelical/Jewish dialogue has been added to an established Liberal/Jewish dialogue. The prospects and advantages have given new direction toward a more balanced Protestant tradition.

Eastern Orthodox Christianity is beginning to interact with Protestantism in a way never thought possible. The orientation of Eastern thought has added a new dimension to Protestant perceptions of the Eastern milieu in which Jesus was born and Christianity first spread. New visions of Western Catholicism have contributed devotional and theological perspective to the background of Protestant growth. For the modern Protestant a balanced treatment of other faiths and religions can only strengthen the value of his or her own tradition, while developing that tradition into an effective witness and world view.

"ALIVE AND WELL"

Martin E. Marty, professor of modern church history at the University of Chicago, concluded his book *Protestantism* in 1972 with these words of warning: "Neither the institutional nor the cultural prospects for Protestantism seem very bright to an observer in the late twentieth century." He did admit in his final reflections: "On the other hand, Protestantism has passed through trial and experienced decline frequently in the past and has followed such phases with renewal. It is possible that surprising forms of new life could present themselves at this century's end."

It is our conviction that such forces of Protestant renewal and rejuvenation are not only present but are actively at work in the world today. Protestantism continues to be an essential witness to order in the midst of chaos, to faith in the midst of faithlessness, to meaning in the face of much that is meaningless in a distrait world. The quest for certitude coupled with the freedom implicit in the Protestant ethic engenders hope and courage amid doubt and despair. These cherished Protestant principles and concepts have not only prevailed historically but are even more powerful, reforming, and creative than at the beginning of the Protestant era.

INDEX

Abbott, Lyman, 94–96, 98, 102, 136
Addams, Jane, 102
Adventist movement, 130
Africa, 157–59, 164–66, 187, 190
African Baptist Society, 164
African Methodist Episcopal
  church, 163–65, 168, 170
African Methodist Episcopal Zion
  church, 163, 167–68
African Society, 162
Albigenses, 11–12
Allen, Richard, 162–63
American Antislavery Society, 166
American Bible Society, 80
American Board of Commissioners
  for Foreign Missions, 79
American Education Society, 80
American Society for the Promotion
  of Temperance, 80
American Society of Church His-
  tory, 182
American Sunday School Union, 80
American Temperance Union, 80
American Tract Society, 80
Amillennialism, 108, 129, 143, 149
Anabaptists, 27, 32–35
Anglicans, 29, 32, 43–47, 55–56, 64,
  69, 72–73, 76, 98–100, 126,
  160–61, 163, 181–82
Anticlericalism, 11, 21–22
Aquinas, Thomas, 188
Aristotle, 67, 188

Arminius, Jacob (Arminianism), 43,
  82
Arndt, Johann, 49
Asbury, Francis, 161–63
Asia, 82–84, 158, 181, 190
Assemblies of God, 190
Association for the Advancement of
  Woman, 80–81
Atheism, 59
Augsburg Confession, 24
Augustine, 6, 29
Azusa Street Revival, 189–90

Babylonian Captivity (of the
  church), 10
Bacon, Francis, 57–58
Bainton, Roland, 71
Balfour Declaration, 141
Baptism, 27, 32–33, 45, 158, 160–61,
  178, 182
Baptists, 45, 48, 76, 78, 81, 83, 97,
  103–4, 110, 125, 127, 142, 161,
  163–66, 168, 190–91, 197
Barmen Declaration, 120
Barnes, Albert, 81
Barnhouse, Donald G., 153
Barth, Karl, 85, 111–12, 120–22
Bartholow, Otho F., 141
Barton, Bruce, 110
Baur, Ferdinand Christian, 86
Bayle, Pierre, 58–60
Beecher, Henry Ward, 94–96, 102